T0301355

Investing in Mortgage-Backed and Asset-Backed Securities

The Wiley Finance series contains books written specifically for finance and investment professionals, as well as sophisticated individual investors and their financial advisors. Book topics range from portfolio management to e-commerce, risk management, financial engineering, valuation and financial instrument analysis, as well as much more. For a list of available titles, visit our website at www.WileyFinance.com.

Founded in 1807, John Wiley & Sons is the oldest independent publishing company in the United States. With offices in North America, Europe, Australia and Asia, Wiley is globally committed to developing and marketing print and electronic products and services for our customers' professional and personal knowledge and understanding.

Investing in Mortgage-Backed and Asset-Backed Securities

Financial Modeling with R and Open Source Analytics + Website

GLENN M. SCHULTZ, CFA

FOREWORD BY
FRANK J. FABOZZI, PH.D., CFA

WILEY

Published by John Wiley & Sons, Inc., Hoboken, New Jersey.
Published simultaneously in Canada.

For general information on our other products and services or for technical support, please contact our Customer Care Department within the United States at (800) 762-2974, outside the United States at (317) 572-3993 or fax (317) 572-4002.

Wiley publishes in a variety of print and electronic formats and by print-on-demand. Some material included with standard print versions of this book may not be included in e-books or in print-on-demand. If this book refers to media such as a CD or DVD that is not included in the version you purchased, you may download this material at http://booksupport.wiley.com. For more information about Wiley products, visit www.wiley.com.

Library of Congress Cataloging-in-Publication Data:

Names: Schultz, Glenn M., author.
Title: Investing in mortgage and asset backed securities, + website :
  financial modeling with r and open source analytics / Glenn M. Schultz ;
  foreword by Frank J. Fabozzi.
Description: Hoboken : Wiley, 2016. | Series: Wiley finance | Includes
  bibliographical references and index.
Identifiers: LCCN 2015035916 (print) | LCCN 2015047714 (ebook) |
  ISBN 9781118944004 (hardback) | ISBN 9781119221531 (ePDF) |
  ISBN 9781119221500 (ePub)
Subjects: LCSH: Mortgage-backed securities. | Securities. | Investments. |
  BISAC: BUSINESS & ECONOMICS / Investments & Securities.
Classification: LCC HG4655 .S387 2016 (print) | LCC HG4655 (ebook) | DDC
  332.63/244—dc23
LC record available at http://lccn.loc.gov/2015035916

Cover Design: Wiley
Cover Image: ©Max Krasnov/Shutterstock

Printed in the United States of America

10 9 8 7 6 5 4 3 2 1

To Missi and Blake

Contents

Foreword

Glenn's 20+ years of experience in structured finance is reflected in this book. Portfolio management, MBS investment banking and structuring, and loan level prepayment modeling are among his expertise. Glenn contributed to *The Handbook of Fixed-Income Securities*, several editions of *The Handbook of Mortgage-Backed Securities*, and *The Handbook of Nonagency Mortgage-Backed Securities*. In 2003, he was honored for his structuring expertise with the IDD/ASR award for the Most Innovative ABS Transaction of the Year.

Glenn's broad experience highlights that investing in mortgage-backed securities requires a multidisciplinary approach including securities law, structuring techniques, and the modeling of econometric data and consumer behavior, both of which fall under the rubric of big data analysis. Furthermore, the proliferation of data and the analysis thereof have brought the concept of reproducible research to the forefront. Ultimately, research or experiments that can be reproduced are more reliable than those which cannot be reproduced. Reproducing the research of others is not only a checking process but it also provides a jump-point for future exploration. *Investing in Mortgage-Backed and Asset-Backed Securities* was written in the spirit of reproducible research and introduces Bond Lab, the first object-oriented and open source software that Glenn created for the analysis of mortgage- and asset-backed securities.

Bond Lab is programmed in R, the statistical computing language of choice, and allows the reader to replicate the analysis presented herein, view the code that created the results, and extend the analysis in any direction one chooses. Furthermore, the commercial acceptance of R on cloud computing platforms offers the investor a promise of unlimited scalability. By harnessing the power of R and open source computing, Bond Lab charts the course for the investor to create a custom technology stack meeting and expressing one's unique view with respect to the mortgage-backed securities market, thereby creating true alpha.

Frank J. Fabozzi, Ph.D, CFA
Professor of Finance, EDHEC Business School
and
Editor, *Journal of Portfolio Management*

Preface

*It is not the critic who counts; ... The credit belongs to the man
who is actually in the arena, ... who spends himself in a worthy
cause; who at the best knows in the end the triumph of high
achievement, and who at the worst, if he fails, at least fails while
daring greatly, so that his place shall never be with those cold and
timid souls who neither know victory nor defeat.*

Theodore Roosevelt

Welcome to the arena of structured finance. The purpose of this book is to hone the skills needed to successfully compete in the arena. Bond Lab and the Companion to Investing in MBS are the training tools, both of which are programmed in the R computing language. This analysis presented in this book is based on Bond Lab version 0.0.0.9000. Bond Lab is, to my knowledge, the first open source object-oriented software designed for the analysis of structured securities. Bond Lab allows the reader to replicate the analysis presented herein, as well as extend the analysis in any direction she chooses thereby creating a richer learning experience and greater understanding of the material.

Investing in Mortgage-Backed and Asset-Backed Securities, was written in the spirit of reproducible research and its underlying philosophy is simple: Mortgage-backed securities are not too complex to understand. In fact, the basic valuation techniques applicable to all fixed-income securities also form the foundation for the valuation of mortgage-backed securities (MBS) and asset-backed securities (ABS). The perceived complexity of investing in structured products, like MBS, can be attributed to four sources:

1. The contingency of residential MBS cash flows, which manifest because the borrower holds the option to prepay and terminate her mortgage obligation early.

2. Cash flow structuring techniques based on the allocation of principal and interest across real estate mortgage investment conduit (REMIC) structures.

3. Credit structuring techniques that allocate losses through the capital structure of a transaction.

4. Valuation techniques that "simulate" the economy—interest rate models.

Organization of the Book

The main goal of this book is to develop a basic framework for the analysis of mortgage- and asset-backed securities using open source software. The financial models presented throughout the book are developed using R [R Core Team 2013], a freely downloaded open source software development environment.

Many people think of R as a statistics package, however it is much more. The R environment is an "integrated suite of software facilities for data manipulation, calculation, and graphical display" [Smith and R Core Team 2013]. As such, R lends itself easily to the development of an integrated financial analysis tool.

Investing in structured products also requires managing large sets of data. Aside from market data, like swap rates and Treasury prices and yields, the structured product investor must also follow borrower transaction data. Examples include voluntary prepayment rates, payment of scheduled principal and interest, and borrower delinquency and default. More often than not the investor must monitor this information at the loan level. Loan level data are becoming more available, and there are a host of vendors that offer the aggregation and delivery of this kind of data. The loan level data that is needed by the investor to monitor collateral performance is also freely available via trustee and/or issuer websites. In this book, we will use MySQL®, also open source, as the data management solution.

Investing in MBS is divided into five parts. Part One, **Valuation of Fixed-Income Securities**, introduces the reader to the techniques used to value all fixed-income securities.

- Chapter 1 begins with the time value of money. It introduces the concept of the present and future value of $1. The concept of the time value of money underlies every investment decision. It is the most basic expression of interest rates that forms the foundation of fixed-income investing.

- Chapter 2 covers the theories of the term structure of interest rates, explaining the coupon, spot rate, and forward rate curves. The chapter numerically illustrates the derivation of both spot and forward rates.

Numerical examples are provided throughout the chapter to assist the reader in gaining a solid understanding of the term structure of interest rates.

- Chapter 3 introduces fixed-income mathematics covering yield to maturity, weighted average life, duration, convexity, and key rate duration. The chapter provides numerical examples as well as the application of each metric.
- Chapter 4 integrates Chapters 1 through 3 into a comprehensive framework for the valuation of fixed-income securities; particular attention is paid to assets whose principal amortizes over the life of the investment. Finally, Chapter 5 illustrates fixed income return analysis. The chapter deconstructs horizon return into its components and illustrates how each contributes to the investor's realized rate of return.

Part Two, **Residential Mortgage-Backed Securities**, introduces the reader to mortgage-backed securities.

- Chapter 6 differentiates the characteristics of residential and commercial real estate. The chapter ends by deconstructing the mortgage loan amortization table and outlining key mortgage servicing activities.
- Chapter 7 extends the concepts presented in Chapter 6, illustrating mortgage cash flow analysis. Specifically, the chapter takes the reader through the amortization and cash flow analysis of a pool of mortgage loans given borrower prepayment.
- Finally, Chapters 8 and 9 provide an overview of the techniques used to analyze the factors influencing mortgage prepayment rates. Chapter 8 illustrates the application of the Cox proportional hazard model to loan level data as a method to explore the drivers of prepayment rates, while Chapter 9 translates the analysis of Chapter 8 into a functioning parametric prepayment model.

Part Three, **Valuation of Mortgage-Backed Securities**, introduces the reader to the basic valuation techniques used to determine relative value in the mortgage-backed securities market.

- Chapter 10 reviews the mortgage dollar roll. The dollar roll is the short-term financing mechanism of the residential mortgage market and represents the starting point of relative value analysis in the residential MBS market.
- Chapter 11 presents the tools investors may use to analyze mortgage-backed securities. The chapter addresses liquidity analysis, static cash flow analysis, and finally the application of return analysis to differentiate the relative value of mortgage-backed securities.

- Chapter 12 introduces option-adjusted spread (OAS) analysis. OAS analysis is perhaps the least understood and most wrongly applied tool in the mortgage valuation arsenal. The chapter guides the reader through the Cox, Ingersoll, Ross single factor term structure model. The chapter illustrates the motivation of the prepayment model presented in Chapter 9 via the interest rate model and ends with a complete treatment of OAS as an investment decision making tool.

Part Four, **Structuring Mortgage-Backed Securities**, introduces the reader to the structuring techniques used in the mortgage-backed securities market. MBS structuring relies on the division of principal and interest to create notes derived from MBS cash flows that are tailored to meet investors' unique risk/reward profiles. Further, the structuring techniques used by dealers alter both the timing and valuation of MBS cash flows. Option-adjusted spread analysis is used throughout the section to explore how the division of principal and interest alter mortgage cash flow valuations.

- Chapter 13 introduces REMICs and explains the rational for their creation, evolution, and legal structure. The chapter closes by outlining the Bond Lab structuring model.
- Chapter 14 kicks off REMIC structuring with stripped mortgage-backed securities (SMBS). A stripped MBS is not a REMIC in terms of its legal formation; however, SMBS are included in the section because they represent the clearest illustration of the division of principal and interest—the key to REMIC structuring and arbitrage.
- Chapter 15 presents the sequential REMIC structure, an example of the division of principal via time tranching, which allows a dealer to create bonds of different maturities thereby exploiting investors' term structure preferences to create a profitable arbitrage.
- Chapter 16 outlines the planned amortization class (PAC)-companion REMIC. The PAC-companion structure is an example of the division of principal. Rather than time tranching, principal is allocated to each bond within the structure based on the prepayment rate of the underlying MBS.
- Chapter 17 completes the sequential REMIC arbitrage illustrating the use of a two-tiered REMIC structure to create an IO class. The structuring difference between the sequential IO and the SMBS IO is explored.
- Chapter 18 outlines the PAC-floater-inverse floater structure and completes the PAC-companion arbitrage illustrating the use of derivative execution to create par priced bonds.
- Chapter 19 illustrates the use of an accrual bond to "clean-up" the companion bond's tail cash flows and create a long duration security.

Part Five, **Mortgage Credit Analysis,** covers default modeling, self-insuring mortgage structures, and the basics of sizing mortgage credit enhancement. A self-insuring structure is one whose credit enhancement is internally created which may subject the investor to principal loss resulting from borrower defaults. Thus, it is imperative that the investor understands default modeling, loss simulation, and the allocation of losses across the transaction's capital structure.

- Chapter 20 illustrates the use of logistic regression analysis to model mortgage default.
- Chapter 21 builds on the analysis presented in Chapter 20 and illustrates the development of a predictive default model.
- Chapter 22 introduces the basics of private-label MBS. The chapter covers alternative subordination structures, cross collateralization, as well as the implication of the third-party credit exposure.
- Chapter 23 illustrates simulation techniques used to determine mortgage credit enhancement levels. The chapter not only focuses on principal subordination but also illustrates how the investor may use simulation to investigate the adequacy of agency guarantee fees and how those fees relate to principal subordination.

Acknowledgments

The Bond Lab® project would not have been possible without the support of my family and friends. To my wife, Missi, thank your for your neverending support, encouragement, and most importantly, your patience throughout the project. Justin D. Wolf, my best friend, thank you for your tireless efforts editing *Investing in Mortgage-Backed and Asset-Backed Securities*. You served as a reliable and trusted consultant and editor, meticulously reviewing each sentence, and the conceptual frameworks presented—any remaining ambiguity or grammatical errors are my full responsibility. Frank J. Fabozzi, PhD, CFA—over the years Frank was kind enough to include me in many of his works and together we edited *Structured Products and Related Credit Derivatives*. This book reflects the insights and experiences gained by working with Frank over many years. Chris J. Carney, your enthusiasm for the Bond Lab project and vision of creating an open source analytic program provided a wellspring of motivation. Steve J. Sinclair, your advice and counsel was invaluable as I navigated the world of object-orientated programming. The R core team, R community, and members of the R-help mailing list provided timely and insightful answers to many of my questions as I developed Bond Lab.

R Software Packages Used

The following R software packages were used for the Bond Lab project. The R packages devtools, roxygen2, and testthat provided the development and documentation environment. In addition, Bond Lab makes use of lubridate, termstrc, and optimx. All the graphics presented herein, with the exception of 13.1, were created using ggplot2 and reshape2, 13.1 was created using GIMP, also open source. I extend my gratitude to the authors and maintainers of these R packages:

- devtools, Hadley Wickham and Winston Chang (2015). devtools: Tools to Make Developing R Packages Easier. R package version 1.7.0. http://CRAN.R-project.org/package=devtools.
- ggplot2, H. Wickham. ggplot2: elegant graphics for data analysis. New York: Springer, 2009.

- lubridate, Garrett Grolemund, Hadley Wickham (2011). Dates and Times Made Easy with lubridate. *Journal of Statistical Software* 40(3), 1–25.
- optimx, John C. Nash, Ravi Varadhan (2011). Unifying Optimization Algorithms to Aid Software System Users: optimx for R. *Journal of Statistical Software*, 43(9), 1–14. URL http://www.jstatsoft.org/v43/i09/.
- reshape2, Hadley Wickham (2007). Reshaping Data with the reshape Package. *Journal of Statistical Software*, 21(12), 1–20.
- roxygen2, Hadley Wickham, Peter Danenberg and Manuel Eugster (2014). roxygen2: In-source Documentation for R. R package version 4.1.0. http://CRAN.R-project.org/package=roxygen2.
- termstruc, Robert Ferstl, Josef Hayden (2010). Zero-Coupon Yield Curve Estimation with the Package termstrc. *Journal of Statistical Software*, 36(1), 1–34. URL http://www.jstatsoft.org/v36/i01/.
- testthat, Hadley Wickham, A testing package specifically tailored for R that's fun, flexible, and easy to set up.
- survival, Therneau T (2015). A Package for Survival Analysis in S, version 2.38, URL http://CRAN.R-project.org/package=survival.

Introduction

The inspiration for Bond Lab arose from the recommendation on the part of the Structured Finance Industry Group to provide mortgage and consumer asset-backed bond payment rules, commonly referred to as the waterfall, in an open source programming language. Although well intended, the recommendation suffered from the following problems:

- First, the waterfall is but one of several structural objects that must come together within the program to define a structured security. Thus, it was rightly pointed out by several providers of commercially available software that a waterfall, in and of itself, is insufficient to analyze structured securities.
- Second, the recommendation mentioned Python as an example of a human readable open source programming language. Although only an example, mentioning Python served to pivot the conversation from the viability of open source deal structures to that of a debate on the choice of programming language.

Bond Lab is an example of open source software designed for the analysis of fixed-income securities with an emphasis on structured securities. It defines the classes, superclasses, structural elements, and methods required to create a structured security before the investor can begin to perform cash flow, relative value, and risk analysis.

The examples used in this book assume securities whose factor or origination date occurred sometime during January 2013, a random choice on my part. Swap rate data, taken from the Federal Reserve's website, is available for the month. The examples are:

Bond ID	Bond Type	Structure
bondlab5	Bond	5-year semi-annual coupon
bondlab10	Bond	10-year semi-annual coupon
bondlabMBS4	Mortgage	30-year pass-through
bondlabMBS5	Mortgage	30-year pass-through
BondLabMBSIO	Mortgage	IO strip
BondLabMBSPO	Mortgage	PO strip
BondLabPAC1	PAC	REMIC tranche

Bond ID	Bond Type	Structure
BondLabCMP1	companion	REMIC tranche
BondLabSEQ1	sequential	REMIC tranche
BondLabSEQ2	sequential	REMIC tranche
BondLabSEQ3	sequential	REMIC tranche
BondLabSEQ4	sequentialIO	REMIC tranche
BondLabPAC2	PAC	REMIC tranche
BondLabFloater	floater	REMIC tranche
BondLabInverse	inverse	REMIC tranche
BondLabPACZ	PAC	REMIC tranche
BondLabCMP_Z	companion	REMIC tranche
BondLabZ	accrual bond	REMIC tranche

Finally, the Bond Lab structuring tool allows the reader to create any structure by defining the REMIC, its tranches, collateral group, and payment waterfall. Thus, the reader may extend her analysis and investigation in any direction she chooses. The Companion to Investing in MBS (companion2IMBS) provides a gentle introduction to BondLab, calling much of the functionality presented herein.

One

Valuation of
Fixed-Income Securities

The Time Value of Money

The chief value of money lies in the fact that one lives in a world in which it is overestimated.

H.L. Mencken (1707–1754)

Chapter 1 outlines the foundation for successful investing irrespective of the asset class under consideration. Namely, the chapter introduces the reader to the concept of the time value of money. Understanding the time value of money is essential for successful investing for the following reasons:

- It allows the investor to measure the value of one asset or portfolio of cash flows relative to another.
- The investor, using the time value of money, can estimate expected holding period returns.

1.1 PRESENT VALUE

Congratulations! You have won $1 million in the "Chances Are Slim Lottery." (They were very slim, but you played anyway, and got lucky.) You now have a choice, either take a lump sum payment of $500,000 or monthly payments of $2,777.78 per month over the next 30 years.

This is a classic time-value-of-money problem. The time value of money postulates that it is preferable to receive a dollar today rather than the same dollar in the future. This is because the dollar received today will have a certain purchasing power over the dollar received in the future.

For example, the dollar received today may be invested in an interest bearing account that will grow over time. Alternatively, one may spend the dollar received today rather than deferring consumption. Either way, one is better off taking the dollar today than at a later date. The winning lottery

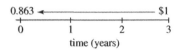

FIGURE 1.1   Present Value of a
Single Payment

problem implies an interest rate: What can be earned on the $500,000 taken today as well as an inflation outlook, or what is the purchasing power of a dollar received at some point in the future?

To answer the winning lottery question we first must understand the concept of present value. The *present value* (PV) equation (1.1) allows a person to determine the value today of a dollar received at some point in the future:

$$\text{Present Value of } \$1 = \frac{1}{(1 + i)^n} \qquad (1.1)$$

where i = Interest rate
$\quad\quad\ n$ = Number of periods

Equation 1.1 states, that given a discount or interest rate (i) and time or number of discounting periods (n) one can determine the value today of a sum received at some point in the future.

Figure 1.1 illustrates the concept. Assuming (i) = 5% annually and (n) = 3 years, the present value of $1, or its value today, is $0.863.

So, if a person were able to invest in a "risk-free" interest bearing account earning 5% interest annually over a three-year period, she would be indifferent, in a purely economic sense, between receiving $0.86 today or a dollar three years from now. Which would you prefer? Your answer is the **time value of money.**

1.2 FUTURE VALUE

Notice that the present value problem implies a *future value* condition. Specifically, the future value is stated as $1. So, it appears that the future value of a dollar is the "tails" side of the present value coin. The future value of a dollar invested in an interest-bearing account is also determined by both the time invested (n) as well as the interest rate earned (i).

$$\text{Future Value of } \$1 = (1 + i)^n \qquad (1.2)$$

where i = Interest rate
$\quad\quad\ n$ = Number of periods

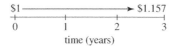

FIGURE 1.2 Future Value of a
Single Sum Today

Equation 1.2 reverses the present value equation and states that given an interest rate (i) and an investment horizon or number of periods (n) the value, at a point in the future, of a sum invested today can be determined.

Figure 1.2 illustrates the concept. Assuming (i) = 5% and (n) = 3 years, the future value of $1 is $1.157.

Together equations 1.1 and 1.2 provide some intuition to solve the winning lottery problem. However, neither equation 1.1 nor 1.2 alone provides the discount rate or (i) used to equate the present value of the annuity payment of $2,777.78 to the $500,000 lump sum offered in the above winning lottery problem.

1.3 PRESENT VALUE OF AN ANNUITY

Before solving the annuity problem, it is important to recognize the difference between an *annuity* and an *annuity due*. An annuity is a group of payments or cash flows to be received at a specific interval (monthly, quarterly, annually) over a specified period of time. An annuity due specifies the payments to be made at the beginning of a period while a regular annuity specifies that the payments are made at the end of a period.

Figure 1.3 illustrates the concept of an annuity. One can simply think of an annuity as a series of payments that are discounted given a rate (i) and a period (n) over which the payments are scheduled to be made. The present value of the annuity is the sum of the present value of the payments. In the example presented in Figure 1.3, the present value of the annuity is $2.72.

Annuity payments may be constant from one period or payment to the next (certain cash flows[1]) or they may vary. Cash flows that vary from one

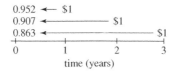

FIGURE 1.3 Present Value of
Annuity Payment

---

[1]The cash flows are certain absent the likelihood of default or early repayment.

period to the next are generally referred to as contingent cash flows. That is, the size of the cash flow may be contingent on exogenous factors. When the annuity payments are constant the present value or future value of the annuity can be calculated using the following closed form solutions:

The present value of an "ordinary" annuity, one under which payments are made at the end of a period, can be expressed as:

$$\text{Present value of annuity} = \frac{1 - \frac{1}{(1+i)^n}}{i} \tag{1.3}$$

where i = Interest rate
$\quad n$ = Number of periods

To adjust for the difference in the timing of the cash flows between an annuity and an annuity due, one simply multiplies the present value of an annuity by $(1 + i)$. Thus, the equation for the present value of an annuity due is:

$$\text{Present value annuity due} = \left[\frac{1 - \frac{1}{(1+i)^n}}{i} \right] \times [(1 + i)] \tag{1.4}$$

where i = Interest rate
$\quad n$ = Number of periods

1.4   FUTURE VALUE OF AN ANNUITY

Of course, you could decide to reinvest (save) the proceeds from your lottery winnings. If this were the case, then the future value of the payments saved is given by equation 1.5.

$$\text{Future value of annuity} = \frac{(1 + i)^n - 1}{i} \tag{1.5}$$

where i = Interest rate
$\quad n$ = Number of periods

1.5   SOLVING FINANCIAL QUESTIONS WITH PRESENT AND FUTURE VALUE

To solve the winning lottery problem all that is left is to determine the appropriate discount rate, or (i). The discount rate (i) is usually determined by a market quoted rate, like the 10-year Treasury yield. So, assuming the 10-year Treasury yield is 3.0%, the present value of the $2,777.78 monthly annuity is $658,859. This is considerably more than the $500,000 lump sum offered by the Chances Are Slim Lottery.

What is the discount rate used by the Chances Are Slim Lottery? We can iteratively solve for this by successively increasing or decreasing the discount rate until the present value of the annuity is equal to the lump sum amount offered. The discount rate used by the Chances Are Slim Lottery is 5.43%. This rate is equivalent to the assumed 10-year Treasury rate of 3% plus a premium or "spread" of 2.43%.

Your analysis, based on the time value of money, indicates you must believe that over the lifetime of the annuity you could earn more than 5.43%—your break-even rate—before accepting the lump-sum payment offered by the Chances Are Slim Lottery.

As you ponder the question, "Can I earn more than 5.43% if I were to take the lump sum payment and invest the proceeds myself?" you receive a call from a well-known and highly successful hedge fund investor who is interested in buying your winning lottery ticket. She indicates that she is willing to purchase your lottery ticket today for $575,000.

You quickly realize that her analysis, investing in or purchasing your winning ticket, is different from your "winning" analysis. She, unlike you, will make a substantial investment to purchase the ticket. What is her return for purchasing the ticket? Her return, or internal rate of return (IRR), is the discount rate that equates the present value of a series of cash flows received in the future to the initial outlay made to purchase those cash flows today. Figure 1.4 graphically illustrates the concept. What is the discount rate or i that equates three equal payments over three years to a $75 outlay today?

Returning to the lottery example, you calculate that the hedge fund investor is willing to accept a annualized return of 4.17% in order to purchase the winning lottery ticket. Her offer to purchase the ticket results in a higher lump sum payment and lower internal rate of return than the Chances Are Slim Lottery is willing to offer you.

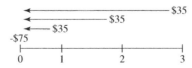

FIGURE 1.4 Internal Rate of Return

1.6   APPLICATION TO FIXED-INCOME SECURITIES

Yield to maturity YTM is the internal rate of return (IRR). It relates the initial cash outlay to purchase a bond for the future cash flow received the—principal and interest earned over the life of the bond.

CONCEPT 1.1

A bond represents both an annuity and a single principal payment. Consider a non-callable bond that pays a 5% coupon semi-annually that matures in 3 years with a principal payment of $1,000. The coupon payment represents an annuity of six equal payments of $25. The principal represents a single lump-sum payment of $1,000 at maturity. Assuming one were to pay $1,000 today for the bond the IRR or yield to maturity is 5%.

The present value of the coupon annuity is:

$$\text{Present value of annuity} = \frac{1 - \frac{1}{(1+(0.05/2))^6}}{(0.05/2)} \times \$25 = \$137.70 \qquad (1.6)$$

The present value of the principal payment is:

$$\text{Present value of } \$1 = \frac{1}{(1+(0.05/2))^6} \times \$1,000 = \$862.30 \qquad (1.7)$$

Said another way, using a 5% discount rate, the present value of a non-callable bond representing an annuity of six equal payments of $25 and a single payment of $1,000 in six years is $1,000.

The time value of money is the basis upon which the valuation of all fixed-income securities rests. In fact, it is the foundation of all investment decisions. Using the time value of money the investor can compare the expected return of one portfolio of assets relative to another portfolio of assets.

CHAPTER 2

Theories of the Term Structure of Interest Rates

Tell me, in four words, what is a forward rate?
Interview Question

Chapter 1 introduced the concept of the time value of money. Key to solving the time value of money is the discount rate *(i)* used to determine either the present or future value of a cash flow occurring at some point in the future *(n)*. Chapter 2 introduces *i* to the reader. By market convention *i* may be referred to as the *yield curve*, the *spot rate*, or the *forward rate*. Spot rates, not the yield curve, are used to price bonds and their related derivative contracts. Thus, understanding the derivation of both forward and spot rates is key to understanding the valuation of fixed-income securities.

Typically, the discount rate or *i*, is derived from a quoted market rate. Given *n* and *i* the present or future value of $1 can be determined. The relationship between the discount rate *i* and the number of periods *n* is often referred to as the yield curve. The most commonly quoted yield curves are the U.S. Treasury yield curve and the interest rate swap or LIBOR curve.

Generally, as *n* increases, *i* also increases but at a diminishing rate. That is, *i* is an asymptotically increasing function of *n*. This is often referred to as an upward-sloping yield curve.

The three theories of the *term structure* of interest rates are:

1. The *rational or pure expectations hypothesis*
2. The *market segmentation theory*
3. The *liquidity preference theory*

Each attempts to explain the following observations with respect to the term structure of interest rates:

- Interest rates across different maturities tend to move together. That is, they are positively correlated.
- The yield curve tends to exhibit a steep positive slope when short-term rates are low and a negative slope when short-term rates are high.
- For the most part, the yield curve exhibits an upward-sloping bias.

Neither the rational expectations nor market segmentation theory fully explain the term structure of interest rates. But, taken together, these theories form the basis of the liquidity preference theory, providing clearer understanding of the term structure of interest rates and the calculation of the discount rates used to value fixed-income securities and their related derivative securities. Thus, the theories of the term structure of interest rates serve as the cornerstone of the relative value analysis that will be presented in following chapters. In the sections that follow, we briefly examine each of these theories.

2.1 THE RATIONAL OR PURE EXPECTATIONS HYPOTHESIS

The rational expectations hypothesis asserts that fixed-income investors do not prefer one maturity bond over another [Muth 1961]. That is, investors are indifferent to holding bonds of different maturities. Thus, under the rational expectations hypothesis, bonds of different maturities are considered to be perfect substitutes for one another. This is because under the rational expectations hypothesis, the return on a long-term bond is equal to the expected average of the returns on short-term bonds (forward rates) over the life of the bond.

To illustrate the expectations hypothesis, assume three investment strategies, each with a three-year investment horizon.

1. Invest $1 in a one-year bond, and when that bond matures, reinvest the proceeds in a one-year bond in the second and third year as each bond successively matures.
2. Invest $1 in a one-year bond, and when that bond matures, reinvest the proceeds in a two-year bond.
3. Invest $1 in a three-year bond.

To make this analysis easier, consider a $1 bond that does not offer a coupon but instead pays $1 of principal at maturity. Simplifying the problem to a series of zero coupon securities allows the investor to apply formula 1.1 to each cash flow individually in order to determine the present value of the series of cash flows. This offers the investor the flexibility to assign a unique discount rate, or i—a non-linear term structure assumption—to each cash flow rather than a single i—a linear term structure assumption—as is the case with yield to maturity or the internal rate of return.

CONCEPT 2.1

A bond that pays no interest is a zero-coupon bond. The rate used to determine the present value of the bond is the spot rate. Zero-coupon bond returns are not subject to reinvestment assumptions to maturity, since the principal value accrues at the *spot rate*.

The *expectations theory* states that long-term bond returns are the product of short-term bond returns. Thus, in our example, the expected return of the first strategy can be written as follows:

$$\text{Horizon return} = \left[\left(1 + s_1\right)\left(1 + f_{(1,1)}\right)\left(1 + f_{(1,2)}\right)\right] - 1 \qquad (2.1)$$

where: s_1 = the 1-year spot rate
$f_{(1,1)}$ = 1-year forward rate, 1 year from today
$f_{(1,2)}$ = 1-year forward rate, 2 years from today

Assume the following spot rate curve given by Table 2.1. The expectations hypothesis states that the two-year spot rate is the product of the one year spot rate and the one year forward rate, one year from today.

TABLE 2.1 Spot Rate Curve (zero coupon yields)

Tenor	Spot Rate Curve
1-year	0.75%
2-year	1.25%
3-year	2.00%

TABLE 2.2 1-Year Forward Rate in 1 Year

Tenor	Spot Rate	$f(1,1)$
1-year	0.750%	
2-year	1.250%	0.496%
3-year	2.000%	0.749%

The two-year spot rate is given by:

$$(1 + s_1)(1 + f_{(1,1)}) = (1 + s_2) \tag{2.2}$$

where: s_1 = the 1-year spot rate
s_2 = the 2-year spot rate
$f_{(1,1)}$ = 1-year forward rate, 1 year from today

Rearranging the terms and solving for the one-year forward rate, one-year from today, results in the following:

$$\left(1 + f_{(1,1)}\right) = \frac{(1 + s_2)}{(1 + s_1)} \tag{2.3}$$

where: s_1 = the 1-year spot rate
s_2 = the 2-year spot rate
$f_{(1,1)}$ = 1-year forward rate, 1 year from today

The expected one-year forward rate, one year forward, is 0.496% and the expected one-year rate, two-years forward is 0.749% (Table 2.2). If the expected forward rates are realized, then the investor's horizon return will be 2%.

$$\text{Horizon return} = \left[(1 + .0075)(1 + .00496)(1 + .00749)\right] - 1 = 2.0\% \tag{2.4}$$

Alternatively, the investor may decide to purchase a bond with a two-year maturity that yields 2% and invest the proceeds in a one-year bond, two years forward. How would you apply equation 2.4 to show that the investor's expected horizon return is 2%?

In the second strategy presented, the investor purchases \$1 of a bond maturing in one year yielding 0.75%, and at its maturity the investor plans to invest the proceeds in a bond maturing in two years. What is the two-year rate, one-year forward?

$$\left(1 + s_1\right)\left(1 + f_{(2,1)}\right) = \left(1 + s_3\right) \tag{2.5}$$

where: s_1 = the 1-year spot rate
s_3 = the 3-year spot rate
$f_{(2,1)}$ = 2-year forward rate, 1 year from today

TABLE 2.3   1-Year Forward Rate in 2 Years

Tenor	Spot Rate	f(1,1)	f(2,1)
1-year	0.750%		
2-year	1.250%	0.496%	1.249%
3-year	2.000%	0.749%	

Rearranging the terms and solving for the two-year rate, one year from today (forward), results in the following:

$$\left(1 + f_{(2,1)}\right) = \frac{(1 + s_3)}{(1 + s_1)} \tag{2.6}$$

where: s_1 = the 1-year spot rate
s_3 = the 3-year spot rate
$f_{(2,1)}$ = 2-year forward rate, 1-year from today

The expected two-year rate, one year forward, is 1.249% (Table 2.3). If the expected two-year forward rate is realized, the investor's horizon return will be 2.0%.

The expectations hypothesis explains the first observation with respect to the term structure of interest rates:

▪ Interest rates tend to move together. For example, if $s_{(t)}$ increases, then $s_{(t+n)}$ also increases, which, in turn, increases the average of the future short-term rates (forwards). Consequently, short-term and long-term interest rates tend to move together.

▪ When short-term rates are low and below their average, the market expects short-term rates to go up, and the yield curve exhibits a positive or upward slope. Conversely, when short-term rates are high and above average, then the market expects short-term rates to go down and the yield curve exhibits a negative or downward slope.

2.2   THE MARKET SEGMENTATION THEORY

The market segmentation theory asserts that the markets for different maturity bonds are segmented. Under this assumption, the interest rate for each bond is determined by the supply and demand for bonds, without consideration given to the expected returns on bonds of other maturities. Stated differently, under this theory bonds are not substitutable and the expected return from a bond of given maturity has no influence on the demand for a bond of another maturity [Vayanos and Vila 2009].

Further, investors are thought to prefer short-term maturity bonds over long-term maturity bonds. Thus, there is greater relative demand for short-term bonds than there is for long-term bonds. As a result, the price of short-term bonds is higher, resulting in a lower yield than that offered on long-term bonds.

The market segmentation theory explains the tendency of the yield curve to exhibit a positive or upward-sloping bias. However, the market segmentation theory cannot explain the tendency of interest rates to move together, or the presence of downward-sloping yield curves.

2.3 THE LIQUIDITY PREFERENCE THEORY

The liquidity preference theory, like the rational expectations hypothesis, also asserts that bonds are perfect substitutes for one another [Keynes 1936]. However, because the investor may be required to sell her bond prior to maturity, thereby assuming interest rate risk, a greater premium is offered to hold longer-term bonds via higher implied forward rates. Simply stated, the liquidity preference theory implies a rational expectation plus a liquidity premium.

In the previous example, the spot rate curve, although upward sloping, implied a lower one-year forward rate. The liquidity preference theory implies higher spot rates than that given by the rational expectations hypothesis. This is because the liquidity premium is assumed to be constant.

Table 2.4 illustrates the derivation of the spot rate curve given a liquidity premium assumption. In the example, the liquidity premium for a "riskless" zero coupon bond with one year to maturity is 0.75%. That is, the one-year spot rate for a risk-free bond is 0.75%. This implies, all else equal, that the one-year spot rate, n periods from today, is also 0.75%. Notice that the spot rate curve implied by the given forward curve in Table 2.4 is steeper than the spot rate curve in the previous example.

TABLE 2.4 1 Year Forward Rate in 2 Years

Tenor	Liquidity Premium	$f(1,n)$	Spot Rate
1-year	0.75%		0.75%
2-year		0.75%	1.50%
3-year		0.75%	2.27%

Since the return on a long-term bond (zero coupon) is equal to the expected average return on short-term bonds (forward rates), one can solve for the spot rate, given a liquidity premium, as follows:

$$s_2 = \left[\left(1 + f_{(1,1)}\right) \left(1 + f_{(1,2)}\right) \right] - 1 \qquad (2.7)$$

where: s_2 = the 2-year spot rate
           $f_{(1,1)}$ = 1-year forward rate, 1 year from today
           $f_{(1,2)}$ = 1-year forward rate, 2 year from today

---

CONCEPT 2.2

A spot rate is the implied rate between two forward rates. The *term structure* of interest rates generally is meant to refer to the to spot and forward rate curves, not the coupon (yield) curve.

The liquidity preference theory incorporates elements of both the rational expectations theory and the market segmentation theory. The liquidity preference theory explains all three observations of the term structure of interest rates:

1. Interest rates across different maturities tend to move together. That is, they are positively correlated.
2. The yield curve tends to exhibit a steep positive slope when short-term rates are low and a negative slope when short-term rates are high.
3. For the most part, the yield curve exhibits an upward-sloping bias.

The use of spot rates to price bonds is complicated by the fact that the market for zero coupon bonds is not liquid. Consequently, it is difficult to observe "market" spot rates. As a result of this, theoretical spot rates are derived from coupon bonds that are quoted along the coupon yield curve. Using the derived spot rates, one is able to price bonds and their related derivatives.

2.4   MODELING THE TERM STRUCTURE OF INTEREST RATES

The remainder of this chapter demonstrates the R package *termstrc* maintained by Josef Hayden and implemented by Bond Lab®. Readers are encouraged to refer to the article written by Ferstl and Hayden supporting the package. The article provides a definitive description of the methods used to fit the term structure of interest rate [Ferstal and Hayden 2010].

The package termstrc includes all the components required to determine theoretical spot rates. The termstrc package implements the McCullough cubic spline model, the Nelson-Siegel model, as well as extensions to the model. The cubic spline model is non-parametric while the Nelson-Siegel model is parametric.

Parametric term structure models employ an indirect method to derive the required discount rates by fitting the forward curve to derive spot rates. A direct method, like the cubic spline approach, solves for the required discount rates to price bonds. Parametric methods, like Nelson-Siegel, yield output that can be interpreted with respect to the level, slope, and shape of the term structure. As a result, the output from these methods provides some intuition to the investor for understanding the evolution of both the forward and spot rates. It is for this reason that the example presented next implements the Nelson-Siegel model for calculating theoretical forward and spot rates.

The Nelson-Siegel approach for modeling the spot rate curve is outlined by Ferstel and Hayden [Ferstal and Hayden 2010].

The instantaneous forward rate is given by the following:

$$f(m_{ij}, \beta) = \beta_0 + \beta_1 exp\left(-\frac{m_{ij}}{\tau_1}\right) + \beta_2 \left[\left(\frac{m_{ij}}{\tau_1}\right) exp\left(-\frac{m_{ij}}{\tau_1}\right)\right] \quad (2.8)$$

where: $\beta_1 > 0$, The long-term forward rate
β_2 = The size and location of the hump in the yield curve
τ_1 = Location parameter for the hump in the yield curve
m_{ij} = Maturity vector

Once solved, the parameter vector $\beta = (\beta_0, \beta_1, \beta_2, \tau_1)$ allows for the calculation of the spot rate as the average of the forward rates as follows, subject to

$$s(m_{ij}, \beta) = \frac{1}{m_{ij}} \int_0^{m_{ij}} f(m_{ij}, \beta) \, dm_{ij} \quad (2.9)$$

which results in the spot rate function below:

$$s(m_{ij}, \beta) = \beta_0 + \beta_1 \frac{1 - exp\left(-\frac{m_{ij}}{\tau_1}\right)}{\frac{m_{ij}}{\tau_1}} + \beta_2 \left[\frac{1 - exp\left(-\frac{m_{ij}}{\tau_1}\right)}{\frac{m_{ij}}{\tau_1}} - exp\left(-\frac{m_{ij}}{\tau_1}\right)\right]$$

$$(2.10)$$

Finally, the discount or present value factor is given by:

$$e^{-m_{ij},s(m_{ij}\beta)/100} \qquad (2.11)$$

The interpretation of the Nelson-Siegel coefficients is as follows:

where: $\beta_0 = \lim_{mj} \rightarrow \infty s(m_{ij}, \beta)$ the long-term interest rate
  subject to: $\beta_1 > 0$ non-negative interest rate constraint
  $\beta_1 =$ the rate at which the spot rate converges to the long-term
    slope of the term strutcure
  if $\beta_1 > 0$, then a downward-sloping term structure
  if $\beta_1 < 0$, then a upward-sloping term strucuture
  $\beta_2 =$ defines the size and location of the hump in the yield curve
  if $\beta_2 > 0$ then the hump occurs at τ_1
  if $\beta_2 < 0$ then the trough occurs at τ_1

2.4.1 Relationship of the Yield Curve to Spot Rates and Forward Rates

The above suggests the following relationship between the yield curve, the spot rate curve, and the forward rate curve.

- When the yield curve is upward sloping, the the spot curve lies above the yield curve and the forward rate curve lies above the spot rate curve.
- When the yield curve is downward sloping, the spot rate curve lies below the yield curve and the forward rate curve lies below the spot rate curve.

2.5 APPLICATION OF SPOT AND FORWARD RATES

Consider the interest rate swap curve quoted as of January 30, 2006, presented in Figure 2.1 [Governors of the Federal Reserve System no date]. Overall, the curve is upward sloping with a inflection point occurring at the two-year maturity. Thereafter, the interest rate swap curve is upward sloping. The 30-year swap rate is 5.08%.

Based on our knowledge of the term structure of interest rates, we would expect the following:

- The forward and spot rate curve should slip below the coupon curve at earlier maturities.
- Given the overall upward-sloping bias, both the forward and spot rate curves should cross over and lie above the coupon curve at the later maturities.

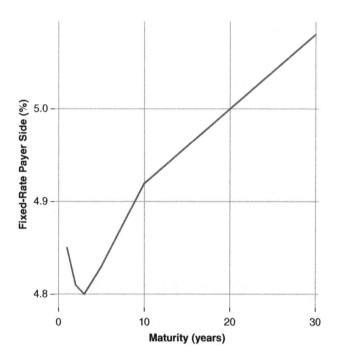

FIGURE 2.1   Interest Rate Swap Curve, Jan. 30, 2006

Figure 2.2 illustrates both the forward and spot rate curve derived from the Jan. 30, 2006, interest rate swap curve. The spot rate curve follows our intuition as well as the coefficients of the Nelson-Siegel terms.

Table 2.5 summarize the model's coefficients. For the most part, the coefficients align with intuition, based on our knowledge of the term structure. The notable exception is β_1, which suggests that the slope of the term structure is modestly negative. Again, this is due to the inversion of the yield curve between the one-month rate and the two-year rate.

The coefficients in Table 2.5 follow our intuition with respect to the relationship between the yield (coupon) curve, spot rate curve, and forward rate curve. However, the valuation of fixed-income securities requires that the investor move beyond simply spot rates and one-month forward rates. Given a spot rate curve any forward rate can be derived. It may be necessary for the valuation of certain fixed-income securities to derive a forward rate curve other than the one-month forward rate.

For example, valuing a floating rate bond whose coupon payment is indexed to a rate whose tenor is greater than one-month, like three-month or six-month LIBOR, requires the computation of a similar forward rate.

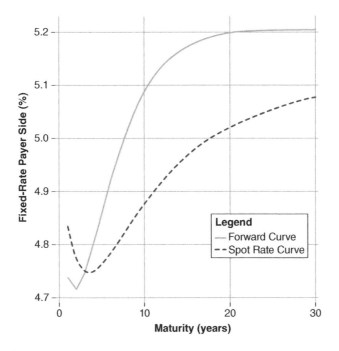

FIGURE 2.2 Forward and Spot Swap Rates, Jan. 30, 2006

TABLE 2.5 Nelson-Siegel Terms

Nelson-Siegel Terms	Value	Interpretation
β_0	5.20	The long term interest rate is 5.20
β_1	-0.35	Implies a downward slope of the term structure
β_2	-0.90	Implies a trough at τ_1
τ_1	3.00	Implies a trough at 2.6 years
$\beta_0 + \beta_1$	4.96	Instantenous short rate

Another example is a mortgage-backed security whose cash flows are contingent on borrower prepayment rates, which are correlated to the prevailing mortgage rate. In the case of a mortgage-backed security, the MBS pool's expected prepayment rate determines the timing of the principal cash flows returned to the investor. The expected prepayment is closely tied to the 10-year swap rate because it influences the prevailing mortgage rate. As a result, the investor is required to calculate the 10-year forward swap rate in order to estimate the forward mortgage rate which in turn motivates her prepayment model (Chapter 9). The above illustrates the extent to which the term structure influences the valuation of structured securities. Indeed, it may be argued, given the extent of the embedded options observed across the structured securities market, a thorough understanding of the term structure is a basic requirement for the valuation thereof.

The forward rate between any two spot rates is given by the equation below:

$$\left[\left(\frac{1+s_2^{t+n}}{1+s_1^t}\right)^{\frac{1}{n}}\right]-1 \qquad (2.12)$$

where: $s_{1,2}$ = The spot rate at t and $t+n$
t = Beginning time period
n = Time interval between spot rates

For example, in Table 2.6 the two-year forward rate in one month (or in the next month) is given by:

$$\left[\left(\frac{1.04769^{2.0833}}{1.049465^{.0833}}\right)^{\frac{1}{2}}\right]-1 \qquad (2.13)$$

$$\text{which results in: } 1.047616, \qquad (2.14)$$

$$f_{(24,1)} = 4.7616\% \qquad (2.15)$$

The two-year forward rate can be confirmed by employing equation 2.1. The horizon return by investing in the one-month spot rate and reinvesting the proceeds at maturity into the two-year forward rate should equal the future value factor of the two-year and one-month spot rate.

$$\text{Horizon return} = (1.004)(1.00975) = 1.10189 \qquad (2.16)$$

The annualized rate of return is:

$$1.10189^{(1/2.0833)} = 4.4768\% \qquad (2.17)$$

The spot rate curve is not easily observed in the market. As a result, spot rates are derived from the coupon or yield curve. The spot rate curve implies both present value and future value factors. The present value factors may be used to value periodic cash flows as zero coupon instruments occurring

TABLE 2.6 Calculation of Forward Rates

Period	Time$_t$	Present Value Factor	Future Value Factor	Spot Rate	1-Month Forward	2-Year Forward
1	0.0833	0.9960	1.0040	4.9465		
2	0.1667	0.9920	1.0081	4.9335	4.9206	4.7616
3	0.2500	0.9881	1.0121	4.9212	4.8966	4.7521
4	0.3333	0.9842	1.0161	4.9095	4.8743	4.7436
5	0.4167	0.9803	1.0201	4.8983	4.8538	4.7361
6	0.5000	0.9764	1.0241	4.8878	4.8349	4.7295
7	0.5833	0.9726	1.0282	4.8777	4.8175	4.7238
8	0.6667	0.9688	1.0322	4.8682	4.8015	4.7189
9	0.7500	0.9650	1.0362	4.8592	4.7870	4.7148
10	0.8333	0.9613	1.0403	4.8506	4.7737	4.7114
11	0.9167	0.9576	1.0443	4.8425	4.7617	4.7087
12	1.0000	0.9539	1.0483	4.8349	4.7509	4.7067
13	1.0833	0.9502	1.0524	4.8277	4.7411	4.7052
14	1.1667	0.9466	1.0565	4.8209	4.7325	
15	1.2500	0.9429	1.0605	4.8145	4.7248	
16	1.3333	0.9393	1.0646	4.8084	4.7180	
17	1.4167	0.9357	1.0687	4.8028	4.7122	
18	1.5000	0.9321	1.0728	4.7975	4.7072	
19	1.5833	0.9286	1.0769	4.7925	4.7030	
20	1.6667	0.9250	1.0811	4.7878	4.6995	
21	1.7500	0.9215	1.0852	4.7835	4.6968	
22	1.8333	0.9180	1.0894	4.7795	4.6947	
23	1.9167	0.9145	1.0935	4.7757	4.6932	
24	2.0000	0.9110	1.0977	4.7722	4.6923	
25	2.0833	0.9075	1.1019	4.7690	4.6920	
26	2.1667	0.9040	1.1061	4.7661	4.6922	
...						
36	3.0000	0.8701	1.1493	4.7484	4.7163	

at each point along the spot rate curve. Conversely, the future value factors define both horizon returns for zero coupon bonds as well as the implied forward rates that can be observed between two spot rates. Because of the above properties, the spot rate curve is used to price fixed-income securities and their related credit derivatives.

CHAPTER 3

Fixed-Income Metrics

But those who came before … will teach you from the wisdom of former generations.

Job 8:10

In this chapter, basic fixed-income mathematics are introduced. The chapter begins with an introduction to the concept of the maturity of a bond, followed by the pricing convention *yield to maturity,* which was briefly discussed in Chapter 1. Following yield to maturity is the concept of weighted average life. Understanding weighted average life is key to understanding the central risk measure of fixed-income securities, namely, *duration* and *convexity.* Duration and convexity measure the price sensitivity of fixed-income securities to changes in interest rates. These risk measures allow the investor to manage the interest rate and term structure risk that is inherent in any fixed-income portfolio.

This chapter is organized to take the reader step-by-step from the simple concept of the maturity of a fixed-income security to the more complex concepts of *effective duration, effective convexity,* and finally *key rate duration*—measures of risk. Key rate duration not only measures the overall sensitivity of the price of a bond to changes in interest rates but also measures the sensitivity of a portfolio of cash flows to changes in the level and slope of the yield curve. Understanding this relationship is critical to successfully investing in mortgage-backed and-asset backed securities.

The term structure of interest rates plays a central role in deriving these risk metrics. It is the basic input for calculating the above measures of risk and thereby provides a link between price and risk.

3.1 MATURITY

The maturity date of a bond is the date on which the principal balance due to the investor is paid. The investor is repaid the amount of principal owed and the borrower's contracted interest payments cease. At this point the bond is said to have *matured*. The concept of maturity is straightforward in the case of a single payment of principal at a specified date.

3.2 YIELD TO MATURITY

The yield to maturity is the discount rate that equates the present value of the cash flow's received from a bond to the price paid for the bond. It is the internal rate of return. From Concept 1.1, a non-callable bond paying a coupon over its term and returning principal at maturity can be priced as a combination of an annuity (the coupon payments) and a zero coupon bond (the principal payment).

The yield to maturity is the discount rate (i) applied to each set of cash flows to determine the sum of the present value—price—of the bond. Thus, the present value of a series of cash flows from a coupon paying bond with a principal payment at maturity can be written as:

$$\text{Present value (price)} = [\text{Coupon}]\left[\frac{1 - \frac{1}{(1+i)^n}}{i}\right] + [\text{Principal}]\left[\frac{1}{(1+i)^n}\right]$$

(3.1)

Bond prices are generally quoted in one of three ways:

- Yield to maturity YTM, which requires the investor to solve for price.
- The spread to the yield curve, which requires the investor to first solve for the YTM by adding the quoted spread to the pricing point on the yield curve and second solve for the price of the bond given its yield to maturity (pricing benchmark + spread).
- Price, which requires the investor to solve for yield to maturity and spread to the coupon curve.

Of the three conventions above, price to yield is the most difficult because the investor is required to iteratively solve for the yield. That is, estimate the yield to maturity, and then either raise or lower her estimate depending on the resultant price. One can begin to solve the yield to maturity calculation with an estimate. Estimating the yield to maturity assures the investor that the initial value used in the process is in the appropriate solution space thereby reducing the number of iterations required to solve for the actual yield to maturity. The estimated yield to maturity is given by equation 3.2. Notice, the numerator measured the value of the annuity received in a given period. The denominator states the amount laid out in a given period to attain the bond annuity. Thus, the estimated yield to maturity is simply a shorthand equation approximating the internal rate of return discussed in Chapter 1.

$$\text{Estimated YTM} = \frac{(c)(fv) + \frac{fv-p}{n}}{\frac{fv+p}{cf}} \qquad (3.2)$$

where: c = coupon rate
       fv = face value "notional principal" balance of the bond
       p = price
       n = number of years to maturity
       cf = frequency of coupon payment

Consider a 5.0% coupon bond priced at par ($100) that pays its coupon semi-annually with a maturity of 10 years. Table 3.1 illustrates the estimated yield to maturity given a price and highlights two important points:

1. There is an inverse relationship between a bond's yield to maturity and its price. That is, as the yield to maturity increases, the bond's price declines. Similarly, as the yield to maturity declines, the price of the bond increases.
2. The further the price of the bond from par, the greater the error in the estimated yield to maturity versus the actual yield to maturity.

TABLE 3.1   Estimated YTM

Price	Est. YTM	Act. YTM
92	6.04%	6.08%
94	5.77%	5.80%
96	5.51%	5.53%
98	5.25%	5.26%
100	5.00%	5.00%
102	4.75%	4.75%
104	4.51%	4.50%
106	4.27%	4.26%
108	4.04%	4.02%

The differences between the estimated and actual yield to maturity presented in Table 3.1 arise because the estimated yield to maturity is a linear approximation, while the bond price to yield to maturity relationship is non-linear (Figure 3.1). As a result, solving for the yield to maturity given price is an iterative calculation. Nonetheless, the estimated yield to maturity provides a precise estimate of the solution space to begin the iteration to solve for the actual yield to maturity.

Figure 3.1 illustrates the point. The price of the bond given yield is not linear. As the yield to maturity declines the price of the bond is less than that expected assuming a linear relationship. Conversely, as the yield to maturity increases the price of the bond is greater than that implied by assuming a linear relationship. Figure 3.1 clearly shows that the relationship of a non-callable bond's price to its yield to maturity is convex. Thus, in this example, the further the price of the bond from par or $100 the greater the difference between the linear approximation and the actual price of the bond. This relationship is referred to as the convexity of a bond.

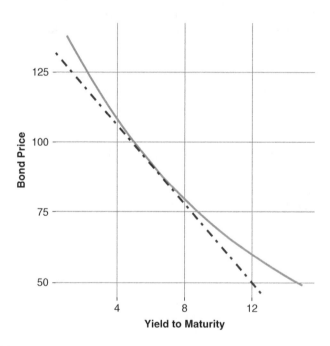

FIGURE 3.1 Price to Yield to Maturity

The relationship between the price of a bond and its yield to maturity is limited by the following boundary conditions:

- An investor generally requires a positive return on her investment. Specifically, the yield to maturity cannot fall below zero percent.[1] The non-negative interest rate assumption results in a upper limit on the price of a bond.
- The price of a bond cannot fall below zero. This is because a creditor cannot by definition owe a debtor. Thus, as interest rates rise the price of the bond falls at a declining rate.

CONCEPT 3.1

In equation 3.1, a bond is presented as a bundle of annuity cash flows (coupon) and a single payment (principal). In practice, all fixed-income securities are not structured in this manner. Fixed-income securities may return principal (amortize) over the life of the investment. Examples are: sinking fund bonds and securities collateralized by consumer loans, like mortgages, whose monthly payment schedules include both interest and principal.

Consider Table 3.2, a fixed-income investment with a term of four years, which pays a 5% coupon semi-annually and $250 annual principal payment. This type of structure is a sinking fund bond.

In the case presented, the cash flow of the bond is such that one may not generalize either the price or yield to maturity as shown in equation 3.1. Consequently, when calculating either the price or yield to maturity the investor must give consideration to both the size and timing of the expected cash flows. Indeed, the nature of MBS and structured securities is such that investors generally recognize both the return of principal, via loan amortization, as well as interest payments on a monthly or quarterly basis. Furthermore, MBS cash flows are contingent in nature. Consequently, the generalized price/yield equation presented in 3.1 is not applicable to

---

[1] The exception to this rule may occur during times of crisis when investors may be willing to accept a modest negative yield from sovereign guaranteed debt in exchange for the certainty of the return of their principal.

TABLE 3.2   Yield to Maturity

Period	Coupon Income	Principal Pmt.	Total Cash Flow
0.5	$25	$0	$25
1.0	$25	$250	$275
1.5	$18.75	$0	$18.75
2.0	$18.75	$250	$268.75
2.5	$12.50	$0	$12.50
3.0	$12.50	$250	$262.50
3.5	$6.25	$0	$6.25
4.0	$6.25	$250	$256.25
Total	$125	$1,000	$1,125

mortgage-backed securities. The equation to determine the price or internal rate of return—yield to maturity—may be rewritten as follows:

$$(FV)\,(Price) = \sum_{t=1}^{n} \vec{CF}_n \frac{1}{(1+i)^n}, n_t \tag{3.3}$$

where: FV = Face value or principal amount
Price = Price expressed as a percentage of the face value (FV)
$\vec{CF}_n$ = Vector of cash flows
i = Discount rate
n = Period

Table 3.3 reports the yield to maturity for the bond cash flows presented in Table 3.2 versus that of bond whose principal is returned at maturity. Notice the following:

- At a price below par—that is, the bond is priced at a "discount"—its yield to maturity increases.
- Conversely, at a price above par—a "premium"—the yield to maturity declines.

TABLE 3.3   Yield to Maturity, Sinking Fund Bond vs. Single Payment at Maturity

Price	Sinking Fund Bond YTM	Single Payment YTM
$97.00	6.35%	5.85%
$100.00	5.00%	5.00%
$103.00	3.72%	4.17%

These two scenarios reflect both the inverse nature of the price-versus-yield relationship but also the impact of the early return of principal on the yield to maturity of a bond that repays principal over its life rather than at maturity. Specifically:

- When a bond is priced at a discount and principal is returned early the yield to maturity increases relative to the "bullet bond" which returns principal at maturity because discount cash flows are returned early at par which is above the price paid for the cash flow.
- Conversely, when a bond is priced at a premium and principal is returned early, the yield to maturity declines relative to the "bullet bond" because premium cash flows are returned early at par which is below the price paid for the cash flow.

CONCEPT 3.2

The early return of principal impacts the investor's realized yield to maturity. When a bond is priced at a discount and principal is returned early, the yield to maturity increases. Conversely, when a bond is priced at a premium and principal is returned early, the yield to maturity declines.

The flaw of the yield to maturity calculation is the assumption that the cash flows received from a bond may be reinvested at a rate that is equal to its yield to maturity. In reality, interest rates may either rise or fall over the investor's holding period. Changing interest rates subject the investor to reinvestment rate risk, or the risk that the investor may have to reinvest coupon and/or principal proceeds at a rate that is different than the yield-to-maturity.

Aside from maturity, the risk measures that define fixed-income securities include: weighted average life, duration, and convexity. The sections that follow outline each.

3.3 WEIGHTED AVERAGE LIFE

How is the investor to think about the maturity of a bond whose return of principal occurs periodically over the term of the bond like the sinking fund example illustrated in Exhibit 3.2? To answer this question, consider the portfolio presented in Table 3.3 consisting of two zero coupon bonds

30   VALUATION OF FIXED-INCOME SECURITIES

each with a face value of $1,000. The average maturity is 2.5 years ($1,000 × 2) + ($1,000 × 5)/$2,000.

The weighted average time to the return of principal of the portfolio in Table 3.4 is 2.5 years. The weights used to compute the weighted average life are the notional principal balance of each zero coupon bond and not the investment proceeds (principal × price) because the investor receives the full principal balance at maturity.

The computation of weighted average life as presented in Table 3.4 can be extended to any fixed-income security that returns some principal over the life of the investment prior to the final or stated maturity. Table 3.5 illustrates the computation of weighted average life for the sinking fund bond example presented in Table 3.2. Like the portfolio of zero coupon bonds the average life is calculated as a weighted average of the return of principal multiplied by the time to receipt of principal. The example suggests that the receipt of principal prior to maturity can be treated like the maturity of a zero coupon bond when calculating weighted average life.

In the case of a bond that periodically returns principal to the investor, like a bond collateralized by consumer installment payments, the "maturity" of the bond is the termination date of the contract, which is

TABLE 3.4 Zero Coupon Bond Portfolio Weighted Average Life

Holding	Face Value	Maturity	Yield to Maturity	Value
Bond 1	$1,000	2 years	2.0%	$980.20
Bond 2	$1,000	5 years	3.0%	$862.60
	$2,000	2.5 years	2.45%	$1,842.80

TABLE 3.5 Weighted Average Life

Period	Coupon Income	Principal Pmt.	Total Cash Flow	Principal × Period
0.5	$25	$0	$25	$0
1.0	$25	$250	$275	$500
1.5	$18.75	$0	$18.75	$0
2.0	$18.75	$250	$268.75	$1000
2.5	$12.50	$0	$12.50	$0
3.0	$12.50	$250	$262.50	$1500
3.5	$6.25	$0	$6.25	$0
4.0	$6.25	$250	$256.25	$2,000
Total	$125	$1,000	Weighted Average Life	2.5 years

defined as the final payment date on which the loan's principal balance is paid in full.

The weighted average life measures the average time the investor's principal is outstanding. In the example presented in Figure 3.2, the weighted average life is 2.5 years. Notice, the return of interest is not part of the weighted average life calculation. Thus, weighted average life speaks only to the timing of the return of principal. When considering the weighted average life of an amortizing asset, the investor must also consider the final payment date. The final payment reports the date or timing of the last principal cash flow to the investor. The cash flow presented in Table 3.2 reports a final payment in the fourth period.

Combining the weighted average life and final payment date allows the investor to assess the average time principal is outstanding as well as the *tail risk* of outstanding cash flows. The formula for weighted average life can be written as follows:

$$\frac{\sum_{i=1}^{n} P_n}{fv}, n \qquad (3.4)$$

where: P_n = The amount of principal returned at period n
fv = The face value of total principal amount of the bond
n_i = the period in which the principal was returned

Because the weighted average life measures the average time that principal is outstanding it may be thought of as a measure of credit risk. Specifically, it measures the average time over which the investor may expect the return of his principal. Credit risk is defined as the risk of loss of principal. Thus, it stands to reason, a bond with a shorter weighted average life carries less relative credit risk than one with a longer weighted average life because a longer maturity bond, all else equal, carries a greater risk of default over time than that of a shorter maturity bond.

3.4 DURATION

There are five measures of duration: Macaulay duration [Macaulay 1938], modified duration, Fisher-Weil duration [Lawrence Fisher 1972], effective duration, and key rate duration [Ho 1992]; each builds on the foundation laid by the prior. The following sections outline lineage of duration.

- Macaulay and modified duration compute duration as a function of the yield to maturity. Because they use the bond's yield to maturity (IRR) these measures are said to assume a *linear* term structure of interest rates—that is, the same discount rate over time.

- Fisher-Weil, effective, and key rate duration are calculated using the spot rate curve. Because they use the spot rate curve to calculate duration, these measures are said to allow for a *non-linear* term structure assumption.

What is duration? Duration is the weighted average time to recovery of principal taking into account all cash flows [Schultz 1986]. It is the sum of the present value of the bond's cash flows weighted by time. It differs from average life in the following ways:

- First, it takes into account the receipt of principal and interest.
- Second, it accounts for the time value of money because the discounted present value of the cash flows are weighted by time rather than the nominal receipt of principal.

3.4.1 Macaulay Duration

Macaulay duration is given by the following equation:[2]

$$\sum_{i=1}^{n} \frac{\frac{cf_n}{(1+i)^n}}{\sum_{i=1}^{n} \frac{cf_n}{(1+i)^n}}, n_i \qquad (3.5)$$

where: cf_n = The cash flow recieved at period n
i = The yield to maturity or internal rate of return
n_i = the period in which the cash flow was received

Consider a 10-year note that pays a 3% coupon semi-annually and is priced at \$100-0/32nds. The duration of the note is 8.71. Table 3.6 illustrates the computation of Macaulay duration:

- The discount factor is computed using the yield to maturity.
- The present value of each individual cash flow is divided by the bond price.
- Finally, the contribution of each individual cash flow to the present value or price of the bond is weighted by time, the sum of which is Macaulay duration.

---

[2]A closed form solution to Macaulay duration exists but it can only be applied to bonds that pay their principal at maturity. As a result, its utility is limited.

TABLE 3.6 Macaulay Duration Calculation

Period	Time	Cash Flow	P.V. Factor	P.V.	P.V. / Price	P.V × Time
1	0.50	15.00	0.9852	14.7782	1.4778	0.7389
2	1.00	15.00	0.9706	14.5597	1.4559	1.4560
3	1.50	15.00	0.9563	14.3445	1.4344	2.1517
4	2.00	15.00	0.9422	14.1328	1.4133	2.8265
5	2.50	15.00	0.9282	13.9234	1.3924	3.4809
6	3.00	15.00	0.9145	13.7181	1.3718	4.1154
7	3.50	15.00	0.9010	13.3157	1.3515	4.7304
8	4.00	15.00	0.8877	13.3149	1.3316	5.3263
9	4.50	15.00	0.8745	13.1189	1.3119	5.9044
10	5.00	15.00	0.8616	12.9250	1.2925	6.4625
11	5.50	15.00	0.8489	12.7340	1.2734	7.0036
12	6.00	15.00	0.8363	12.5458	1.2546	7.5275
13	6.50	15.00	0.8240	12.3604	1.2360	8.0342
14	7.00	15.00	0.8118	12.1777	1.2177	8.5244
15	7.50	15.00	0.7998	11.9978	1.1998	8.9983
16	8.00	15.00	0.7879	11.8204	1.1820	9.4563
17	8.50	15.00	0.7763	11.6458	1.1645	9.8989
18	9.00	15.00	0.7648	11.4738	1.1437	10.3263
19	9.50	15.00	0.7535	11.3041	1.1304	10.7389
20	10.00	1015.00	0.7424	753.6075	75.3607	753.6075
					Duration	8.71

■ Macaulay duration may be thought of as the half-life, not the average life, of a bond. It measures the investor's time to recovery of the initial principal investment. Macaulay duration is quoted in years. For example, the Macaulay duration presented in Table 3.6 is quoted in years (8.71).

CONCEPT 3.3

Unlike weighted average life, Macaulay duration makes no distinction between coupon interest and the payment of principal. Rather, like the yield to maturity calculation, cash flows are not discriminated with respect to interest or principal. The indiscriminate treatment of cash flows not only sets the foundation for the valuation of fixed-income securities but is central to the structuring and securitization of consumer installment contracts.

Macaulay duration is somewhat analogous to weighted average life in that it is a measure of the return of the investor's initial investment. Thus, Macaulay duration can be thought of as an alternative measure to credit risk. Specifically, once the investor recoups her initial investment the risk of loss due to default is limited to opportunity cost or loss of investment return that she expected to receive on her initial investment.

3.4.2 Modified Duration

Modified duration differs from Macaulay duration in that modified duration indicates the approximate percentage change in the price of a bond given a 100 basis point change in the yield to maturity [Sack and Wright 2006]. Because modified duration estimates the change in price given a change in yield it is a common measure of risk used across the fixed-income markets.

The equation for modified duration is:

$$\frac{\text{Macauley Duration}}{1 + \left[\frac{ytm}{n}\right]} \tag{3.6}$$

Where: n = number of coupon payments per year

         ytm = the yield to maturity

Returning to the example presented in Table 3.6 the modified duration of a 10-year note that pays a 3.0% coupon semi-annually and priced at par to yield 3.0% is:

$$8.58 = \frac{8.71}{1 + (0.03/2)} \tag{3.7}$$

Equation 3.8 states duration as the percentage change in price given a 1% or 100-basis-point change in the interest rate. In the case of the 10-year note above the expected price change given a 1% change in interest rates is 8.58%. The equation for the percentage change in price given a change in the interest rate is:

$$\Delta \text{Bond price} = -\text{Duration} \times \Delta(i/100) \tag{3.8}$$

Using the example in equation 3.8, the percentage change in price is 8.58% given a 1% change in the assumed interest rate. For example, a 100-basis-point decline in the interest rate results in a 8.58% increase in the price of the bond.

$$0.0858 = -8.58 \times -0.01 \tag{3.9}$$

In the case of a 100-basis-point decline in the prevailing interest rate, the predicted price of the bond is:

$$\text{Bond price} = 100 + (-0.0858 \times -100)$$

$$\text{Bond price} = \$108.58$$

In the case of a 100-basis-point increase in the prevailing interest rate, the predicted price of the bond is:

$$\text{Bond price} = 100 + (-0.0858 \times 100)$$

$$\text{Bond price} = \$91.42$$

Duration is inversely related to both the bond's coupon rate and its yield to maturity. Figure 3.2 graphically depicts the relationship between the coupon and duration of a 10-year note priced at par. The figure demonstrates the following points:

- When the bond is a zero coupon bond, it makes no periodic coupon payments, and its duration is equal to its maturity. Because duration is

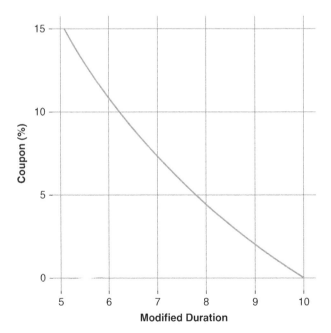

FIGURE 3.2 Coupon versus Duration

a measure of the time to recovery and a zero coupon bond returns all of its expected cash flow at maturity, the time to recovery is equal to the time to maturity.

Extending this concept further, the duration of a spot rate is equal to its tenor along the term structure of interest rates.

■ There is an inverse relationship between the coupon a bond pays and its duration. As the coupon received by the investor increases, the duration of the bond decreases because the present value of the cash flows are weighted by time, and as the coupon increases a greater share of the investor's return is derived from the coupon income rather then the return of principal.

For example, in the case of the 3% 10-year note, the coupon return over the life of the bond is $300, which represents 23% of the total cash flow paid to the investor. In the case of a 6% coupon bond, the coupon income earned over the life of the bond is $600, representing 37.5% of the total cash flow paid to the investor. Simply stated, the more coupon income received by the investor, the less time it takes for the investor to recuperate her initial investment resulting in a shorter duration.

There is a positive relationship between the maturity of a bond and its duration. All else equal, modified duration increases with maturity. Figure 3.3 illustrates the relationship between maturity and the modified duration's of two 10-year notes—one that pays a 3% coupon and the other that pays a 6% coupon.

■ Modified duration increases as the maturity of the bond increases. However, the rate of increase in modified duration is asymptotic. Meaning, modified duration increases at a decreasing rate as maturity increases.

■ The coupon of the bond determines the rate at which duration increases with yield to maturity. Figure 3.3 shows that the 6% note reaches its asymptote much sooner than the note that pays a 3% coupon. Recall from Figure 3.2 the inverse relationship between coupon and duration. As a result, the 6% coupon bond will reach its asymptotic inflection point much sooner.

■ Extending the intuition above, a zero coupon bond's duration moves one-for-one with changes in maturity.

In summary:

■ Macaulay duration is the half-life of a bond. It measures the time until the investor recovers her initial investment. As such, Macaulay

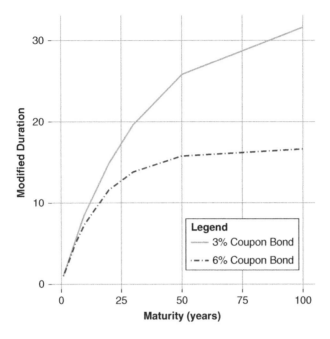

FIGURE 3.3 Maturity versus Duration

duration can be interpreted as a measure of credit risk because it is a measure of time.

- Modified duration measures the percentage change in the price of a bond given a 1% change in interest rates. It is widely used as a measure of price risk in the fixed-income markets.
- The approximation of price given $\Delta(i)$ is local, so it is most accurate at the tangent to the actual price yield relationship. It is also most accurate when $\Delta(i)$ is smaller because it is a linear approximation and does not take into account convexity of bond prices.

3.5 CONVEXITY

From equation 3.8 it is clear that modified duration is a linear approximation of the change in the price of a bond given a change in interest rates. The graphical representation presented in Figure 3.1 shows that the price to yield relationship of a bond is not linear. Rather, the relationship between a bond's change in yield and change in price is convex. The convexity of a bond measures the second order change in the price of a bond given a change in the interest rate. The formula for convexity is [Sack and Wright 2006]:

$$\left(\frac{1}{2}\right)\frac{\sum_{i=1}^{n} n(n+1)\left[\frac{cf_n}{(1+i)^{(n+2)}}\right]}{\sum_{i=1}^{n}\frac{cf_n}{(1+i)^n}} \tag{3.10}$$

where: cf_n = The cash flow recieved at period n
i = The yield to maturity or internal rate of return
n_i = the period in which the cash flow was received

Table 3.7 illustrates the calculation of convexity for the 10-year note presented in Table 3.6. Convexity is calculated in much the same manner as duration:

- Convexity "time weight" is $n(n+1)$.
- Convexity present value weight is $(1+i)^{(n+2)}$.
- Present value weight is applied to the cash flow and multiplied by the time weight.

TABLE 3.7 Calculation of Convexity

Period	Time	Cash Flow	CVX. Time	CVX. CF	CVX. CF ×Time
1	0.5	15.00	0.75	1.3923	1.0442
2	1.0	15.00	2.00	1.3718	2.7436
3	1.5	15.00	3.75	1.3515	5.0682
4	2.0	15.00	6.00	1.3315	7.9894
5	2.5	15.00	8.75	1.3118	11.4790
6	3.0	15.00	12.00	1.2925	15.5100
7	3.50	15.00	15.75	1.2734	20.0560
8	4.0	15.00	20.00	1.2545	25.0916
9	4.50	15.00	24.75	1.2360	30.5920
10	5.0	15.00	30.00	1.2177	36.5332
11	5.5	15.00	35.75	1.1997	42.8920
12	6.0	15.00	42.00	1.1820	49.6459
13	6.5	15.00	48.75	1.1645	56.7731
14	7.0	15.00	56.00	1.1473	64.2525
15	7.5	15.00	63.75	1.1304	72.0637
16	8.0	15.00	72.00	1.1137	80.1868
17	8.5	15.00	80.75	1.0972	88.6026
18	9.0	15.00	90.00	1.0810	97.2928
19	9.5	15.00	99.75	1.0650	106.2392
20	10.0	1015.00	110.00	71.004	7810.4078
				Convexity	43.12

Convexity is related to duration, much like duration is related to maturity. Specifically, as the duration of a bond increases its convexity also increases. Figure 3.4 shows that, holding all else equal, the convexity of a bond increases by the square of its duration. From Figures 3.3 and 3.4 we can reason the following relationships:

- Holding maturity constant, a bond with a lower coupon will have greater convexity than one with a higher coupon.
- Since, duration increases at a decreasing rate with maturity, convexity must also do the same.

Using both modified duration and convexity one can estimate the change in the price of a bond given a change in interest rates as follows:

$$\Delta \text{Bond price} = -\text{Duration} \times \Delta(i/100) + \text{Convexity} \times \Delta(i/100)^2 \quad (3.11)$$

Using the example of 10-year bond that pays a 3% coupon semi-annually and priced at par; the predicted price change given a 1% or 100 basis change in interest rates is:

$$\text{Bond price} = -8.58 \times .01 + 43.12 \times 0.01^2$$
$$\text{Bond price} = -0.0858 + 0.0043$$
$$\text{Bond price} = -0.0815$$

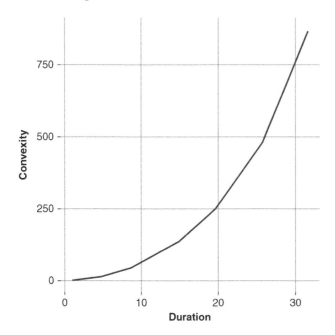

FIGURE 3.4 Convexity versus Duration

In the case of a 100-basis-point decline in interest rates the predicted price is:

$$\text{Bond price} = 100 + (-0.0815 \times -100)$$

$$\text{Bond price} = \$108.15$$

In the case of a 100-basis-point increase in interest rates the predicted price is:

$$\text{Bond price} = 100 + (-0.0815 \times 100)$$

$$\text{Bond price} = \$91.85$$

The Macaulay duration, modified duration, and convexity calculations presented in equations 3.5, 3.6, and 3.10 assume a flat term structure of interest rates. Specifically, they use the bond's yield to maturity or internal rate of return as the discount factor in their computation.

3.6 FISHER-WEIL DURATION AND CONVEXITY

Lawrence Fischer and Roman Weil proposed an alternative measure of duration and convexity based on the spot rate curve [Lawrence Fisher 1972]. *Fisher-Weil duration* and convexity are calculated the same way as Macaulay duration. However, rather than using the bond's yield to maturity as the discount factor, Fisher-Weil proposed using the spot rate curve, the term structure of interest rates. Assume the yield curve presented in Table 3.8. The resulting spot and forward rate curves are depicted in Figure 3.5.

3.6.1 Fisher-Weil Duration

Returning to the example of a 10-year note that pays a 3% coupon semi-annually, the note is priced at par with a yield to maturity of 3.0%.

TABLE 3.8 Hypothetical Yield Curve

Tenor	1-yr.	2-yr.	3-yr.	5-yr.	10-yr.	20-yr.	30-yr.
	1.00%	1.50%	1.75%	2.15%	3.00%	3.60%	3.75%

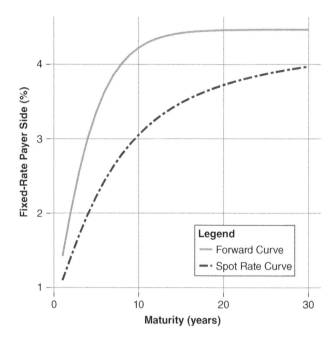

FIGURE 3.5 Hypothetical Spot and Forward Rate Curves

From equations 3.6 and 3.10 we know that the modified duration of the note is 8.58 and the convexity is 43.12. Table 3.9 illustrates the calculation of Fisher-Weil duration using the hypothetical spot rate curve presented in Figure 3.5.

Given a yield to maturity of 3.0%, the present value of the cash flows is $1,000 and the price of the bond is par. However, discounting the cash flows along the spot rate curve results in a present value of $1,004.59 for a price of $100.459.

The higher price of the bond using the spot rate curve implies a lower yield to maturity, and as a result, the modified and Fisher-Weil duration measures are not comparable. To correct this situation and create directly comparable duration measures, the present value along the spot rate curve must equal the present value of the cash flows using a discount rate of 3.0%. To equate the bond's price, discounting along the spot rate curve, to the yield to maturity price of the bond the investor must solve for a constant spread to the spot rate curve that equates the spot rate price to the yield to maturity price.

TABLE 3.9 Fisher-Weil Duration

Period	Time	Cash Flow	Spot Rate	P.V. Factor	P.V.	P.V. / Price	P.V. × Time
1	0.50	15.00	0.9929	0.9951	14.9261	0.0149	0.0075
2	1.00	15.00	1.1543	0.9886	14.8288	0.0148	0.0148
3	1.50	15.00	1.3140	0.9806	14.7091	0.0147	0.0221
4	2.00	15.00	1.4701	0.9712	14.5685	0.0146	0.0291
5	2.50	15.00	1.6210	0.9606	14.4089	0.0144	0.0360
6	3.00	15.00	1.7659	0.9488	14.2326	0.0142	0.0427
7	3.50	15.00	1.9041	0.9361	14.0417	0.0140	0.0491
8	4.00	15.00	2.0353	0.9226	13.8385	0.0138	0.0554
9	4.50	15.00	2.1592	0.9083	13.6252	0.0136	0.0613
10	5.00	15.00	2.2761	0.8936	13.4036	0.0134	0.0670
11	5.50	15.00	2.3860	0.8784	13.1755	0.0132	0.0725
12	6.00	15.00	2.4891	0.8628	12.9427	0.0129	0.0777
13	6.50	15.00	2.5857	0.8471	12.7065	0.0127	0.0826
14	7.00	15.00	2.6761	0.8312	12.4682	0.0125	0.0873
15	7.50	15.00	2.7607	0.8153	12.2289	0.0122	0.0917
16	8.00	15.00	2.8398	0.7993	11.9895	0.0120	0.0959
17	8.50	15.00	2.9138	0.7834	11.7508	0.0118	0.0999
18	9.00	15.00	2.9829	0.7676	11.5135	0.0115	0.1036
19	9.50	15.00	3.0475	0.7519	11.2781	0.0113	0.1071
20	10.00	1015.00	3.1079	0.7363	747.3902	0.7474	7.4737

Fisher-Weil Duration   8.69

CONCEPT 3.4

Spread to the Spot Rate Curve: The present value of the cash flows using the spot rate curve is equalized by iteratively solving for a spread to the spot rate curve that equates the spot rate present value to the yield to maturity present value.

Comparing Tables 3.6 (Macaulay duration) and 3.9 (Fisher-Weil duration) nets the following observations given an upwardly sloping yield curve:

- The Fisher-Weil duration measure of 8.68 is higher than that of the modified duration measure of 8.58. The difference is largely due to the application of present value weights used by each measure.

- The Fisher-Weil calculation uses higher present value weights or lower discount rates *(i)* on the earlier cash flows. As a result, the Fisher-Weil duration assigns a greater relative weight to the earlier cash flows. For example, the Fisher-Weil calculation assigns a higher present value factor to the cash flow received at period six than does the Macaulay duration: 0.9488 in Table 3.9 versus 0.9145 in Table 3.6.
- Conversely, the Fisher-Weil calculation uses lower present value factors on the later cash flows than does the Macaulay duration. The Fisher-Weil present value factor applied to the cash flow received at period 20 is 0.7363 versus the Macaulay duration present value factor applied at year 20 of 0.7424.

3.6.2 Fisher-Weil Convexity

Fisher-Weil convexity is calculated in Table 3.10. Like Fisher-Weil duration, it is calculated using the spot rate curve rather than the note's yield to maturity.

TABLE 3.10 Fisher-Weil Convexity

Period	Time	Cash Flow	CVX.Time	CVX.CF	CVX.CF × Time
1	0.50	15.00	0.7500	0.0146	0.0110
2	1.00	15.00	2.0000	0.0145	0.0290
3	1.50	15.00	3.7500	0.0143	0.0537
4	2.00	15.00	6.0000	0.0141	0.0849
5	2.50	15.00	8.7500	0.0140	0.1221
6	3.00	15.00	12.0000	0.0137	0.1649
7	3.50	15.00	15.7500	0.0135	0.2130
8	4.00	15.00	20.0000	0.0133	0.2658
9	4.50	15.00	24.7500	0.0131	0.3231
10	5.00	15.00	30.0000	0.0128	0.3844
11	5.50	15.00	35.7500	0.0126	0.4493
12	6.00	15.00	42.0000	0.0123	0.5175
13	6.50	15.00	48.7500	0.0121	0.5886
14	7.00	15.00	56.0000	0.0118	0.6623
15	7.50	15.00	63.7500	0.0116	0.7382
16	8.00	15.00	72.0000	0.0113	0.8162
17	8.50	15.00	80.7500	0.0111	0.8959
18	9.00	15.00	90.0000	0.0109	0.9770
19	9.50	15.00	99.7500	0.0106	1.0594
20	10.00	1015.00	110.0000	0.7030	77.3286
			Fisher-Weil Convexity		42.84

Given a positively sloped yield curve, one would expect Fisher-Weil convexity to be less than that calculated using the yield to maturity. This is because the earlier duration and hence lower convexity cash flows are given a greater relative present value factor in an upwardly sloping yield curve environment.

3.6.3   Fisher-Weil vs. Modified Duration and Convexity

The Fisher-Weil duration and convexity measures overcome the flat term structure imposed by Macaulay duration and, like modified duration, measure a bond's price risk relative to the spot rate curve. For a bond that pays principal at maturity the time weighted present value is mostly at the maturity of the bond. Thus, Fisher-Weil duration will closely match that of the bond's maturity tenor along the spot rate curve. For example, the time-weighted present value contribution of principal in Table 3.9 is:

$$\text{Principal contribution} = \frac{\frac{(1,000)(0.7376)}{(1000)} \times 10}{8.69}$$

$$= \frac{0.7376 \times 10}{8.69}$$

$$= \frac{7.376}{8.69}$$

$$= 84.46\%$$

The price of a non-callable bond that pays 100% of its principal at maturity is most sensitive to a change in the spot rate tenor or point on the curve that matches its maturity date. Table 3.11 compares the modified duration and convexity to the Fisher-Weil duration and convexity of a 3.0% 10-year bond priced at par. Both measures are close to one another, which suggests that the prices of non-callable bonds (those that return principal at maturity) are not overly sensitive to changes in the shape of the spot rate curve.

In contrast to the single bond example, consider a portfolio of non-callable bonds each with a different maturity date. Individually, they

TABLE 3.11   Parametric Comparison of Yield to Maturity vs. Spot Rate Curve Valuation

Method	Yield to Maturity	Nominal Spread[a]	Modified Duration	Convexity
Yield to Maturity	3.0%	0 basis points (bps)	8.58	43.11
Spot Rate Curve	3.0%	N/A	8.69	42.84

[a]Nominal Spread is defined as the yield to maturity minus the pricing benchmark

will exhibit price sensitivity to a change in the interest rate of the closest comparable tenor on the spot rate curve. And, as in the example of the single bond, each one will individually exhibit a modest degree of sensitivity to the changes in the shape of the spot rate curve. However, the portfolio will exhibit a greater degree of sensitivity to changes in the shape of the spot rate curve than will the individual bonds that constitute the portfolio the degree to which is dependent on the maturity distribution of the portfolio.

Indeed, Fisher-Weil duration was initially conceived to *immunize* a portfolio of bonds against a known set of liability cash flows. By implementing a non-linear term structure, Fisher-Weil enables the investor to begin to assess the yield curve risk of a portfolio of bonds relative to a portfolio of liabilities.

In the case of structured investments, such as MBS, Fisher-Weil duration enables the investor to assess the overall yield curve risk of a series of amortizing cash flows that are derived from a pool of installment loans. More importantly, Fisher-Weil provides a bridge between modified duration and convexity, which assumes a flat term structure, to effective and key rate duration and convexity, which assume a non-linear term structure—*the spot rate curve.*

CONCEPT 3.5

A mortgage- or asset-backed security can be thought of as a portfolio of amortizing bonds, mortgage or consumer loans, that return principal over the term of the security. As a portfolio of amortizing loans (bonds), the value of a mortgage- or asset-backed security will exhibit a greater degree of sensitivity to a change in the spot rate curve than a comparable non-callable bond.

3.7   EFFECTIVE DURATION

If the investor can determine the price of a bond given a change in the interest rate then it stands to reason that she can determine the duration of a bond given its price change with respect to a change in the discount rate or *(i)*. Rearranging the terms in equation 3.8 the duration of a bond given a change in *i* is:

$$(-\text{Duration})\Delta\ (i) = \frac{P_{(\Delta i)} - P_{(0)}}{P_{(0)}}$$

Isolating the duration term given Δi is positive results in the following:

$$-\text{Duration}_{(+)} = \frac{P_{(+)} - P_{(0)}}{P_{(0)}\Delta i}$$

Similarly, one can compute the duration of a bond given Δi is negative as follows:

$$-\text{Duration}_{(-)} = \frac{P_{(-)} - P_{(0)}}{P_{(0)}\Delta i}$$

One must measure the change in price given both the up and down interest rate scenarios. This is because in some cases, like mortgage-backed securities or bonds with embedded options, the investor's expected cash flow may change as the interest rate environment changes.

For example, lower interest rates create a greater economic incentive for the home owner to refinance, which results in higher mortgage prepayment rates to the mortgage bond holder. This scenario, in turn, results in a shorter modified duration. Conversely, a higher interest rate environment reduces the incentive for the homeowner to refinance, slowing down mortgage prepayment rates and the return of principal to the mortgage bond holder resulting in a longer modified duration.

Effective duration measures the price change across both the Δi positive and Δi negative scenarios. Combining these equations and eliminating common terms results in equation 3.12:

$$\text{Effective duration} = \frac{P_{(+)} - P_{(-)}}{2P_{(0)}\Delta i} \qquad (3.12)$$

where: $P_{(+)}$ = The price of the bond given a shift up in the discount curve
$\quad\quad P_{(-)}$ = The price of the bond given a shift down in the discount curve
$\quad\quad P_{(0)}$ = The price of the bond
$\quad\quad \Delta i$ = The amount of the interest rate shift

Effective duration is calculated using the following steps:

1. First, beginning with the spot rate curve, solve for the spread over the spot rate curve that equates the present value of the bond's cash flows to the present value of the bond's cash flows discounted using the internal rate of return. The spot rate curve plus the spread is the discount curve that will be used to calculate the effective duration of the bond. In the example of the 10-year bond presented earlier, the spread over the spot rate curve is 5.4 basis points.

2. Next, shift the discount curve up and down by a specified number of basis points—a parallel shift of the yield curve. In this example the discount curve is shifted by 50 (bps).
3. Finally, determine the price of the bond for each interest rate shift and apply equation 3.14.

Using the hypothetical yield curve presented in Table 3.8, the effective duration of the 10-year note is −8.42. effective duration is calculated as follows:

$$\text{Effective duration} = \frac{(958.94 - 1{,}043.20)}{2 \times 1000 \times 0.005}$$

$$= -8.42$$

3.8 EFFECTIVE CONVEXITY

Effective convexity, like effective duration, can be determined by shifting the spot rate curve. Effective convexity measures the $P_{(+)}$ and the $P_{(-)}$ duration separately and calculates the rate of change in duration given each shift in the spot rate curve. Measuring duration across the $P_{(+)}$ and the $P_{(-)}$ to changes in the spot rate curve results in equation 3.13:

$$\text{Effective convexity} = \frac{P_{(+)} + P_{(-)} - 2(P_{(0)})}{2 \times P_{(0)} \times \Delta\ (i)^2} \qquad (3.13)$$

Using the example:

$$\text{Effective convexity} = \frac{(958.94 + 1{,}043.20 - (2 \times 1000))}{(2 \times 1000 \times 0.005^2)}$$

$$= \frac{2.14}{0.05}$$

$$= 42.80$$

3.9 SUMMING THE AFOREMENTIONED MEASURES OF DURATION AND CONVEXITY

Both duration and convexity may be approached assuming a linear term structure of interest rates as in the cases of the Macaulay and modified measures. Alternatively, one may assume a non-linear term structure of interest rates. In this case, the discount function used is the spot rate curve.

TABLE 3.12 Comparison of Duration and Convexity Measures

Method	Duration	Convexity	Term Structure
Macaulay	8.71		Linear
Modified	8.58	43.11	Linear
Fisher-Weil	8.69	42.84	Non-linear
Effective	8.42	42.80	Non-linear

Approaching these measures assuming a non-linear term structure is preferable to that of the linear assumption because the spot rate curve assigns the proper present value factor to each cash flow. Table 3.12 compares the duration measures presented in the previous sections. The Macaulay duration measure is the longest because it is not adjusted by the discount factor. Modified duration and convexity lie between the Fisher-Weil and effective measures. Both the Fisher-Weil and effective measures use the spot rate curve, whereas modified uses a linear term structure assumption, which accounts for the difference.

Of the measures presented, effective duration and convexity are preferable to Macaulay, modified, or Fisher-Weil. Effective duration and convexity provide a more accurate measure of price risk because they are based on the spot rate curve—which is used to price bonds. Ultimately, effective duration and convexity relate the price risk of a bond to the term structure of rates.

3.10 KEY RATE DURATION

Key rate duration is the fifth and final generation of duration and is addressed as a separate section simply because the aforementioned measures represent the legacy leading to its concept. The lineage of duration is Macaulay, modified, Fisher-Weil, effective, and key rate duration.

Key rate duration, introduced by Thomas Ho, takes the concept of Fisher-Weil duration one step further and computes the duration of a bond relative to key rates along the spot rate curve. Ho's original work specified 11 key rates across the spot rate curve. They are: 3-month, 1-, 2-, 3-, 5-, 7-, 10-, 15-, 20-, 25-, and 30-year maturities [Ho 1992]. To illustrate the calculation, Table 3.13 provides a hypothetical coupon curve and its associated spot rate curve for the computation of key rate duration.

The key rate duration for each point along the spot rate curve is calculated by shifting the tenor "key rate" up and down by a number of basis points, in this case 25 bps. The change in the spot rate curve between each key rate is calculated using linear interpolation.

TABLE 3.13 Hypothetical Coupon and Spot Rate Curve

Tenor	3-mo.	1-yr.	2-yr.	3-yr.	5-yr.	10-yr.	20-yr.	30-yr.
Coupon Curve		1.00%	1.50%	1.75%	2.15%	3.00%	3.60%	3.75%
Spot Rate Curve	1.76%	3.31%	3.90%	4.10%	4.27%	4.39%	4.46%	4.48%

For example, to calculate the 10-year key rate duration one follows the steps outlined below:

■ **Key Rate Up**
— The 10-year spot rate is shifted up by 25 basis points.
— The up 25-basis-point shift is linearly interpolated between the 5-year and 10-year spot rates and the 10-year and 15-year spot rates.

■ **Key Rate Down**
— The spot 10-year key rate is shifted down by 25-basis-points.
— The down 25-basis-point shift is linearly interpolated between the 5-year and 10-year spot rates and the 10-year and 15-year spot rates.

■ **Key Rate Duration**
— The cash flows are then repriced along both the up and down 25-basis-point spot rate curves.
— Equations 3.12 and 3.13 are applied to determine both the key rate duration and key rate convexity. Key rate duration and convexity can be calculated for either a single bond or a portfolio of bonds.

In the case of a non-callable bond that pays its principal at maturity the key rate that will have the greatest overall impact on the price of the bond is the key rate tenor that matches the timing of the principal repayment. This is because the return of principal contributes the most to the bond's duration as shown in Tables 3.6 and 3.9. However, for structured securities, like mortgage-backed securities (MBS), key rate duration can provide valuable insight regarding the security's price sensitivity given a change in the level or slope of the yield curve.

Consider a 4.00% 30-year pass-through MBS priced at par assuming a 100 PSA[3] prepayment assumption. The key rate durations for the points

---
[3]Public Securities Association mortgage prepayment model.

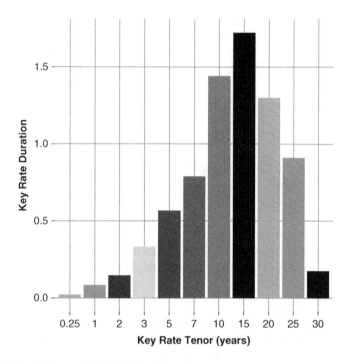

FIGURE 3.6   30-Year 4.0 MBS% Key Rate Duration

on the spot rate curve are shown in Figure 3.6. In the key rate duration framework, effective duration is the sum of each key rate duration. For our example, 4.00% MBS priced at par and assuming a 100 PSA, the effective duration, based on the hypothetical curve presented in Table 3.13, is 7.86. Key rate duration analysis illustrates the contribution to the overall effective duration given by each "key rate" along the spot rate curve.

- The 3-month (0.022), 1-year (0.083), and 2-year (0.147) tenors contribute 0.253 duration units or 3.37% of the overall effective duration of the security.
- The 3-year (0.336) and the 5-year (0.567) tenors contribute 0.904 duration units or 12.04% of the overall effective duration of the security.
- The 7-year tenor contributes 0.791 duration units, or 10.54% of the overall effective duration of the security.
- The 10-year tenor contributes 1.443 duration units, or 22.96% of the overall effective duration of the security.
- The 15-year tenor contributes 1.724 duration units, or 23.55% of the overall effective duration of the security.

- The 20-year tenor contributes 1.301 duration units, or 17.33% of the overall effective duration of the security.
- The 25-year tenor contributes 0.911 duration units, or 12.14% of the overall effective duration of the security.
- Finally, the 30-year tenor contributes 0.177 duration units, or 2.36% of the overall effective duration of the security.

The key rate analysis highlights the yield curve exposure of a 4.0% 30-year MBS. From the key rate analysis, the 10- and 15-year tenors contribute just over 46% of the overall duration of this MBS, suggesting that its price is particularly sensitive to interest rate changes along the intermediate and long end of the spot rate curve.

- For example, assume the yield curve shifts at the 5-year tenor with short rates falling and long rates rising by an equal amount, a *"bearish twist of the yield curve."* Under this scenario, the price of the MBS will decline because the longer key rates contribute more than the shorter key rates to the overall duration of the security.
- The short-term rate exposure, 5 years and less, is equal to a little more than one-third the spot rate exposure of the 10-, 15-, and 20-year tenors combined.

Key rate duration analysis extends our understanding of the yield curve risks associated with investing in a portfolio of fixed-income securities. Because structured securities may be thought of as a "portfolio" of loans, key rate duration analysis is particularly helpful in assessing the yield curve risk that may be embedded in these securities. Through key rate duration analysis the fixed-income investor can gain insight into the overall interest rate risk of her portfolio, via its effective duration, as well as a means to measure the portfolio's term structure risk.

By measuring the investor's risk exposure to specific points along the term structure of interest rates key rate duration analysis provides an intuitive risk measure that relates both the level and slope of the term structure of interest rates to the expected timing of cash flows. Understanding this relationship is the foundation for understanding the valuation framework of structured securities.

The Valuation of Fixed-Income Securities

What is a cynic? A man who knows the price of everything and the value of nothing.

Oscar Wilde

Chapter 4 presents a valuation framework using the concepts present in chapters 2 and 3 in a valuation framework that may be applied to structured investments like MBS.

- Chapter 2 demonstrates that fixed-income securities are priced using the spot rate curve. That is, one may think of the cash flows derived from any fixed-income security as a series of zero coupon bonds.
- Chapter 3 presents the parametric analysis of fixed-income securities. It illustrates that the measures of interest rate risk, namely effective duration and effective convexity, and key rate duration and convexity are derived by "shocking" the spot rate curve along the key rates and revaluing the expected cash flows given the simulated change in the spot rate curve.

By measuring a security's risk along the yield curve, key rate duration provides the intuition to value structured securities by relating both the level and slope of the term structure to the expected timing of the security's cash flows, and ultimately its value.

CONCEPT 4.1

The "term structure" of interest rates generally is meant to refer to the term structure of the spot and forward rate curve, not the yield curve.

The yield curve defines the relationship between the yield of a coupon bearing bond and its maturity. As such, the yield curve can only be used to price a bond that is quoted at its tenor on the yield curve. On the other hand, the spot rate curve may be used to price any bond.

4.1   A VALUATION FRAMEWORK FOR FIXED-INCOME SECURITIES

The prices of structured securities, like most fixed-income securities, are quoted as a spread to the weighted average life over the yield curve. Usually, the yield curve quoted is either the interest rate swap curve or the U.S. Treasury curve. Structured security cash flows, like those shown in Figure 3.7, are distributed along the spot curve due to both the amortizing nature of the underlying assets and the borrower's option to repay the loan, either partially or fully, at any time prior to maturity. This introduces a greater amount of term structure risk relative to a non-callable bond. In addition to introducing term structure risk, the timing of the cash flows along the spot rate curve creates a series of "cheap" (under-priced) or "rich" (over-priced) cash flows that are asymmetrically distributed on either side of the security's average life.

4.2   APPLICATION OF THE FRAMEWORK TO STRUCTURED SECURITIES

Figure 4.1 shows that the valuation of structured securities begins with solving for the spread over the spot rate curve, or ZV spread[1] by treating each cash flow as a zero coupon bond and discounting them along the spot rate curve. The spot spread is the constant spread that, when added to the spot rate curve, equates the present value of the security's cash flows to the proceeds or price of the security.

The *nominal spread* in Figure 4.1 is the difference between the yield to maturity, the linear discount rate, used to price each individual cash flow less the yield to maturity of the pricing benchmark. For example, if the bond's yield to maturity is 4.0% and the yield to maturity of the pricing benchmark on the yield curve is 3.0%, then the nominal spread is 1.0%.

---

[1]The term ZV-spread refers to option adjusted spread analysis (OAS). Assuming 0% volatility the OAS is equal to the spread over the spot rate curve. Hence the term zero volatility spread, or ZV-spread.

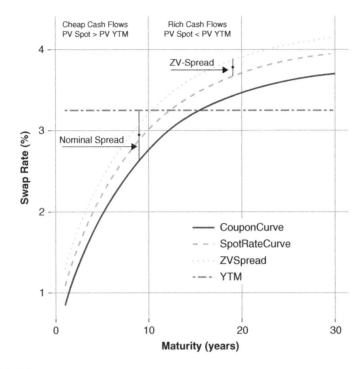

FIGURE 4.1 The Valuation Framework for Fixed-Income Securities

Notice that the valuation framework begins with two term structure assumptions. The first is a non-linear term structure (the spot rate curve) and the second, a linear term structure (yield to maturity). By comparing the valuation of cash flows under each term structure assumption the investor can gauge the relative "richness" or "cheapness" of the cash flows. This is done as follows:

- First, compute the nominal spread over the spot rate curve by subtracting the flat term structure (yield to maturity) from the pricing benchmark on the yield curve.
- Second, determine the relative "richness" or "cheapness" of each cash flow by subtracting the *ZV-spread* from the nominal spread. Cash flows are considered to be priced "cheap" when the nominal spread is greater than the ZV spread. Conversely, cash flows are considered to be priced "rich" when the nominal spread is less than the ZV-spread.

From the first and second observations above we can formulate the following rules:

- If the ZV spread is less than the nominal spread then the "rich" cash flows outweigh the "cheap" cash flows. Therefore, the nominal maturity on the yield curve used to price the cash flows or the "pricing benchmark" is too short relative to the weighted average life of the cash flows.
- If the ZV spread is greater than the nominal spread then the "cheap" cash flows outweigh the "rich" cash flows. Therefore, the pricing benchmark used to price the cash flows is too long relative to the weighted average life of the cash flows.
- If the ZV spread is equal to the nominal spread then the valuation of the cash flows is balanced. Therefore, the pricing benchmark is accurate relative to the weighted average life of the cash flows.

The valuation framework presented in Figure 4.1 is simplified to the degree that expected cash flows are more or less "deterministic." For example, the principal contribution of a non-callable 10-year note to the present value or price of the note is 74% (Table 3.6). Thus, the key rate risk and by extension the yield curve risk is predominately the 10-year tenor on the spot rate curve. Conversely, the key rate and yield curve risk of a 4.00% 30-year MBS pass-through is distributed across the spot rate curve (Figure 3.6). To the extent that cash flows are more or less distributed across the term structure key rate and yield curve risk are increased or decreased.

The valuation framework outlined above together with the key rate duration analysis presented in Chapter 3 suggests that changes in either the level or slope of the yield curve can alter the valuation of structured securities due to the following:

- Structured securities, unlike a non-callable bond whose term structure exposure is largely the tenor along the spot rate curve that matches its maturity, are exposed, to one degree or another, to all key rates across the spot rate curve.
- Changes to either the level or slope of the yield curve often influence consumer tendencies to terminate a loan early, either through voluntary repayment or default. In turn, the timing of the expected cash flows and key rate exposure along the term structure is altered.

4.3 TWIST AND SHIFT: CHARACTERIZING CHANGES IN THE LEVEL, STEEPNESS, AND CURVATURE OF THE TERM STRUCTURE

The yield curve may shift in a number of ways resulting in changes to its shape which may be defined by the following characteristics: level, steepness, and curvature [Ho 1992]:

- *Parallel shift*: Changes to the level of the yield curve are a result of all rates moving by the same amount. These shifts are classified as either up or down:
  - Parallel shift up: Interest rates go up by the same amount across the term structure. Under this scenario, the market's long-term expectation of prepayment rates declines and cash flow maturities extend along the curve. As a result, key rate durations become more heavily weighted to the longer maturities. This is referred to by investors as extension risk.
  - Parallel shift down: Interest rates go down by the same amount across the term structure. Under this scenario, the market's long-term expectation of prepayment rates increases, cash flow maturities shorten along the term structure, and key rate durations become more heavily weighted to the shorter maturities. This is referred to by investors as contraction risk.
- *Twist shift*: Changes to the curvature of the yield curve are characterized by movements in both short and long rates. These movements are classified as follows:
  - Twist flatten: the short end twists up and the long end twists down. Under this scenario, the market's long-term prepayment expectation increases and cash flow maturities contract along the term structure. The short dated cash flows decline in value while the valuation of the long dated cash flows increases. Under this scenario, key rates become more heavily weighted to the shorter maturities.
  - Twist steepen: The short end twists down and the long end twists up. Under this scenario, the market's long-term prepayment expectation declines and cash flow maturities extend along the term structure. The short dated cash flows increase in value while the long dated cash flows decrease in value. Under this scenario, key rates become more heavily weighted to the longer maturities.

Finally changes to the steepness of the coupon curve are characterized by either short rates or long rates moving by a greater or lesser amount than the other. Shifts are classified as follows:

— Bull flatten: The short end remains unchanged and the long end twists down. Under this scenario, the market's long-term prepayment expectation increases and cash flow maturities contract along the term structure. The valuation of the short dated cash flows is unchanged while the valuation of the long dated cash flows increases.

— Bear steepen: The short end remains unchanged and the long end twists up. Under this scenario, the market's long-term prepayment expectation declines and cash flow maturities extend along the term structure. The valuation of the short dated cash flows increases while the valuation of the long dated cash flows declines.

4.4 CASE STUDY: 4.00% 30-YEAR MBS

To evaluate the impact that changes in both the level and slope of the term structure have on the valuation of structured securities, consider the aforementioned 4.00% 30-year MBS pass-through security presented in Chapter 3 and summarized below in Table 4.1.

The parametric analysis yields the following observations:

- The average life of 11.3 years is close to that of the pricing benchmark; the 10-year swap rate (1.92%).
- The YTM is 3.31% at a price of $105.75, resulting in a spread to the 10-year swap of 139 bps.
- The effective duration is 7.13, suggesting that a (+/−) 100 bps parallel shift in the term structure will result in approximately a (+/−) 7.13% change in the price of the MBS.

TABLE 4.1 MBS Base Case Parametric Analysis

Note Rate	4.75%
Net Coupon	4.00%
Term	360 mos.
Loan Age	0 mos.
Weighted Average Life (WAL)	11.30 years
Price	$105.75
Yield to Maturity	3.31%
YTM (nominal) Spread	1.39%
Effective Duration	7.13
ZV-Spread	1.22%
12-mo. Hrz. Return	2.02% −

- The ZV spread of 1.22% is less than the nominal spread, indicating that given the slope of the term structure and the timing of the cash flows, the rich cash flows outweigh the cheap cash flows.

The base case interest rate scenario is the Jan. 10, 2013, curve presented in Table 4.2. The yield curve assumptions of steepen 50 basis points and flatten 50 basis points are used to illustrate how changes in the level and slope of the term structure affect the valuation of structured securities and are presented in Table 4.3. Both the steepen and flatten scenarios are based on the following assumptions:

- A steepening of the yield curve between the 2- to 10-year tenors of 50 basis points is centered around the 5-year.
- A flattening of the yield curve between the 2- to the 10-year of 50 basis points is centered around the 5-year.
- The Bond Lab generic FHLMC prepayment model (FH30.Generic) is used.[2]

4.4.1 Swap Curve Twist Steepen Scenario

Under the swap curve twist steepen scenario shown in Table 4.3, the 10-year swap rate increases by 25 bps while the 2-year swap rate falls by 25 bps—a

TABLE 4.2 Base Case Yield Curve—Jan. 10, 2013

Tenor	1-yr.	2-yr.	3-yr.	5-yr.	10-yr.	20-yr.	30-yr.
	0.31%	0.38%	0.50%	0.91%	1.92%	2.40%	2.88%

TABLE 4.3 Yield Curve Scenarios

Tenor	1-yr.	2-yr.	3-yr.	5-yr.	10-yr.	20-yr.	30-yr.
Swap Curve Steepens	0.06%	0.13%	0.25%	0.91%	2.17%	2.65%	3.13%
Swap Curve Unchanged	0.31%	0.38%	0.50%	0.91%	1.92%	2.40%	2.88%
Swap Curve Flattens	0.56%	0.63%	0.75%	0.91%	1.67%	2.40%	2.63%

---

[2]A full treatment of mortgage prepayment modeling is presented in Part 2.

steepening of the swap curve between the 2- and 10-year swap rate of 50 bps. The steeper swap curve produces the following effects:

- *Long term:* Figure 4.2 shows that the steeper swap curve results in higher forward rates. As a result, the market's expectation of future interest rates goes up and by extension the expected future mortgage rate also goes up.
- *Near term:* The higher spot 10-year swap rate, which influences the level of mortgage rates, results in a higher mortgage rate and a near term slow down in expected mortgage prepayments as borrowers adjust their behavior in response to the higher interest rate environment (Figure 4.3).

Figure 4.3 illustrates the effect of a steeper swap curve. Higher spot and forward rate curves extend the expected cash flow maturities along the swap curve resulting in the following:

- Expected cash flows become more heavily backloaded and are repriced to a higher discount rate due to the steepening of yield curve.

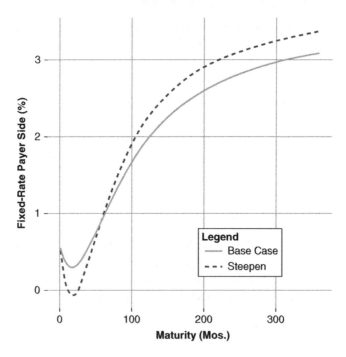

FIGURE 4.2   Yield Curve Steepens 50 Basis Points

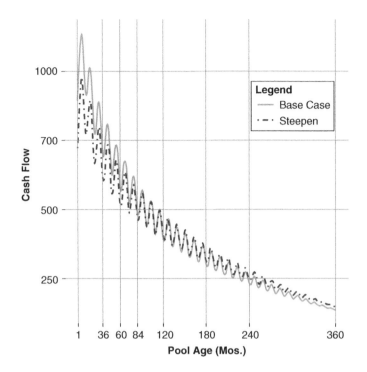

FIGURE 4.3   Cash Flow Comparison—Swap Curve Steepens 50 Basis Points

▦ Extension of the cash flow maturities along the swap curve shifts key rate duration, increasing the price sensitivity of these cash flows to interest rate changes on the long end of the swap curve.

The ending key rate durations shown in Figure 4.4 are used to reprice the security, given a 50 bps steepening of the swap curve. Table 4.4 shows that using the 4.00% 30-year MBS key rate durations, the expected price change given the steepening of the swap curve is 1.41%. One can translate this relationship to an effective duration by multiplying the result (1.41%) by four (1.0%/0.25%). Therefore, the twist duration given a 50 bps steepening scenario around the five-year swap rate, based on the given prepayment assumptions, is 5.62.

The effective duration under the steepening scenario is considerably less than the effective duration assuming a parallel shift in the yield curve. The swap curve steepening example using key rate duration implies another concept of duration, namely, that of *twist duration*. Twist duration measures a bond's price change given a change in the curvature of the swap curve. In the above case, the twist duration is 5.62 meaning that given a

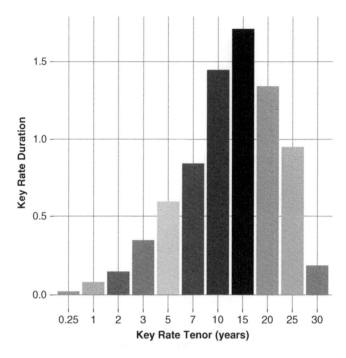

FIGURE 4.4 Key Rate Duration—Swap Curve Steepens 50 Basis Points

TABLE 4.4 Effective Duration—Swap Curve Steepens 50 Basis Points

Key Rate	Duration	Interest Rate Shift	Price Change
0.25	0.32	−0.25	0.00
1-yr.	0.11	−0.25	0.03
2-yr.	0.17	−0.25	0.04
3-yr.	0.36	−0.25	0.09
5-yr.	0.61	0.00	0.00
7-yr.	0.87	0.25	−0.21
10-yr.	1.18	0.25	−0.23
15-yr.	1.64	0.25	−0.38
20-yr.	1.37	0.25	−0.33
25-yr.	1.02	0.25	−0.24
30-yr.	0.21	0.25	−0.05
		Steepening Duration	1.41

(+)100-basis-point twist in the swap curve, centered around the five-year tenor, the expected price change of the MBS is 5.62%. Although swap rates on the short end of the curve in Table 4.3 went down, which, in turn, increased the value of the short dated cash flows, the value of the MBS declined from $100.00 to $98.59 due to the following:

- A greater share of a 30-year mortgage's cash flows are weighted to the long end of the swap curve (Figure 3.6).
- Lower prepayment expectations under the steepening scenario extend a greater share of the expected cash flows to the "rich cash flow" region along the spot rate curve (Figure 4.1), where the present value of the spot rate is greater than the present value of the yield to maturity discount rate (the flat term structure assumption), a phenomenon commonly referred to as "extension risk" in the structured securities market.
- As shown in Figure 4.4 the key rate durations shifted, adding greater weight to the longer maturities relative to the base case (Figure 3.6).

Table 4.5 summarizes the change in valuation. Together, the changes in both the level and slope of the swap curve, as well as the expected cash flow profile due to changes in prepayment expectations, alter the valuation of the MBS.

- The price declines according to the key rate durations. The overall price decline is less than that predicted by the effective duration, which is based on the assumption of a parallel shift in the swap rate curve.
- The yield to maturity spread widens from 139 to 142 basis bps, reflecting the longer cash flows and effective duration, which increases to 7.60.
- The expected 12-month horizon return declines to 0.41% from the base case—no change expected return of 2.02%.

TABLE 4.5 MBS Steepen Parametric Analysis

Note Rate	4.75%
Net Coupon	4.00%
Term	360 mos.
Loan Age	0 mos.
Weighted Average Life (WAL)	11.89 years
Yield to Maturity	3.34%
YTM (nominal) Spread	1.42%
Effective Duration	7.60
12-mo. Hrz. Return	0.41%

Both the average life and effective duration extend while the swap rate curve becomes steeper, led by long rates rising and short rates falling, which results in slower long-term prepayment expectations. As a result, the cash flow maturities extend, pushing a greater share of the cash flows further along term structure. Consequently, the yield to maturity increases and expected 12-month horizon return declines.

4.4.2 Swap Curve Twist Flatten Scenario

Under the swap curve twist flatten scenario shown in Table 4.3, the 10-year swap rate declines by 25 basis points while the 2-year swap rate goes up by 25 basis points—a flattening of the swap curve between the 2- and 10-year swap rate of 50 basis points. The flatter swap curve produces the following effects:

■ *Long term:* Figure 4.5 shows that the flatter swap curve results in lower forward rates. As a result, the market's expectation of future interest rates goes down and by extension the expected future mortgage rate goes down.

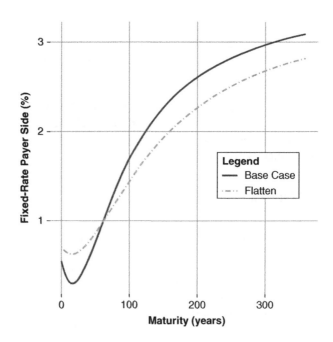

FIGURE 4.5 Yield Curve Flattens 50 Basis Points

■ *Near term:* The lower 10-year swap rate results in a lower mortgage rate and a near-term speed-up in the mortgage prepayment rate as borrowers adjust their behavior in response to the lower interest rate environment.

Figure 4.6 illustrates the effect of a flatter swap curve. The lower spot and forward rate curves cause the expected cash flow maturities to contract along the swap curve, resulting in the following:

■ The expected cash flows become more heavily front loaded while they are priced to a relatively lower discount rate because the swap curve is upward sloping.
■ The contraction of the cash flow maturities along the swap curve shifts the key rate durations to the left, increasing the price sensitivity of the cash flows to interest rate changes on the short end of the swap curve, a phenomenon commonly referred to as *call risk* in the structured securities market.

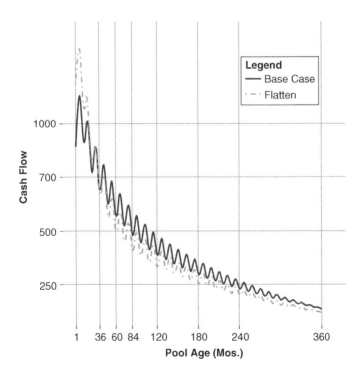

FIGURE 4.6 Cash Flow Comparison—Swap Curve Flattens 50 Basis Points

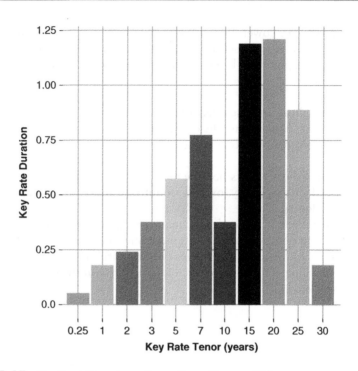

FIGURE 4.7 Key Rate Duration—Swap Curve Flattens 50 bps

The ending key rate durations, shown in Figure 4.7, are used to reprice the 4.00% 30-year MBS given a 50 bps flattening of the swap curve. Table 4.6 shows that using the key rate durations the expected price change given a 50-basis-point flattening of the swap curve is −0.94%. As in the previous example, one can translate the result to an effective duration by multiplying it (−0.94) by four, yielding twist effective duration of 3.76.

Although the cash flow maturities shortened due to faster long-term prepayment expectations, a greater share of the cash flows remained at the longer key rate durations, resulting in a price increase.

Table 4.7 summarizes the parametric statistics given the swap curve flattening scenario:

- The cash flows are more heavily loaded to the earlier maturities and both the average life and effective duration shorten to 10.21 years and 6.04, respectively.
- The accelerated return of the cash flow causes the yield to maturity to decline to 3.25% and the nominal to increase to 1.33%.
- The 12-month horizon expected return goes up to 3.41% due to the influence of the lower interest rates along the longer tenors of the swap curve.

TABLE 4.6 Effective Duration—Swap Curve Flattens
50 Basis Points

Key Rate	Duration	Interest Rate Shift	Price Change
0.25	0.05	0.25	−0.01
1-yr.	0.18	0.25	−0.03
2-yr.	0.24	0.25	−0.05
3-yr.	0.37	0.25	−0.09
5-yr.	0.57	0.00	−0.00
7-yr.	0.77	−0.25	0.21
10-yr.	0.37	−0.25	0.23
15-yr.	1.18	−0.25	0.38
20-yr.	1.21	−0.25	0.33
25-yr.	0.89	−0.25	0.24
30-yr.	0.18	−0.25	0.05
		Flatten Duration	−0.94

TABLE 4.7 MBS Flattening Parametric Analysis

Note Rate	4.50%
Net Coupon	4.00%
Term	360 mos.
Loan Age	0 mos.
Weighted Average Life (WAL)	10.21 years
Yield to Maturity	3.25%
YTM (nominal) Spread	1.33%
Effective Duration	6.04
12-mo. Hrz. Return	3.41%

4.5   SCENARIO COMPARATIVE ANALYSIS

The comparative analysis presented in Table 4.8 illustrates the influence that changes in both the level and slope of the swap curve exert on structured investments like mortgage-backed securities.

- Under the steepen scenario, the yield increases modestly due to the MBS premium price and slower prepayment speeds. Relative to the base case, the MBS weighted average life and effective duration extends while the 12-month horizon return goes down.
- Under the flatten scenario the yield decreases due to the MBS premium price and faster prepayment speeds. Relative to the base case, the MBS weighted average life and effective duration shortens while 12-month horizon return goes up.

TABLE 4.8   Comparative Analysis of Scenario Outcomes

Note Rate:	4.75%
Net Coupon:	4.00%
Term:	360 mos.
Loan Age:	0 mos.

Scenario	YTM	WAL	Eff. Dur.	YTM Spd. vs. 10-yr. Swap	12-month Hrz. Return
Steepen	3.34%	11.89 yrs.	7.60	0.97%	0.41%
Unchanged	3.31%	11.30 yrs.	7.13	1.39%	2.02%
Flatten	3.25%	10.21 yrs.	6.04	1.58%	3.41%

Notice, the nominal spread tightens as yields on the pricing benchmarks (swap rates) rise and prices fall. Both the nominal and ZV-spread tighten because the value of the investor's short option to refinance, held by the borrower, declines in value. Similarly, when yields on the pricing benchmark fall and prices go up, both the nominal and ZV-spreads widen as the investor's short option to the borrower to refinance increases in value. The nominal spread behavior is a reflection of MBS negative convexity.

Changes in both the level and slope of the swap curve alter the cash flow timing (actual and expected) of securities that are collateralized by either consumer or commercial installment loans. To the degree that cash flows are contingent on the prevailing interest rate, the impact of changes in the term structure will have a greater or lesser impact on the valuation of the structured security. For example, residential mortgage prepayment rates are highly contingent on many variables, including the level and slope of the swap curve (the general level of interest rates). Thus, changes in the level, curvature, or steepness of the term structure influence borrower prepayment behavior, which in turn alters the timing of the cash flows along the term structure changing the price of the MBS. Conversely, commercial MBS prepayments are far less sensitive to these influences and as a result the valuation of CMBS is greatly simplified with respect to borrower prepayment.

Fixed-Income Return Analysis

Price is what you pay. Value is what you get.

Warren Buffet

Chapter 5 extends the valuation framework presented in Chapter 4 to *return analysis*. The metrics presented in Chapter 3 are often referred to as *parametric* because they represent a set of measurable factors that define a fixed-income security and may be classified as either valuation measures related to the price or risk of a fixed-income security.

- The valuation measures that define the price of a bond are:
  1. The yield to maturity
  2. Nominal spread to the coupon curve
  3. Spread to the spot rate curve (*zero volatility* OAS)
  4. Option-adjusted spread (OAS)[1]
- The risk measures that define the price risk of a bond are:
  1. Effective duration and effective convexity
  2. Key rate duration and key rate convexity

5.1   RETURN STRATEGIES

Individually, neither the valuation measures nor the risk measures provide a sense of the expected return of a fixed-income security. Return analysis combines both the valuation and risk measures to inform the investor of a fixed-income investment's potential return profile given her expectation of the future evolution of interest rates.

---

[1]A complete review of Option-Adjusted Spread is presented in Chapter 12.

At first blush, one may argue that return analysis is not pertinent to the *buy-and-hold investor* since the investment horizon is equal to the maturity of the bond, which is not the case for the following reasons:

- First, for a buy-and-hold investor, the holding period return or terminal value is dependent on the future path of interest rates because the investor must reinvest coupon income at the prevailing market rate—which more likely than not will be different from the yield to maturity assumption used to price the bond, subjecting the buy-and-hold investor to reinvestment rate risk. Generally speaking, the longer the holding period, the greater role of the reinvestment rate in determining the investor's horizon return.
- Second, the investor for any number of reasons may be "forced" to sell prior to maturity under an adverse interest rate environment resulting in a principal loss. Alternatively, the investor may be "forced" to sell under a favorable interest rate environment resulting in principal gain.
- Finally, asset allocation strategies often look to the relative return of one asset class versus another to determine the proper allocation between any number of potential investments. Return analysis is a critical input to the asset allocation decision.

Aside from the buy-and-hold strategy discussed above, return strategies may be classified in one of two ways [Waring and Siegel 2006]:

1. *Total rate of return* strategies are relative strategies in the sense that the return of the asset under consideration is measured relative to the return of others. For example, the return of bond A may be measured against that of bond B, or a prescribed performance benchmark index, or liability stream as in the case of portfolio immunization strategies. The goal of a total return strategy is to "beat the benchmark," thus generating excess return, or *alpha*. In the total return case, negative returns are acceptable so long as they are less than that of the relative benchmark.
2. *Absolute return* strategies shun the concept of a performance benchmark to measure alpha. The absolute return investor's strategies are designed to seek a positive return under any market condition. The goal is to produce a consistent return that is above that of the market return—alpha. For example, a stated return of 1-month LIBOR plus 250 bps would represent the goal of an absolute return investor. The absolute return investor, unlike the total return investor, may take a short position against a comparable long position to capture alpha.

The above descriptions illustrate that the differences between a buy and hold, total return, and absolute return investor are those of the investment time horizon and/or the direction of the position taken by the investor (i.e., long or short). Both the buy-and-hold and total-return investors are by definition long only investors. The difference between these two investors is their investment time horizons. Specifically, a total return investor typically has a shorter horizon than that of the buy-and-hold investor. The absolute return investor differs from the total investor only in the sense that she may take a short position against a long position in an attempt to capture alpha. Conversely, the total return investor is long only, seeking to create alpha against a specific performance benchmark.

5.2 THE COMPONENTS OF RETURN

There are three components to the return realized by the fixed-income investor:

1. *Coupon income*—the interest rate that is paid to the investor for lending the money to the borrower.
2. *Reinvestment income*—the income earned through the investment of the coupon income.
3. *Price change*—the appreciation or decline (principal gain or loss) of the fixed-income security relative to its purchase price.

5.3 THE BUY-AND-HOLD STRATEGY

The following example illustrates the buy-and-hold return analysis, the simplest of the three return strategies discussed above. Consider a 3.0% five-year bond priced at par to yield 3.0% to maturity. To understand how the coupon and reinvestment income components contribute to the investor's total return, Table 5.2 presents a return matrix. The return matrix allows for the systematic calculation of the investor's horizon total return. The assumptions used in the return analysis matrix are:

1. The investor reinvests her cash flow receipts to match the time to the next coupon payment. In this case, six-month intervals.
2. The reinvestment rate is assumed to be constant at 0.25% (25 basis points).
3. The investor's holding period is to maturity (implicit in the buy-and-hold strategy).

5.3.1 Coupon Income

The investor receives coupon income, which is calculated by multiplying the bond's coupon by the principal balance outstanding at the time of the last payment date. The coupon accrues according to the bond basis that is one of the following:

- Actual days/Actual days
- 30 days/360 days
- Actual days/360 days

Table 5.1 shows the timing of the investor's expected coupon income. In this case, she expects to earn $150 of coupon income over her anticipated holding period.

TABLE 5.1   Return Matrix Input—Coupon Income

1	2	3	4	5	6	7	8	9	10	Total
$15	$15	$15	$15	$15	$15	$15	$15	$15	$15	
						Coupon Income				$150

TABLE 5.2   Return Matrix: Coupon Income plus Reinvestment

1	2	3	4	5	6	7	8	9	10
$15	$15.04	$15.08	$15.11	$15.15	$15.19	$15.22	$15.26	$15.30	$15.34
	$15	$15.04	$15.08	$15.11	$15.15	$15.19	$15.22	$15.26	$15.30
		$15	$15.04	$15.08	$15.11	$15.15	$15.19	$15.22	$15.26
			$15	$15.04	$15.08	$15.11	$15.15	$15.19	$15.22
				$15	$15.04	$15.08	$15.11	$15.15	$15.19
					$15	$15.04	$15.08	$15.11	$15.15
						$15	$15.04	$15.08	$15.11
							$15	$15.04	$15.08
								$15	$15.04
									$1,015.00
						Total Coupon + Reinvestment			$151.70

Coupon Income	$150.00
Reinvestment Income	$1.70
Return of Principal	$1,000.00
Total Return	$1,151.70

5.3.2   Reinvestment Income

▪ In the first period, the investor receives her scheduled coupon payment of $15 and reinvests it at the six-month rate of 25 basis point annually.
▪ In the second period, she receives her next coupon payment of $15 and the maturation of her reinvestment of the previous coupon payment of $30.01875.
▪ In the third period, she again receives her next scheduled coupon payment of $15 as well as the return of her reinvestments, a total of $45.06.

The investor's annualized return is given by the following:

$$\text{Annualized return} = \left(\left[\frac{\text{Ending portfolio value}}{\text{Initial investment}} \right]^{\frac{1}{n}} - 1 \right) \times \text{Frequency} \quad (5.1)$$

Where: n = Number of periods
        Frequency = Payment frequency of the bond

The investor's annualized return in this example above is:

$$\text{Annualized return} = \left(\left[\frac{1{,}151.70}{1{,}000} \right]^{\frac{1}{10}} - 1 \right) \times 2$$

$$= \left(1.15170^{\frac{1}{10}} - 1 \right) \times 2$$

$$= (1.014224125 - 1) \times 2$$

$$= 2.844\%$$

▪ Initially, one may notice that the annualized holding period return to maturity (2.844%) is not equal to the bond's yield to maturity (3.0%). The difference is because the short-term reinvestment rate of 0.25% is considerably less than the yield to maturity. Yield to maturity is an internal rate of return calculation and as such assumes the cash flows are reinvested at the internal rate of return (section 3.2). More often than not, this assumption is violated. Cash flows may be reinvested at a higher or lower rate, depending on the path of future interest rates.
▪ Furthermore, in this example the reinvestment income contributes very little to the investor's overall return, which is typically the case, particularly when interest rates are low or the horizon period is short.

5.4   TOTAL AND ABSOLUTE RETURNS

Unlike the case of the buy-and-hold investor, the total or absolute return investor may sell her bond investment prior to maturity. In the case of either the total or absolute return investor, the holding period is generally shorter than the maturity of the bond. Indeed, even a buy-and-hold investor may be required to sell her investment in order to raise cash to meet an unexpected out flow from the portfolio. As a result, a price change that is due to a change in the yield maturity as well as a shorter time maturity, due to the passage of time, affects her realized holding period return.

5.4.1   Price Change

The price change is given by the following:

$$\Delta \text{Bond price} = \frac{P_h - P_0}{P_0} \qquad (5.2)$$

where: P_h = Horizon price
P_0 = Initial investment price

Revisting equation 3.11:

$$\Delta \text{Bond price} = -\text{Duration} \times \Delta(i/100) + \text{Convexity} \times \Delta(i/100)^2$$

the modified duration of a five-year, 3.0% bond is 4.61 and its convexity is 12.95. Thus, given an instantaneous (+/−) 100 bps change in the term structure the expected price change of a 3.0% five-year bond priced at $100 is 4.74%.

$$\Delta \text{Bond price} = -4.61 \times 0.01 + 12.95 \times 0.01^2$$

$$\Delta \text{Bond price} = -0.0461 + 0.0013$$

$$\Delta \text{Bond price} = -0.0474$$

The duration and convexity profile of a bond indicate the bond's price risk given a change in the term structure. However, that profile does not indicate the return an investor may expect to realize, given a holding period that is shorter than the bond's maturity date.

5.5   DECONSTRUCTING THE FIXED-INCOME RETURN PROFILE

The return analysis presented in this section continues with the hypothetical yield curve used in Chapter 3 and is presented again in Table 5.3. Given an

TABLE 5.3 Hypothetical Swap Rate Curve

Tenor	1-yr.	2-yr.	3-yr.	5-yr.	10-yr.	20-yr.	30-yr.
	1.00%	1.50%	1.75%	2.15%	3.00%	3.60%	3.75%

investment horizon that is less than the time to maturity of the bond, the expected return is calculated using equation 5.1.

The assumptions used are:

- A 3.0% five-year bond priced at par.
- Yield to maturity is 3.0%.
- The nominal spread over the five-year benchmark is 85 basis points.
- A holding period (investment horizon) is two years.
- The nominal spread on a comparable three-year bond is 65 bps.

Two years forward, assuming both the swap curve and nominal spreads are unchanged the price of the bond is $101.72875. The pricing inputs are:

- A three-year maturity bond with a 3.0% coupon.
- The yield to maturity is 2.40% (1.75% + 0.65%).
- The price of a three-year, 3% coupon bond two years forward yielding 2.40% is $101.72875.

What is the investor's realized return? From Table 5.2, the coupon income plus reinvestment (two years) is equal to $60.23. The price of the bond increased $101.72875. The investor's proceeds from the sale of the bond after two years is equal to $1,017.2875 plus the coupon and reinvestment income, totaling $1,077.517.

From equation 5.1 the investor's annualized return given a two-year holding period assuming that the swap curve remains unchanged is:

$$\text{Annualized return} = \left(\left[\frac{1,077.517}{1,000} \right]^{\frac{1}{4}} - 1 \right) \times 2$$

$$= \left(1.077517^{\frac{1}{4}} - 1 \right) \times 2$$

$$= (1.01884 - 1) \times 2$$

$$= 3.768\%$$

Given a two-year horizon, the investor's realized annual return is more than that which would have been achieved under the buy-and-hold strategy due to the following:

- In all, the yield to maturity declined 60 basis points from the time of the initial investment, raising the price of the bond:
  - First, the bond price went up because it is priced relative to the three-swap rate, a lower yielding benchmark than the five-year swap rate that was used at the point of the initial investment.
  - Second, the nominal spread also fell from 85 bps to 65 bps, a decline of 20 bps.
- However, the reinvestment rate, 25 bps, is lower than that assumed by the yield to maturity calculation (3.0%), which reduces realized income.

The metrics used to describe the risk of the bond also changed at the two-year horizon. The duration and convexity of the bond at the end of the two-year horizon are 2.86 and 5.46, respectively. Substituting the change in the yield to maturity, the horizon duration, and the horizon convexity into **equation** 3.11 yields a predicted price change:

$$\Delta \text{Bond price} = -2.86 \times -0.006 + 5.46 \times -0.006^2$$
$$= 0.01712 + 0.00019$$
$$= 0.01735$$

Using the risk measures of duration and convexity observed at the end of the two-year investment horizon and given the swap curve presented in Table 5.3 the estimated change price is 1.735%, close to the observed price change of the bond at the end of the two-year horizon.

Together, the measures that define the price of a bond and those that define the risk of a bond can be used to estimate the return of a bond given an investment horizon, a horizon yield to maturity, and the horizon duration and convexity.

5.6   ESTIMATING BOND RETURNS WITH PRICE AND RISK MEASURES

CONCEPT 5.1

The coupon income (interest) is an annuity payment. The investor can calculate the price of a bond as the present value of an annuity (coupon) + the present value of the principal payment at maturity, as presented in Concept 1.1. Alternatively, the investor can calculate the expected return of a bond as the future value of an annuity + the principal repayment at maturity relative to the purchase price of the bond. Again, as stated in Chapter 1.2 the future value of $1 is the "tails" side of the present value coin. Simply stated, present value is future value, and future value is present value; each is tied to the other by i, the discount rate.

The estimated return is calculated by using equation 1.5 and assuming a annual reinvestment rate of 25 basis points as illustrated in Table 5.2. The return attributable to both coupon and reinvestment income is:

$$\text{Coupon plus reinvestment} = \text{Coupon} \times \frac{(1+i)^n - 1}{i} \qquad (5.3)$$

$$\text{Coupon plus reinvestment} = \$15 \times \frac{(1+0.000208)^3 - 1}{0.000208} + \$15$$

$$= \$15 \times \frac{(1.00624 - 1)}{0.000208} + \$15$$

$$= \$15 \times 3.00624 + \$15$$

$$= \$60.09$$

$$= \frac{\$60.09}{\$1,000}$$

$$= 0.06009$$

In the above example, the investor received a three-payment annuity of $15 and a final payment at the horizon date of $15. The total coupon income plus reinvestment income received by the investor at the end of the two year horizon is $60.09. The estimated price change at the end of the two-year horizon assuming the swap curve presented in Table 5.1 is given by the following:

$$\Delta \text{Bond price} = -\text{Duration} \times \Delta(i/100) + \text{Convexity} \times \Delta(i/100)^2 \qquad (5.4)$$

$$= -2.86 \times -0.006 + 5.46 \times -0.006^2$$

$$= 0.01712 + 0.00019$$

$$= 0.01735$$

The investor's holding period return is 7.74%. The investor's estimated annualized return is 3.76%. The example above illustrates an important point; individually the measures that define price or risk tell the investor little about the expected return of a fixed-income security. However, together they provide the investor with some insight regarding the expected return over a given investment horizon. Return analysis examines each of the three components of total return presented in section 5.2.

1. Coupon income: In the simplest sense the investor may consider the coupon income as an annuity.
2. Reinvestment income: The income generated by reinvesting the coupon income. To estimate the reinvestment income the investor may assume a constant reinvestment rate—a flat term structure assumption. Alternatively, the investor may assume a reinvest rate that follows the forward rate curve—a non-linear term structure assumption.
3. Price change: The gain or loss realized by the investor due to a change in the price of the bond over the investment horizon. It is determined by the principal balance outstanding at the end of the investment horizon and pricing the security based on the simulated changes the level, steepness, and curvature of the term structure as described in section 4.3 and illustrated throughout the previous chapter. Both sections 5.2.3 and 5.2.4 show that the price change based on the given scenario is determined by *rolling the security forward*.

Return analysis blends the measures that define both the price and risk of a bond to provide the investor with an understanding of its expected return given the following inputs:

- The investor's holding period.
- A term structure assumption at the end of the holding period.
- A reinvestment assumption over the holding period.
- In the case of an MBS or ABS security, a prepayment assumption.

Return analysis allows the investor irrespective of her strategy (buy and hold, total return, or absolute return) to assess the return potential of a fixed-income security. Indeed, using this analysis she is able to select a portfolio that meets her unique risk/reward profile regardless of the strategy that she chooses.

Two

Residential Mortgage-Backed Securities

CHAPTER 6

Understanding Mortgage Lending and Loans

The surest way to ruin a man who doesn't know how to handle money is to give him some.

George Bernard Shaw

A mortgage note represents a pledge of real estate to secure a loan. The mortgagee (borrower) pledges the property to the mortgagor (lender) as collateral to secure repayment of the loan. Thus, the loan is said to be *secured* by the pledged property. Ownership of the property rests with the borrower throughout the term of loan. However, the lender holds a lien against the property and if the borrower is unable to repay the loan according to its terms, then the ownership of the property is transferred to the lender to settle the outstanding debt.

6.1 CLASSIFICATION OF REAL ESTATE

Generally, real estate is classified as follows:

■ **Residential real estate.** The term *residential real estate* refers to property used as a place of residence. Residential real estate may be subdivided in the following ways:
— Primary residence: The owner spends most of his time living at the residence.
— Secondary residence: The owner spends some, but not the majority, of his time living at the residence. Often, this is vacation property.
  Residential real estate can be further subdivided based on the property type:
— Single-family detached
— Planned unit development

81

— Condominium
— Two-to-four unit

■ **Commercial real estate.** The term *commercial real estate* refers to property used to conduct commerce and may be subdivided as follows:

— Farm
— Commerce

Property used for commerce may be further subdivided as follows:

— Commercial residential (apartment complex)
— Retail, shopping mall
— Industrial
— Hospital
— Hospitality, hotel

The mortgage loan is the basic input of the mortgage securtitization process. Thus, it is important that the investor understand how the loan is structured from the borrower's point of view:

■ The origination and underwriting practices of the lender.
■ The terms of the loan: the amortization schedule and the note rate (fixed or floating).
■ The servicer's policies and procedures.

6.1.1 Residential Mortgage Origination and Underwriting

A borrower that is interested in a mortgage must meet certain credit standards set by the lender in order to qualify for the loan. The lender's underwriting practices seek to determine the borrower's willingness and ability to repay the loan. Typically, the lender follows an underwriting matrix that measures the credit quality of the borrower across several metrics.

■ **Borrower's willingness to repay.** The underwriter will typically measure the borrower's willingness to repay with the following criteria:

— Credit score. Credit reporting agencies typically score borrowers. The credit score is an attempt to summarize the borrower's repayment history, outstanding obligations, and open lines of credit into a single metric.
— Repayment history. The lender will typically consider the borrower's past repayment performance. For example, the lender considers the number of 30-, 60-, and 90-days past due notations in the borrower's credit report. Often, the lender sets a maximum number of allowable reported delinquencies (derogatories) in the past 12 months.

— Notice of default or foreclosure. The lender will typically check whether the borrower has defaulted on a debt obligation in the past seven years.

▪ **Borrower's ability to repay.** The underwriter may measure the borrower's ability to repay the loan based on the following:

— Current amount of credit lines outstanding. A borrower with numerous open lines of credit may be overleveraged, thereby impairing his ability to repay the loan on a timely basis.

— The debt to income ratio, or DTI. DTI measures the borrower's current monthly debt payment relative to monthly gross income and is normally measured as a "front-end" ratio and a "back-end" ratio.

  • The front-end ratio measures the mortgage payment (principal and interest) relative to the borrower's gross monthly income. The most disciplined underwriting standard is a maximum of a 25% front-end DTI.

  • The back-end ratio measures the mortgage payment plus other housing expenses, taxes, insurance, utilities, and maintenance, relative to the borrower's monthly gross income. Disciplined underwriting standards typically establish a maximum of a 33% back-end DTI.

The borrower is also required to make a down payment between 5% and 25% of the purchase price of the home when seeking to qualify for a mortgage, which is often referred to as the borrower's or homeowner's equity. Homeowner's equity is calculated as follows:

$$\text{Homeowner's equity} = MV - CB \qquad (6.1)$$

Where: MV = Market value of the property
CB = Outstanding current balance of the loan

Homeowner's equity is often expressed as a percentage of the current outstanding balance of the loan. The homeowner's equity as a ratio is:

$$\frac{MV - CB}{CB} \qquad (6.2)$$

The loan-to-value (LTV) ratio used by the lender when underwriting a loan, is defined as:

$$\text{Loan-to-value ratio} = \frac{CB}{MV} \qquad (6.3)$$

and it is the complement of homeowner's equity, as illustrated in equation 6.4.

$$1-\text{Homeowner's equity} \tag{6.4}$$

The homeowner's equity stake minimizes the risk of default. In the event that the lender is forced to foreclose on the property, the homeowner's equity provides a cushion to the lender that, upon liquidation, there will be sufficient proceeds to recover the balance of the debt owed by the borrower.

Table 6.1 illustrates the economics of foreclosure. The appraised value of the home at time of purchase was $200,000 and the borrower made a 20% down payment. After three years, the borrower defaults but had made timely payments up to this point. The outstanding balance of the loan at the time of default is $152,135.52.

The value of the home has fallen by 10% and the lender is able to sell the home for $180,000. The costs associated with foreclosure and liquidation represent 20% of the sale price, and include legal fees, real estate brokerage commissions, maintenance and repair costs, property taxes, and capitalized interest costs. Notice that the costs associated with liquidation are both fixed and variable. The variable costs include both capitalized interest and ongoing maintenance costs ongoing maintenance costs. Variable costs generally increase as the time to liquidation increases. Thus, variable costs, and by extension, loss severity, may be lower in areas where the housing market is stronger and higher in areas where the housing market is weaker.

After expenses the liquidation proceeds to the lender amounted to $144,000 and the current balance of the loan outstanding was $152,135.52, producing a loss on liquidation of ($8,135.52). The liquidation loss is often

TABLE 6.1 Economics of Foreclosure Liquidation

Appraised Value at Purchase	$200,000
Borrower Down Payment	20% ($40,000)
Original Loan Balance	$160,000
Note Rate	4.5%
Monthly Pmt.	$810.70
Loan Age	36 mos.
Remaining Balance	$151,895.3
Sale Price	$180,000
Liquidation Costs	20% ($36,000)
Liquidation Proceeds	$144,000
Gain (Loss) on Liquidation	($8,135.52)
Loss Severity	5.36%

referred to as loss severity and is calculated as follows:

$$\text{Loss severity} = \frac{LP - CB}{CB} \qquad (6.5)$$

Where: LP = Liquidation proceeds
$\quad\quad\; CB$ = Outstanding current balance of the loan

From the lender's perspective, homeowner's equity provides protection against loss in the event of default. As shown above, even given a 20% down payment, the lender may incur a loss in the event the borrower defaults and the lender is forced to foreclose in the attempt to recover the amount owed by the borrower. Thus, should a borrower attempt to qualify for a loan with less than a 20% down payment, the lender generally requires private mortgage insurance, or PMI. The lender takes out the PMI policy but the borrower pays the policy premium via a higher note rate. The PMI policy protects the lender and guarantees that in the event of default the policy provider will pay the lender the insured amount.

Consider the analysis presented in Table 6.2. In this case, the borrower's down payment is 5% ($10,000) and the lender takes out a PMI policy for 20% of the purchase price. Assuming the cost of the policy is 0.25% annually, the borrower's note rate increases from 4.50% to 4.75%. The combination of the higher loan balance and the higher note rate results in an increase of the borrower's monthly payment from $810.70 to $991.13.

TABLE 6.2 Economics of Foreclosure Liquidation with PMI

Appraised Value at Purchase	$200,000
Borrower Down Payment	5% ($10,000)
Original Loan Balance	$190,000
Note Rate	4.75%
Monthly Pmt.	$991.13
Loan Age	36 mos.
Remaining Balance	$180,770.60
Sale Price	$180,000
Liquidation Costs	20% ($36,000)
Liquidation Proceeds	$144,000
Gain (Loss) on Liquidation	($36,770.6)
Loss Severity	20.34%
PMI Claim	$40,000
Gain (Loss) with PMI	$3,229.4

The borrower defaults after making 36 monthly payments. As in the prior example, the value of the home falls by 10%. Without PMI protection, the lender faced a potential loss upon liquidation of $36,770.6, a loss severity of 20.34%. The lender claims the PMI provider for $40,000. In this scenario, PMI coverage afforded the lender the ability to net a gain of $3,229.4 upon liquidation.

6.1.2 Commercial Mortgage Origination and Underwriting

Commercial mortgage underwriting is less concerned about the borrower's willingness to repay since the loan is made to a corporation. A corporate entity, as a point of renegotiation of a loan's terms, may be more inclined to strategically default or file for bankruptcy protection than a homeowner. As a result, commercial mortgage loan underwriting focuses exclusively on the borrower's ability to repay the loan. The borrower's ability to repay a loan is demonstrated by the ongoing cash flow potential of the property, and is measured by the following four key underwriting ratios:

- The combined loan-to-value ratio, CLTV, is expressed as the total debt outstanding against the property relative to its market value. Generally, lenders underwrite loans to a maximum combined loan-to-value ratio of 80%. The combined loan-to-value ratio is given by the following:

$$CLTV = \frac{\sum_{i=1}^{n,lien} CB, n}{MV} \qquad (6.6)$$

where: $\sum_{i=1}^{n,lien} CB, n$ = sum of all debt taken against the property

MV = current market value of the property

- The loan-to-cost ratio, LTC, is used in cases when the borrower's commercial property project involves an initial construction phase. The LTC is expressed as the ratio of the construction loan to the total cost of the construction project. Generally, lenders underwrite these loans to a loan to cost ratio at or below 85%.

$$LTC \text{ ratio} = \frac{CL}{TPC} \qquad (6.7)$$

where: CL = construction loan amount
TPC = total project costs

A project's total cost includes: land costs, fixed and variable construction costs, as well as reserves.

■ The debt service coverage ratio, DSCR. It is likely the most important ratio to understand when making a commercial loan. The debt service ratio is calculated as follows:

$$DSCR = \frac{\text{Net operating income (NOI)}}{\text{Total debt service}} \qquad (6.8)$$

The net operating income is the income produced from a commercial property "net" of all operating expenses. Consider the simplified pro-forma statement of a rental property presented in Table 6.3.

Next, assume a commercial loan with the following characteristics: a 5.0% note rate, 30-year amortization, and $3,000,000 original balance. The monthly payment is $8,339.56. The annual payment is $100,062.70. The DSCR is:

$$DSCR = \frac{\$130,000.00}{\$100,062.70}$$
$$= 1.299$$

■ Capitalization rate, or *cap rate,* is the investor's return on her money. If the investor purchased the property for cash, the cap rate is:

$$\text{Capitalization rate} = \frac{\text{Net operating income}}{\text{Purchase price}} \qquad (6.9)$$

TABLE 6.3 Net Operating Income

Gross Scheduled Rents	$200,000
Less 5% Vacancy Assumption	($10,000)
Gross Operating Income	$190,000
Operating Expenses	
Property Taxes	
Insurance	
Maintenance	
Management Fees	
Reserves for Replacement	
Total Operating Expenses	$60,000
Net Operating Income (NOI)	$130,000

Continuing with the above example:

— The annual net operating income, or NOI, is $130,000.
— The loan amount is $3,000,000.
— Assuming an 80% loan-to-value ratio, the purchase price of the property is:

$$\text{Purchase price} = \frac{\$3,000,000}{0.80}$$
$$= \$3,750,000$$

Given a $3,750,000 purchase price, the capitalization rate is:

$$\text{Capitalization rate} = \frac{\$130,000}{\$3,750,000}$$
$$= 3.46\%$$

6.2 RESIDENTIAL MORTGAGE LOAN AMORTIZATION

The most common type of residential mortgage is a fixed-rate mortgage. Although the term may vary, the most common term chosen by borrowers is a 30-year, fixed-rate loan. For the most part, a mortgage requires monthly payments of principal and interest. Throughout the remainder of this book a standard mortgage is defined as a fixed-rate mortgage with a 30-year term requiring monthly payments of principal and interest. The monthly payment of a standard mortgage is obtained using the following formula [McDonald and Thornton 2008]:

$$\text{Monthly payment} = \left[MB_0(1 + i)^{term} \right] \times \left[\frac{i}{(1 + i)^{term} - 1} \right] \qquad (6.10)$$

Where: MB_0 = Original mortgage balance
$term$ = Mortgage term in months
i = Mortgage note rate/12

The formula for a mortgage loan payment may be deconstructed as follows:

1. The first quantity, $MB_0(1 + i)^{term}$, is the future value of the amount borrowed (equation 1.2) and is the amount to which the borrowed sum will grow, assuming the borrower made no payments to the lender over the life.

2. The second quantity determines the level annuity payment, both principal and interest, that reduces principal amount owed to $0.00 over the term of the loan.

Table 6.4 provides a partial amortization table for a standard loan. The monthly payment is $1,013.67. Working across the table, in the first month the scheduled interest is $750 and the scheduled principal is $263.37. By month 12, the scheduled interest has fallen to $738.93 and the scheduled principal has increased to $274.44.

TABLE 6.4 Mortgage Amortization Table

Original Bal: $200,000
Note Rate: 4.50%
Term: 360 mos.

Period	Begin Bal.	Monthly Pmt.	Sch. Interest	Sch. Principal	Ending Bal.
1	200000.00	1013.37	750.00	263.37	199736.63
2	199736.63	1013.37	749.01	264.36	199472.27
3	199472.27	1013.37	748.02	265.35	199206.92
4	199206.92	1013.37	747.03	266.34	198940.58
5	198940.58	1013.37	746.03	267.34	198673.23
6	198673.23	1013.37	745.02	268.35	198404.89
......					
10	197593.80	1013.37	740.98	272.39	197321.40
11	197321.40	1013.37	739.96	273.42	197047.99
12	197047.99	1013.37	738.93	274.44	196773.55
......					
24	193685.92	1013.37	726.32	287.05	193398.87
25	193398.87	1013.37	725.25	288.12	193110.75
26	193110.75	1013.37	724.17	289.21	192821.54
33	191063.39	1013.37	716.49	296.88	190766.51
34	190766.51	1013.37	715.37	298.00	190468.51
35	190468.51	1013.37	714.26	299.11	190169.40
36	190169.40	1013.37	713.14	300.24	189869.16
......					
180	132982.60	1013.37	498.68	514.69	132467.91
181	132467.91	1013.37	496.75	516.62	131951.29
182	131951.29	1013.37	494.82	518.55	131432.74
......					
357	4015.76	1013.37	15.06	998.31	3017.45
358	3017.45	1013.37	11.32	1002.06	2015.40
359	2015.40	1013.37	7.56	1005.81	1009.58
360	1009.58	1013.37	3.79	1009.58	0.00

6.3 DECONSTRUCTING THE AMORTIZATION TABLE

The scheduled principal is calculated as follows:

$$\text{Scheduled principal} = MP - (i \times CB) \qquad (6.11)$$

Where: MP = Mortgage payment
i = Note rate/12
CB = Current balance outstanding

A *loan amortization* table like the one presented in Table 6.4 is calculated using equations 6.10 and 6.11. Alternatively, equation 6.12 yields the scheduled principal in any given period without the use of an amortization table.

$$\text{Scheduled principal} = CB \left[\frac{i \times (1 + i)^{period-1}}{(1 + i)^{term} - 1} \right] \qquad (6.12)$$

Where: CB = Current mortgage balance
i = Mortgage note rate/12
$period$ = Payment period
$term$ = Mortgage term in months

The scheduled ending balance is calculated from the amortization table as follows:

$$\text{Scheduled ending balance} = MB_0 - \sum_{i=1}^{n} SP \qquad (6.13)$$

Where: MB_0 = Original mortgage balance
SP = Scheduled principal

Similarly, one can calculate the remaining balance, in the absence of prepayment, without an amortization schedule, using the following formula.

$$\text{Ending balance} = MB_0 \left[\frac{(1 + i)^{term} - (1 + i)^{period}}{(1 + i)^{term} - 1} \right] \qquad (6.14)$$

Where: MB_0 = Original mortgage balance
i = Mortgage note rate/12
$period$ = Payment period
$term$ = Mortgage term in months

6.4   MORTGAGE SERVICING

Mortgage lenders must also perform other duties after the loan is closed and funded. These duties can be classified as follows:

- Loan Maintenance
  1. Send payment notices and remind the borrower when the payment is due.
  2. Make sure the borrower sends timely and accurate payments.
  3. Accurately record the borrower's payment.
- Loan Administration
  1. Administer escrow accounts for the payment of taxes and insurance.
  2. In the absence of escrow, verify the borrower has paid her property taxes and insurance coverage is maintained on the property.
  3. Send the borrower tax information at the end of the year.
- Delinquency Management and Loss Mitigation
  1. Contact and counsel delinquent borrowers.
  2. Implement loss mitigation strategies. These strategies are designed to aid delinquent borrowers to return to current payment status.
  3. Initiate foreclosure proceedings if the borrower cannot return to current status.
  4. Maintain and liquidate foreclosed properties.

The servicer receives a *servicing fee* in exchange for the above activities. The servicing fee typically ranges between 0.25% and 0.50%. In addition to the servicing fee, the servicer is also allowed to retain any late fees paid by the borrower, foreclosure penalties, and prepayment penalties. The amounts and fees that a servicer is entitled to collect and retain is set forth in the *servicing agreement* between the owner of the loan (lender) and the servicer.

CONCEPT 6.1

By investing in a MBS transaction the investor agrees to the financial relationship between the original mortgage lender and the loan servicing agent. In addition, the investor may be subject to loss in the event the servicer is deemed to have violated "good" servicing practices thereby harming the homeowner. Thus, it is imperative that the investor monitor the servicer's business practices throughout the life of the transaction.

At first blush, investing in a mortgage- or asset-backed security appears to be an "arm's length" transaction in that the investor provides "term funding" to the originator of the loan, which is not the case. In practice, the investor may incur losses due to either of the following:

- Loan performance, both voluntary prepayment and default, that is incongruent, with the lender's *underwriting* matrix, which suggests an inordinate amount of exceptions to the underwriting matrix.
- Loss due to poor servicing practices. The servicing agreement sets forth the amounts and fees that are received by the servicer. However, the trust (investor) may be liable for servicing violations that harm the consumer; especially if the lender is no longer an ongoing concern.

As a result, the investor must closely monitor the following:

1. The expected collateral performance (prepayment, delinquency, and default) given the originator's underwriting matrix versus the actual collateral performance.
2. The servicer's administration, collection, and loss mitigation practices.
3. The financial strength of the lender and servicer.
4. In the case of a securitization conduit—an entity that originates loans for the purpose of securitization—the consistent application of its underwriting standards as outlined in the prospectus is important to protect the investor from incurring greater than expected losses.

CHAPTER 7

Modeling Cash Flows

If a measurement matters at all, it is because it must have some conceivable effect on decisions and behaviour.

Douglas W. Hubbard

The investor in a MBS transaction is exposed to prepayment risk, or the early termination of the loan. There are two types of prepayment risk:

- **Voluntary repayment** occurs when the borrower exercises his right to prepay the loan at any time. Voluntary repayments occur due to the following:
  - *Refinancing*—in this case, the borrower may be seeking to obtain a lower rate and/or extract equity from the property.
  - *Turnover*—the sale of property, which is typically related to relocation, family formation, or a life event such as death or divorce.
- **Involuntary repayment**, in this case the borrower defaults on the loan. Defaults occur due to the following:
  - *Life event*—a job loss, illness, or family break-up, etc.
  - *Strategic*—the value of the property has fallen below the amount owed on the loan.

7.1   PREPAYMENT CONVENTIONS

Because a borrower may terminate his loan at anytime, the lender (investor) is said to be "short" the prepayment option to the borrower. In the case of commercial real estate lending, the loans are structured with a make-whole prepayment penalty and as a result, voluntary repayment occurs less frequently, simplifying the analysis and valuation of these securities. On the other hand, residential real estate loans typically do not carry prepayment penalties, and as a result are subject to greater voluntary prepayment risk than commercial real estate. Since residential real estate carries greater prepayment risk, Part Two focuses exclusively on residential real estate prepayment rates.

The cash flow analysis presented next extends the concept of mortgage prepayment to a securitization pool of residential loans. A mortgage-backed security, MBS, represents a pool of many residential mortgage loans each of which may terminate, *a prepayment*, either voluntarily, *refinance or move*, or involuntarily, *default*, at any time. Consequently, the cash flow profile of a mortgage securitization is not a binary outcome. This changes the MBS cash flow profile.

7.1.1 Single Monthly Mortality Rate

The monthly prepayment rate, or single monthly mortality rate (SMM) measures the percentage of a pool's principal balance that has prepaid in the current month. It is based on the change in the pool's factor (survival factor) from one period to the next, and is given by the following [Corporation no date]:

$$SMM = \frac{\text{Scheduled balance} - \text{Ending balance}}{\text{Scheduled balance}} \times 100 \qquad (7.1)$$

Equation 7.1 can be rewritten:

$$SMM = \frac{\text{Beginning balance} - \text{Scheduled principal} - \text{Ending balance}}{\text{Beginning balance} - \text{Scheduled principal}} \times 100$$
$$(7.2)$$

7.1.2 Conditional Prepayment Rate

The market convention is to state the single monthly mortality rate, or SMM, as an annualized measure, known as the *conditional prepayment rate* (CPR) [Corporation no date]. The formula for CPR is:

$$CPR = 1 - (1 - SMM)^{12} \times 100 \qquad (7.3)$$

7.1.3 Public Securities Association Model

The *Public Securities Association (PSA) model* was developed to describe how mortgage prepayments evolve as a function of loan age. The PSA model specifies the mortgage prepayment loan age (seasoning) function as follows:

- Begins at 0.2% CPR the first month,
- Increases by 0.2% CPR per month, and
- Reaches a maximum of 6.0% CPR in month 30.

Figure 7.1 illustrates the application of the PSA model. For example, at 100 PSA the investor is assuming that the pool's prepayment rate will follow the seasoning ramp described above.

- A 150 PSA assumption multiplies the PSA model by 150%. Under this assumption, the pool's prepayment rate will begin at 0.3% in the first month, season 0.3% per month, and reach a peak of 9.0% in month 30.
- A 50 PSA assumption multiplies the PSA model by 50%. Under this assumption, the investor believes that the pool's prepayment rate will begin at 0.1% in the first month, season 0.1% per month, and reach a peak of 3.0% in month 30.

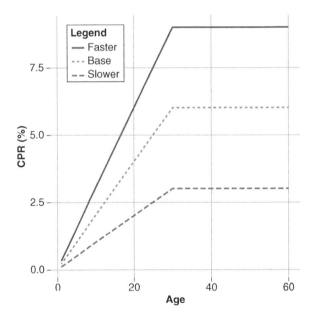

FIGURE 7.1 PSA Mortgage Prepayment Assumption

7.1.4 Prospectus Prepayment Curve, PPC

Figure 7.1 generalizes the PSA model. Issuers of non-agency residential MBS typically price their transactions using a generalization of the PSA model presented in equation 7.4. For example, a prime non-agency issuer may price its transaction to a PPC ramp that begins at 3.0% CPR in the first month, increasing by 3.0% per month for 11 months, reaching 36% CPR in month 12, the peak seasoning age.

$$\text{PPC} = \text{Min}\left[\text{Start CPR} + \left[(\text{Age} - 1) * \frac{(\text{End CPR} - \text{Start CPR})}{(\text{Peak seasoning age} - 1)}\right], \text{End CPR}\right] \quad (7.4)$$

CONCEPT 7.1

The *prospectus prepayment curve* was created to provide dealers with greater deal pricing flexibility than that provided by PSA assumption. The use of the PPC is more prevalent in the non-agency MBS sector.

7.2 MODELING MBS CASH FLOWS

Table 6.4 provides the amortization schedule of a 4.50%, 30-year level payment (amortization) mortgage. The inputs required to calculate the scheduled payment (scheduled interest and principal) are as follows:

- Original balance of the mortgage
- Borrower's note rate
- Term of the mortgage
- Loan age

In the case of a mortgage securitization, the cash flow analysis is complicated by the presence of any or all of the following: servicing fees, guarantee fees (GFee), private mortgage insurance (PMI). These costs are subtracted from the borrower's note rate. The net of the borrower's note rate less servicing, GFee, and PMI is the net note rate, or *net weighted average coupon* (NWac).

- The servicing fee compensates the servicer on a monthly basis for the administration duties outlined in Chapter 6 (section 6.4).

- The PMI fee protects the lender from loss in the event that the borrower defaults and there is insufficient equity in the home to cover the outstanding balance of the note (see Table 6.2).
- The guarantee fee is a premium paid by the borrower to the guarantor, typically the party that securitized and sold the MBS pool, for its guarantee of timely principal and interest to the investor.

The NWac, scheduled principal, and prepaid principal are "passed through" to the investor, hence, the term *pass-through security*.

7.2.1   0% PPC Assumption—*No Prepayment*

Figure 7.2 illustrates the cash flow profile of a 4.0% MBS pool assuming a 0% PPC—*no prepayments*.

- In the absence of prepayments, the investor receives a level cash flow over the life of the pool. In this case, the investor receives $609.13 per $100,000 invested.

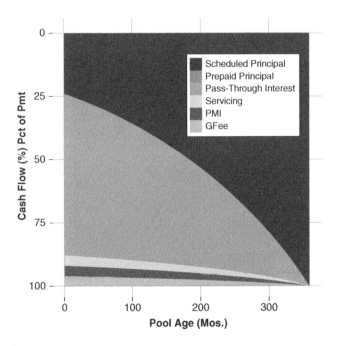

FIGURE 7.2   Cash Flow Share Assuming 0% PPC

- Early in the life of the pool, a greater share of the mortgage payment consists of interest. As the loans underlying the pool amortize, the share of scheduled principal, as a percentage of the borrower's scheduled payment, increases.
- About halfway through the life of the loan the amount of scheduled principal paid is greater than the amount of interest paid. This accelerates the amortization of the loans underlying the pool as it approaches its final payment *maturity* date.

7.2.2 100% PPC Assumption

The borrower's option to prepay his loan at anytime alters the timing of the cash flows received by the investor because prepayments are passed through as the *unscheduled* return of principal. The example presented in Figure 7.3 uses a 100 PPC assumption and shows that as the borrowers in the pool exercise their option to prepay the principal returned to the investor becomes *front loaded*.

Figure 7.3 illustrates how the application of a prepayment assumption changes the share of principal and interest paid to the investor.

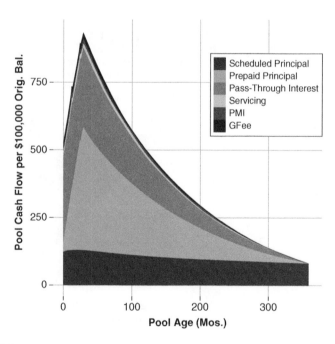

FIGURE 7.3   Pool Cash Flow Assuming 100% PPC

For example, at month 100 the share of principal paid—both scheduled and prepaid—account for around 75% of the total principal received. In contrast, Figure 7.2 shows that in the absence of prepayments, scheduled principal accounts for around 50% of the total principal received by the investor.

7.2.3 Applying Prepayment Assumptions

From the cash flow analysis presented in the previous section, one can see that the derivation of MBS cash flows is dependent on the investor's underlying prepayment assumption. As a result, it is important to understand both the nomenclature used in the description of structured security cash flows as well their practical application.

The foundation of all prepayment applications is the single monthly mortality rate (SMM) presented in 7.1. The SMM is the percentage of the outstanding balance that prepays. However, most investors annualize measures of prepayment rates. In the case of MBS, the measure quoted is the conditional prepayment rate (CPR). The CPR is an annualized expression of the SMM. It refers to the amount of prepaid principal an investor would receive over a 12-month period assuming the SMM remains constant.

To calculate a prepaid principal amount, one may be tempted to simply take the CPR or SMM and multiply it by the period's beginning balance—an incorrect application of the concept. The amount of prepaid principal is calculated only after giving credit to the scheduled principal paid in the period. Table 7.1 provides the derivation of the cash flows of a mortgage pass-through security, including the allocation of servicing, the guarantee fee, and PMI. To calculate the pass-through security's cash flows using the example introduced in section 7.2.1, the following steps are taken:

- First, calculate the scheduled principal due (equation 6.11).
  - For example, the scheduled principal due based on the beginning balance in Nov. 2013 and assuming 100% PPC is $273.83.
- Second, determine the appropriate CPR.
  - For example, a loan age of 10 along the 100 PPC assumption is equal to 2.2% CPR.
  - Then, de-annualize the CPR to an SMM—this is the monthly principal prepaid.

$$SMM = \left(1 - (1 - .020)^{(1/12)}\right) = 0.001682$$

TABLE 7.1 MBS Cash Flow Table

Original Balance: $100,000
NWac: 4.00%
Gross WAC: 4.75%
Term: 360 mos.
PPC Assumption: 100

Pmt. Date	Begin Bal.	Sched. Prin	Prepaid Prin.	Investor Interest	Servicing	PMI	G-Fee
2013-02	100000.00	275.80	16.63	333.33	20.83	20.83	20.83
2013-03	99707.55	275.77	33.20	332.35	20.77	20.77	20.77
2013-04	99398.57	275.69	49.69	331.32	20.70	20.70	20.70
2013-05	99073.18	275.56	66.10	330.24	20.64	20.64	20.64
2013-06	98731.51	275.39	82.42	329.10	20.56	20.56	20.56
2013-07	98373.69	275.17	98.64	327.91	20.49	20.49	20.49
......							
2013-11	96784.04	273.83	162.34	322.61	20.16	20.16	20.16
2013-12	96347.86	273.38	177.93	321.15	20.07	20.07	20.07
2014-01	95896.54	272.88	193.38	319.65	19.97	19.97	19.97
......							
2015-01	89377.15	263.45	364.54	297.92	18.62	18.62	18.62
2015-02	88749.15	262.38	377.42	295.83	18.48	18.48	18.40
2015-03	88109.34	261.27	390.06	293.69	18.35	18.35	18.35
......							
2028-01	21621.48	119.03	110.58	72.07	4.50	4.50	4.50
2028-02	21391.86	118.42	109.40	71.30	4.45	4.45	4.45
2028-03	21164.03	117.81	108.24	70.54	4.40	4.40	4.40
......							
2042-12	95.26	47.63	0.24	0.31	0.01	0.01	0.01
2043-01	47.38	47.38	0.00	0.15	0.00	0.00	0.00

- Third, after giving credit to the scheduled principal due, calculate the prepaid principal.
  - (Beginning balance − Scheduled principal) × SMM

$$\text{Prepaid principal} = \$96{,}784.04 - \$273.84 = \$162.34$$

- Finally, allocate interest. First, pay the investor interest amount, servicing, PMI, and G-Fee.

A mortgage pass-thorough security is the simplest expression of structuring a pool of mortgage loans. The MBS pool illustrates both the division of principal and interest.

- In the case of a pass-through security the principal—both scheduled and prepaid—is allocated 100% to the pass-through security.
- The interest is allocated first to the servicer plus lender paid PMI. The servicer remits the remaining interest to the trustee and the trustee allocates interest as follows:

    — The investor—in the case of guarantee the G-fee provider advances full and timely payment to the investor.
    — The G-Fee provider.

Notice, with the exception of the G-fee provider, the investor's interest priority payment is last in the waterfall. Understanding the cash flow dynamics of the underlying collateral is the key to the valuation of structured securities irrespective of the type of loans (residential mortgage, commercial mortgage, auto loan, etc.). The valuation of structured securities, like residential MBS, requires deriving the timing of the return of principal and timely payment of interest. Modeling expected cash flows provides the foundation for discounting along the spot rate curve.

Cash flow modeling drives the valuation of all structured securities. It establishes a framework that defines the following:

- Timing of the return of principal
- Payment of interest to the investor
- Allocation of losses due to borrower default
- Recovery of principal following the liquidation of defaulted loans

CHAPTER 8

Mortgage Prepayment Analysis

It ain't what you don't know that gets you into trouble. It's what you know for sure that just ain't so.

Mark Twain

In order to properly value a residential mortgage, a commercial mortgage, or a consumer asset backed security the investor must generate a prepayment estimate. Typically a model that estimates both voluntary and involuntary repayment is used for this purpose. Before one can "build" a prepayment model, an understanding the fundamental drivers of mortgage prepayments is essential. For this reason, mortgage prepayment analysis is treated as a separate topic from modeling. Prepayment data and the analysis thereof fall under the rubric of *big data* and *statistical learning*.

8.1 BIG DATA—WHAT IS IT?

The definition of *big data* remains somewhat elusive. Some consider big data as a data set that is too large to be processed with realistically available memory, while others may consider big data as large data sets representing complex relationships or interactions. The conceptualization of big data can be characterized as a "mile wide and inch deep" or "half as wide but ten miles deep."

Rejecting the notion of big data in terms of its overall size leads to the following definition of big data: *a complex data set requiring advanced methods of statistical computing to both understand its structure and produce reliable model estimates of future behavior.* Using this definition, mortgage prepayment data, although not big data in terms of the number of rows (observations) or absolute size (terabytes), qualifies as big data in that the interactions between variables (the data structure) is complex.

8.2   THE STATISTICAL LEARNER

Statistical learning refers to "a set of tools for *understanding data*" [Tibshirani 2013]. The goal of statistical learning is to estimate a function f describing the relationship between the response variable and the predictor variable(s). The function is estimated for either inference or prediction.

Estimating f for inference seeks to answer the following questions:

- Is the change in the response variable explained by the change(s) in predictor variable(s)?
- If so, to what degree, and what is the functional form of the relationship between the two?

When estimating f for prediction, the value of the response (y) variable is not known. However, the value(s) of the predictor variable(s) are known. In this case, one estimates the value of $\hat{Y}$ given an estimate of $f(x)$, that is:

$$\hat{Y} = \hat{f}_{(x)} \tag{8.1}$$

Estimating $f(x)$ may be done using parametric, semi-parametric, or non-parametric methods.

- A parametric method assumes a functional form of $f(x)$. For example, a common assumption is that $f(x)$ is linear. Once the functional form is decided, the training data are used to "fit" the model. A well-known parametric method is least squares regression.
- A non-parametric method will not assume a functional form of $f(x)$. Rather, these methods seek to produce an estimate of $f(x)$ that is as close as possible to the observed data while minimizing the roughness of the function. A non-parametric method, by avoiding the assumption of a functional form of $f(x)$, offers the potential to fit a much broader range of $f(x)$ than does a parametric method.

Finally, statistical analysis may fall under the rubric of supervised or unsupervised learning.

- In the case of supervised learning, a training data set is provided, and for each observation of the predictor variable(s), there is a value of the response variable.
- Unsupervised learning attempts to find the hidden structure in unlabeled data, no supervising function or underlying distributional assumption is inferred. For example, cluster analysis seeks to determine whether or not observations of the data fall into distinct groups.

Modeling mortgage prepayment relies on both supervised and unsupervised statistical learning. The investor uses both parametric and non-parametric techniques to explore the predictors of mortgage prepayments. However, the model deployed is usually based more on the techniques of parametric statistical learning than on those of non-parametric statistical learning because the model is often required to predict borrower prepayment rates outside the boundaries of the training data.

This chapter is organized as a case study of prepayment analysis leading to the construction of a predictive prepayment model (Chapter 9). There are three reasons for treating the chapter as a case study:

1. Enumerating the prepayment characteristics of all the outstanding mortgage loan types would easily fill hundreds of pages.
2. The mortgage lending market is dynamic and new loan structures and lending practices continually evolve. Thus, it is important to understand the basic framework for exploring and understanding mortgage prepayments.
3. The techniques presented are applicable to all mortgage-and asset-backed securities and provide a solid applied framework for the analysis of prepayments.

8.3 SURVIVAL ANALYSIS

The analysis of mortgage repayment, delinquency, and default is the analysis of time to failure data. *Survival analysis* follows each individual loan up to the time of the failure—voluntary prepayment or default. The time to event is recorded as the response variable. The loans that survive to the end of the study period may experience a failure event at an unknown time beyond the end of the study while others may be lost to follow-up during the study these loans are said to be *censored* [Crawley 2013].

8.3.1 Working with Censored Data

Survival, or life length data, has two components that must be clearly defined [David. W. Hosmer and Lemeshow 1998]:

- A start: the point in the study where time $(t) = 0$.
- An end: the point where time (t) is the time at failure.

In the case of a mortgage loan, the reason for the end is a voluntary or involuntary prepayment of the loan prior to its scheduled final payment.

Thus, when analyzing and modeling loan level data, the event under study is whether the loan terminates before the scheduled final payment (1 = yes and 0 = no). Given the length of time to the scheduled final payment of most loans, the analyst is often unable to observe the survival time of a cohort or portfolio of loans through their scheduled final payment. As a result, the survival time is partially observable. Consequently, at the end of a study a loan may survive, terminate, or possibly be lost (incomplete observation of survival time). Observations may be either right or left censored. Following is a brief explanation of the most commonly encountered censoring when performing loan level prepayment analysis.

8.3.2 Right Censored Data

Right censoring, the most commonly encountered form of censoring. A right censored observation is one in which the study begins at $t = 0$ and ends before the event under study is observed. The observation is referred to as right censored because the incomplete observation occurs in the right tail of the time axis. In a study where right censoring is the only type of censoring possible, the observation of the subjects may begin at the same time or varying times. For example, a loan level prepayment study allowing only right censored data includes loans originated on or after a certain date.

8.3.3 Left Truncation (Delayed Entry)

In some instances there is a clear definition of the beginning point of the prepayment study. However, some loans may not fall under observation until that time has passed. For example, assume the study date begins at time t. If the study covered a 10-year period the loans in the study would have a maximum loan age of $t + 120$. Furthermore, suppose that after the start of the study there are loans originated prior to the study date with an age of 60 months added to sample and prior to their inclusion were still active. Thus, the analyst knows that the loans were at risk of termination for 60 months prior to the beginning of the study.

8.3.4 Left Censored Data

Finally, the analyst may experience left censored data. An observation is left censored if the event of interest has already occurred when the study begins. For example, a loan is included in a study that has just started with a loan age of 60 months and has already prepaid.

8.3.5 Kaplan-Meier Survivorship Analysis

Survival analysis requires an understanding of the following functions:

- The *probability density function* The probability density function is the probability of a continuous random variable time (T). In the case of a loan level prepayment model, the density function describes the percentage of loans that will likely prepay from the initial loan cohort in a given instant of time.
- The *survival function* The survival function is the likelihood that the loan will survive and remain current beyond (T). The survivor function plots the natural log of the proportion of a cohort of loans beginning at time T_0 that are still alive at t_n. It is given by:

$$S_t = P(T > t) \tag{8.2}$$

CONCEPT 8.1

The survival function can be estimated as follows:

$$\frac{\text{Number of loans that survived}}{\text{Number of loans at risk}} \tag{8.3}$$

The *hazard function* is the likelihood that a loan will not survive beyond (T) and is given by:

$$\frac{\text{Number of loan that prepaid}}{\text{Number of loans at risk}} \tag{8.4}$$

The cumulative survival function is:

$$\prod_{t_{(t)\leq t}} \frac{n_i - d_i}{n_i} \tag{8.5}$$

where: n_i = The number of loans at risk
d_i = The number of loans that prepaid (failed) at period n_i

TABLE 8.1   Kaplan-Meier Survivorship

Loan Age	Number at Risk	Events	Censored	Hazard	Survival	Cum. Survival
0	584,717	1,308	0	0.002	0.998	0.998
1	583,409	2,131	9	0.004	0.996	0.994
2	581,269	3,702	20	0.006	0.994	0.988
3	577,547	5,250	27	0.009	0.991	0.979
4	572,270	5,752	5,043	0.010	0.990	0.967
5	561,475	6,375	4,759	0.011	0.989	0.958
6	550,341	6,738	4,039	0.012	0.998	0.946

The above equations provide the foundation of the simplest case of survival analysis, the Kaplin-Meier survivorship function also known, in the absence of predictor variables, as the *product limit* estimator.

Table 8.1 numerically illustrates the Kaplan-Meier survivorship:

- The study begins with 584,717 loans at risk. Of those loans, 1,308 experienced voluntary prepayment and at loan age 0 no loans were lost to follow-up.
- The hazard or mortality rate at loan age 0 is $0.002 = 1,308/584,717$. The survival rate is $0.998 = 1 - .002$. The hazard (mortality) rate is equivalent to the single monthly mortality rate (SMM). It can be expressed as the constant prepayment rate (CPR) observed at loan age (n) using equation 7.3 as shown:

$$CPR = 1 - (1 - 0.0022)^{12}$$

$$= 0.0237$$

$$= 2.37\%$$

- The cumulative survival rate, given by equation 8.4, at loan age 6, is 0.946, or 94.6% of the loans under study have survived to loan age 6. The cumulative survival is equivalent to the MBS pool factor.

Figures 8.1 and 8.2 further illustrate the relationship between the cumulative survival function, the monthly mortality rate, and the monthly CPR. Figure 8.1 shows that the cumulative survival function closely resembles the MBS pool factor. In fact, the MBS pool factor is simply the ratio of the current balance outstanding relative to the original balance of the pool. As such, the MBS pool factor reports the percentage loan balance that has survived, after giving consideration to scheduled principal through loan or pool age (n).

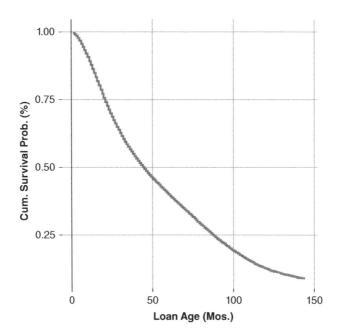

FIGURE 8.1   FH 30-yr. Cum. Survival

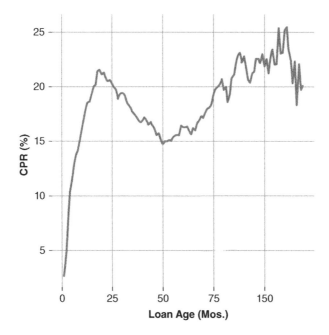

FIGURE 8.2   FH 30-yr. CPR

CONCEPT 8.2

- The n survival probability is given by:

$$\text{CumSurv}_n = \text{CumSurv}_{n-1} \times \text{Surv}_n$$

Rearranging the terms:

$$\text{Surv}_n = \frac{\text{CumSurv}_n}{\text{CumSurv}_{n-1}}$$

- The hazard (mortality) rate at n is:

$$\text{Hazard}_n = 1 - \text{Survival Prob.}_n$$

- Finally, substituting the Hazard_n into equation 7.3

$$\text{CPR} = 1 - (1 - \text{Hazard}_n)^{12}$$

8.4   THE COX PROPORTIONAL HAZARDS MODEL

For some the preferred framework for the analysis of mortgage prepayment data is the *Cox proportional hazards model*. The analysis of mortgage voluntary repayment, delinquency, and default is the analysis of time to failure, or survival time data, and the Cox proportional hazards model is one of the most widely accepted statistical techniques used to model the relationship between a set of predictor variables and survival outcomes [Therneau and Gambash 2000].

The Cox model is semi-parametric in that it does not assume an underlying error structure. However, it does assume the hazard multiplier (risk score) of a given predictor variable is constant over time (equation 8.9). The model is particularly well suited to perform the analysis of repayment, delinquency, and default data. The hazard function [Crawley 2013] is given by:

$$\lambda(t; Z_i) = \lambda_0(t) r_t(t) \tag{8.6}$$

where: Z_i = the covariates for the individual$_i$ at $_t$

The risk score for the individual is given by:

$$r_i(t) = \exp^{\beta Z_i(t)} \qquad (8.7)$$

The above can be rewritten:

$$\lambda_0(t)\exp^{\beta Z_i(t)} \qquad (8.8)$$

where: $\lambda_0(t)$ = an unspecified baseline hazard function

Finally, consider the concept of a hazard ratio [Therneau and Gambash 2000] [David. W. Hosmer and Lemeshow 1998]. Given two subjects with covariate vectors Z_1 and Z_2, the hazard ratio is given by:

$$\frac{\lambda_0(t)\exp^{\beta Z_1(t)}}{\lambda_0(t)\exp^{\beta Z_2(t)}} = \frac{\exp^{\beta Z_1(t)}}{\exp^{\beta Z_2(t)}} \qquad (8.9)$$

8.5 DATA TYPES

The analysis and modeling of mortgage prepayment data require the analyst to work with categorical, continuous, and time-dependent variables. The aforementioned data types as well as strategies for working with each are discussed below.

8.5.1 Categorical Variable

A *categorical variable* is a descriptive variable like loan purpose or property type. A categorical variable may have more than one possible value. For example, loan purpose may be *purchase, refinance,* or *cash-out refinance.* It may also be binary in nature such as *yes* or *no.*

A categorical variable *(factor)* with more than one level, denoted n, may be modeled using an $n - 1$ design strategy. The most common method used for the coding of categorical design variables is the *referent cell coding method.* Using this method the analyst selects a level, typically the most frequently observed, as the reference level against which all others are measured. An example of the referent cell coding method is provided below. As shown in Table 8.2, the loan purpose factor is coded on three levels using two design variables d_1 and d_2.

The loan purpose factor design suggests that the hazard ratios of the levels refinance and cash-out refinance are measured against the purchase level. In this case, the purchase level defines the baseline hazard function $\lambda_0(t)$.

TABLE 8.2   Referent Cell Coding

Level	d_1	d_2
Purchase	0	0
Refinance	0	1
Cash-out Refinance	1	0

8.5.2   Continuous Variable

A *continuous variable* is one that takes on an indiscrete value. Examples of continuous variables include: loan-to-value ratio, the borrower's credit score, and loan balance. An important part of working with a continuous variable is to determine its functional form, which can be done using several methods. Two of the most common are described below:

- The simplest method is to transform the continuous variable into a categorical variable. The transformation is accomplished using quartiles, or intervals, and estimating the each interval's hazard ratio. The hazard ratios are then plotted against the mid-point of each interval. If the correct form is linear in the log hazard then the points will connect to form a straight line. In the event that the plot deviates from a straight line, its form may be used to suggest a suitable transformation of the variable.
- The second method involves fitting a model excluding the predictor variables—a null model. The null model residuals are then smoothed and plotted versus the predictive variable. The shape of the plot of the smoothed values results in an estimate of the functional form of the predictor variable. Once the functional form is identified, a suitable transformation may be applied.

8.5.3   Time-Dependent Variable

A *time-dependent variable* is a variable whose value changes as a function of time. The value of the hazard function is dependent on the current value of the variable rather than its value at the beginning of the study $t = 0$. A time-dependent variable may be either internal or external. An internal time dependent variable's value changes as a function of time. For example, loan age is an internal time-dependent variable and requires direct observation of the loan in the study. An external time-dependent variable's value does not require the loan to be under direct observation. An external time-dependent variable measures environmental factors that apply to all the loans in the study. Examples of external time-dependent variables include: the prevailing mortgage rate and home price inflation or deflation.

8.6 CASE STUDY: FHLMC 30-YEAR LOAN LEVEL PREPAYMENT ANALYSIS

This case study uses FHLMC's sample loan level data set as of August 2013. The sample data set contains 50,000 loans randomly selected from each full vintage year from 2000 through 2011 and a proportionate share of loans from each partial vintage year 1999 and 2012. In all, the data set used for this case included 675,000 loans originated between January 1999 and July 2012.

This case study highlights the analysis of voluntary prepayment rates. Many variables influence mortgage prepayment rates [Schwartz and W. N. Torous 1989] [Stanton 1995] [Peristiani 1998] [Michale, Marschoun, and Maxam 2002]. The study illustrates the analysis and modeling of voluntary prepayments based on the following predictor variables:

- External Time Dependent Variables
  — The housing turnover rate. *Turnover*
  — Seasonal factors; *Seasonals*
- Internal Time Dependent
  — Loan age; *Seasoning*
  — The current mortgage rate vs. the borrower's note rate. *Borrower Incentive*
- Categorical Variables
  — Loan Purpose; Loan purpose consists of three levels:
    • Purchase
    • Refinance
    • Cash-out Refinance

To avoid potential left censoring of the data, only loans with an origination date occurring on or after December 2012 are included in the modeling data set. The censor coding is as follows:

- open loan = 0,
- voluntarily repayment = 1,
- involuntary repayment = 2.

8.6.1 Borrower Economic Incentive to Refinance

The borrower's economic incentive to refinance refers to the borrower's option to prepay and is likely the first internal time dependent predictor variable encountered by the analyst. There are several ways to measure the borrower's incentive to refinance. [Michale, Marschoun, and Maxam 2002] [Stanton 1995] [Schwartz and W. Torous 1992] [Peristiani 1998]. Recall that a mortgage is simply a self-amortizing annuity. Thus, the borrower's decision to refinance is one of retiring the existing mortgage annuity with a value of X and taking out a new mortgage annuity with a value of Y. Presumably, the value of the mortgage annuity Y is less than that of the mortgage annuity X after transaction costs. The following methods may be used to measure the borrower's economic incentive to refinance.

- Measuring the ratio of the present value of the current mortgage annuity to that of the new mortgage annuity.

$$\text{Annuity ratio} = \left[\frac{(1 + \text{Note rate})^{-n}}{(1 + \text{Mortgage rate})^{-n}} \right] \qquad (8.10)$$

- Related to the above is measuring the log ratio of the borrower's note rate to the prevailing or lagged mortgage rate.

$$\text{Log ratio incentive} = \ln \left[\frac{\text{Note rate}}{\text{Mortgage rate}} \right] \qquad (8.11)$$

- Measuring the spread between the borrower's note rate and the prevailing or lagged mortgage rate.

$$\text{Incentive spread} = \text{Note rate} - \text{Mortgage rate} \qquad (8.12)$$

The homeowner may face a positive economic incentive to refinance due to declining mortgage rates. For example, assume a homeowner carrying a 5.0% 30-year loan with 24 months of seasoning. If the prevailing 30-year mortgage rate falls from 5.0% to 4.0% then the homeowner faces a positive economic incentive of 1.0% to refinance his existing loan. Similarly, a homeowner may face a negative economic incentive to refinance due to rising mortgage rates. Assume the homeowner in the above example. If the prevailing mortgage rate were to go up from 5.0% to 6.0%, then the homeowner faces a negative economic incentive of 1.0% to refinance his loan.

Modeling the borrower's economic incentive to refinance is a classic example of using histograms. The analysis begins by binning the incentive spread measure (Note rate - Mortgage rate), in this case by 50 basis points, and plotting the distribution. Figure 8.3 shows, that the borrower incentive within this data set is modestly skewed to the right—the mean incentive is 1.19 bps and the median incentive is 1.27 bps. The are a few extreme outliers to the right.

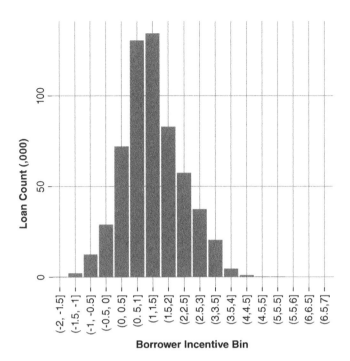

FIGURE 8.3   Distribution of Borrower Incentive

Given that the distribution of incentive spread is near normal, the next step is to explore the functional form. The steps are:

1. First, using the survival regression package which can be downloaded from the R CRAN website fit a null model to the loan level data set.
2. Second, using the predict function extract the residuals. The predict function in R has two options to return the overall number of events E_i and the linear predictor $X_i \beta$ for each individual. The option for type "expected" will return the E_i of the martingale residual.
3. Plot the residuals x versus the incentive spread y. In this case, the model was fit over $584,717$ loans, which results in too much density with respect to the residual plot. As a result, every $1,000^{th}$ observation was extracted and plotted.
4. The final step is to employ local regression smoothing R *function loess* to tease out the function form.

Figure 8.4 presents the results of the analysis and suggests that the incentive spread function is a sigmoid curve. That is, the functional form has the shape of the letter S hence the term *S-curve* when referring to the borrower's propensity to refinance given a positive economic incentive.

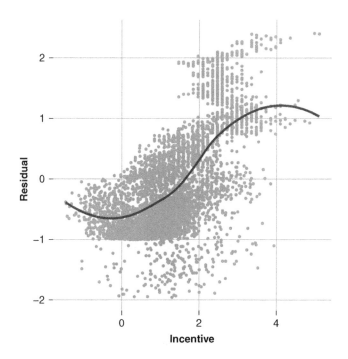

FIGURE 8.4 *Loess Model*—Functional Form of Borrower Incentive

Did this technique yield the correct functional form of the borrower's propensity to refinance when faced with a positive economic incentive? To answer this, one can turn to the MySql® loan level database. A query of the database based on incentive spread by 50 bps yields the result presented in Figure 8.5. The actual data also report a sigmoid function. The loan level data suggest that the prepayment rate is expected to drop to around 5.0 CPR when the borrower incentive spread is negative. As the borrower incentive spread increases, the expected prepayment rate also goes up, reaching a peak above 30.0 CPR. Again, Figure 8.6 presents the results of a loess fit across the predicted values of the null model. Figure 8.6 supports the notion of sigmoid function.

The functional form above encourages the use of smoothing splines to capture the influence of incentive on the expected mortgage prepayment rate. Table 8.3 provides summary statistics of the Cox model fit given the predictor variable *Incentive*.

- Borrower incentive is significant predictor of the voluntary prepayment, the descriptive statistics presented in Table 8.3 suggest that borrower incentive explains 38% of the variance in mortgage prepayment rates.

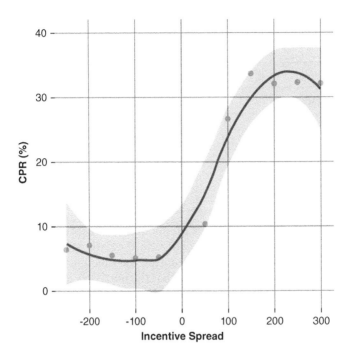

FIGURE 8.5 *Actual Data—CPR*

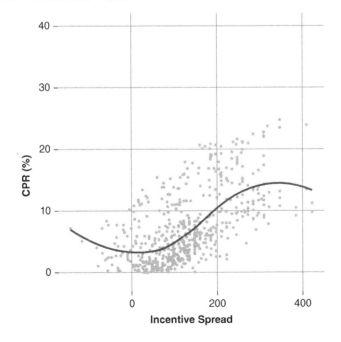

FIGURE 8.6 *Loess Data Fit—CPR*

TABLE 8.3 Cox Model—Incentive

	coef	exp(coef)	se(coef)	z	p
smooth(Incentive)	−0.9344	0.3928	0.0018	−519	0.00

Descriptive Statistics			
Concordance	0.775		se = 0.001
Rsquare	0.3928		
Likelihood Ratio Test	284,420	1 df	p =0
Wald Test	269,320	1 df	p =0
Score	280,588	1 df	p =0

A smoothing spline is used in the modeling to capture the functional form of the predictor variable *Incentive*. In the early stages of analysis, a simple null model works well for exploring the functional form of a given predictor variable. It is for this reason that the borrower incentive, arguably the more complex of the predictor variables, was presented first.

8.6.2 Loan Seasoning

Loan seasoning is not seasonality, it is an internal time dependent variable. The PSA model presented in section 7.1.3 and equation 7.4 (PPC curve) both represent an example of loan seasoning. A seasoning ramp defines the rate at which a pool of *at-the-money*[1] residential mortgage loans converge to the long-term expected housing turnover rate. One may argue that because loan seasoning is tied to housing turnover that it is an external time dependent variable—this is incorrect—unlike housing turnover, direct observation of the borrower is required to measure loan seasoning.

8.6.2.1 Housing Turnover Housing turnover measures the rate at which the nation's housing stock *turns over* on an annualized basis. It is measured by the ratio of existing home sales to the stock of existing homes. Housing turnover may be calculated using census data as follows:

$$\text{Turnover} = \frac{\text{Annual single-family home sales}}{\text{Owner-occupied housing stock}}$$

Figure 8.7, using recent Census data, illustrates the housing turnover rate from 2005 through 2010. Leading up to the peak of the U.S. residential

---

[1]An *at-the-money* loan is defined as a loan with a note rate of (+/−) 25 bps around the current mortgage rate.

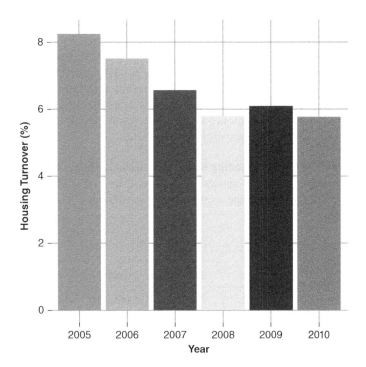

FIGURE 8.7 Housing Turnover

real estate bubble, the housing turnover rate was 8.2% (2005). Following the real estate bubble, the turnover rate fell to 5.7%. The ebb and flow of the housing turnover rate is affected by economic and social factors:

- *Relocation*, homeowner migration between counties, states, and regions. Typically, homeowner migration is driven by employment opportunities. For example, consider a situation in which the economic conditions in State A have declined but those in State B have increased. The stronger economic growth in State B versus State A may induce some homeowners to migrate from State A to State B in search of greater opportunity thereby creating higher housing turnover rates in States A and B.
- *Changes in home prices* may contribute to housing turnover. For example, strong home price appreciation may cause some home owners to trade up. That is, use their home equity gain to purchase a larger home. Conversely, home price declines that place the home owner in a negative equity position may trigger a strategic default

when the home is worth less than the outstanding note or reduce the homeowner's mobility. In either case, turnover rates are affected.

■ *Family formation or break-up*: home owners with children may trade-up to a larger home as the family grows or move to a neighboring school district that is deemed more desirable. Alternatively, families whose children have reached adulthood may down-size as the children leave home and form their own households. Finally, a family break-up or death will also contribute to the housing turnover rate.

8.6.2.2 The Mortgage Seasoning Ramp The baseline hazard ($\lambda_0(t)$) defines the turnover rate. Table 8.4 shows the results of the Cox model fit including incentive spread and loan age as the predictor variables. The results of the model fit are:

TABLE 8.4 Cox Model—LoanAge, Incentive

	coef	exp(coef)	se(coef)	z	p
smooth(LoanAge)	−1.234e-01	8.893e-01	2.844e-04	−434.1	0.00
smooth(LoanAge^2)	−4.710e-01	1.000e-00	2.832e-06	166.3	0.00
smooth(Incentive)	−5.764e-01	5.619e-01	2.054e-03	−280.6	0.00

Descriptive Statistics				
Concordance =		0.967		se = 0.001
Rsquare =		0.797		
Likelihood Ratio Test =		931,691	3 df	p =0
Wald Test =		124,914	3 df	p =0
Score =		807,192	3 df	p =0

Including the variables LoanAge and LoanAge^2 significantly improved the model's fit. The model's *R*-square increases to 0.797, suggesting that together loan age and incentive explain 79.7% of the variance in mortgage prepayment rates. Finally, analysis of variance (ANOVA) is used to compare the two models. The Incentive, LoanAge model is superior to the Incentive model (p < 0.0000). The variables LoanAge and LoanAge^2 successfully captured the functional form of the seasoning ramp.

Figure 8.8 presents a plot of the baseline hazard (Incentive = 0). The plot of the baseline clearly suggests a function that is similar to the concept of the PPC ramp. Namely, the prepayment rate increases over a seasoning period. The Cox model suggests that "at-the-money" borrowers, those with 0 bps incentive, season over 30 months reaching a peak CPR just above 8.0%. The seasoning ramp illustrated by the Cox model fit follows the PPC model

TABLE 8.5 ANOVA—Incentive vs. LoanAge, Incentive

	loglik	Chisq	Df	P(> | Chi |)
1	−4,290,191.09			
2	−3,958,555.63	663,270	2	0.0000

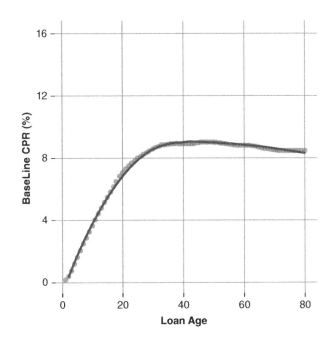

FIGURE 8.8 *Model Fit—CPR*

presented in section 7.1.3 seasoning to a peak around month 30. However, the peak seasoning just above 8.0% CPR versus the PPC maximum CPR assumption of 6.0% CPR, suggesting a modestly faster housing turnover rate:

■ The plot of the baseline hazard function suggests that the probability of prepayment increases linearly as function of time as the loan age approaches 30 months.
■ Given loan seasoning greater than 30 months the probability of prepayment tends to stabilize and then decline.

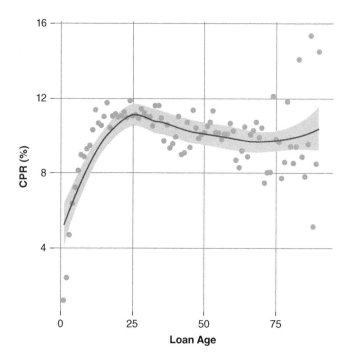

FIGURE 8.9   *Actual Data*—CPR

The rate at which a pool of loans converges to the national turnover rate is influenced by both demographic and economic factors. Typically, a homeowner remains in his residence for an average of 10 years [Paul Emrath 2009]. Figure 8.9 presents the "near-the-money" (+/– 25 bps) loan seasoning ramp from the FHLMC loan level data set. The loan seasoning ramp begins at 1.3 CPR in the first month and increases by about 0.408 CPR per month for 24 months, reaching a peak CPR of 11% around month 25—in line with PSA model assumption. Both the housing turnover rate and loan seasoning are intimately related. The basic questions the investor must address are at what rate will the loan seasoning function converge to the housing turn over rate? What is the expected housing turnover rate?

8.6.3 Seasonality

Seasonality is an example of an external time dependent variable that is modeled as a categorical factor rather than a continuous variable. The housing turnover rate tends to follow a seasonal pattern. Typically, more homes are available for sale in the spring and summer months than in the fall and winter months.

- A household with children may defer their planned home sale until the spring and summer months to avoid disrupting their children's education.
- A single household or those without children may remain in the market irrespective of the time of year.
- The better weather of the spring and summer months is more conducive to both house hunting and moving.

Table 8.6 shows the result of the ANOVA test between the previous model (1) and the model including month (2) as a seasonal component:

TABLE 8.6 ANOVA—Incentive, LoanAge vs. Incentive, LoanAge, Month

	loglik	Chisq	Df	P(> | Chi |)
1	−3958556			
2	−3909559	97994	11	0.0000

Including a seasonal component improves the model. The R-square increases to 0.828 from 0.797; indicating the predictor variables Incentive, LoanAge, and Seasonality explain 82.8% of the variance in mortgage prepayments. Overall, the inclusion of seasonality increases the model's fit versus the competing model of Incentive and LoanAge. For the most part, the seasonality coefficients for each month follow the pattern that one would expect. Figure 8.10 presents the results of the seasonality analysis. The referent level in this model is June (coefficient = 1.0) and the model's coefficients are exponentiated and applied as multipliers on the baseline hazard (see equations 8.6 to 8.9).

- Relative to June, prepayment rates in December, January, and February are lower—the hazard multipliers are less than 1.0.
- Prepayments tend to pick up somewhat in the second and third quarters (May, June, July, and August). Assuming a one-month lag between the sale of an existing home and its closing (a prepayment) implies greater home sales in April, May, June, and July. This pattern is consistent with expectations regarding the home selling season.
- The seasonal factor increases in October suggesting a pattern of late home sales in September.

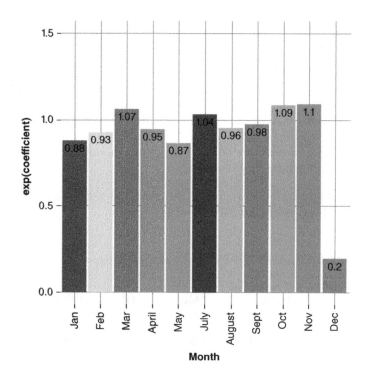

FIGURE 8.10 Seasonal Factors

8.7 SURVIVAL ANALYSIS—MODELING LOAN COHORTS

Once the investor has controlled for the influence of loan age, borrower incentive, and seasonality, the next task is to determine which loan cohorts may be modeled together. That is the likelihood of prepayment between loan cohorts is not significantly different. The goal is to identify those cohorts that should be treated as significantly different, possibly requiring a separate prepayment model. Through this process the investor gains both an understanding of the predictors that influence mortgage prepayments as well as sound modeling strategies. To illustrate the technique, the analysis is limited to loan purpose.

8.7.1 Loan Purpose

The first step is to determine the referent level for modeling purposes. The referent level of a categorical factor is typically the level with the

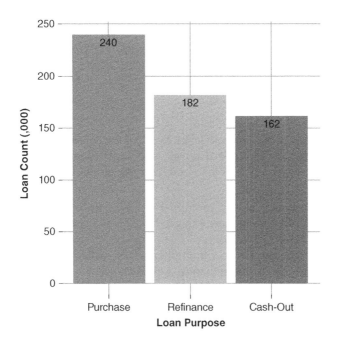

FIGURE 8.11 Loan Purpose

greatest number of observations. Figure 8.11 shows that the purchase cohort accounts for 240,000 loans (41%) followed by refinance and cash-out refinance. The levels of the factor loan purpose are ordered as follows: purchase, refinance, cash-out refinance.

ANOVA (Table 8.7) shows that including loan purpose improves the model's fit. Including loan purpose reduces the standard error of the coefficients more so than increasing the R-square of the model. The analysis thus far supports the notion of including loan purpose as part of the prepayment model. The question is how to incorporate loan purpose into the prepayment model. A general approach to the aforementioned problem is outlined in Table 8.8.

TABLE 8.7 ANOVA Loan Purpose

	loglik	Chisq	Df	P(> | Chi |)
1	−3,909,558.56			
2	−3,908,819.26	1,478.60	2	0.0000

TABLE 8.8 Loan Purpose Coefficient Analysis

Level	Coefficient	Std. Dev.	exp (Coeff.)	Lower 95%	Upper 95%
Refinance	0.1206	0.004	1.13	1.12	1.14
Cash-out	0.1495	0.004	1.16	1.15	1.17

- Assess the results of the model fit. Specifically, consider the loan purpose coefficients, their standard errors, and most importantly, their confidence intervals. Table 8.8 summarizes the model fit statistics for loan purpose.
  - The refinance hazard multiplier is 1.13—meaning that loans originated as a refinance are expected to prepay at a rate 13% faster than the baseline (purchase).
  - The cash-our refinance multiplier is 1.16—meaning that loans originated as a cash-out refinance (i.e., the borrower extracts equity from his home), are expected to prepay at a rate 16% faster than the baseline.
  - Finally, examination of the confidence intervals. Notice in this case, the confidence intervals do not overlap. This suggests that the hazard ratios of refinance and cash-out refinance are significantly different.

  Indeed, the analysis thus far supports the following modeling strategy:
  - Include loan purpose as a predictor variable in the model.
  - Treat each level (purchase, refinance, and cash-out) separately, potentially building a prepayment model for each.
- Next, how should loan purpose be incorporated into the model? To answer this, examine the assumption of proportionality of the hazard. Is the hazard ratio stable over time? The assumption of the Cox model is that the hazards are proportional. This means that any two subjects—in this case by loan purpose—obey the relationship expressed in equation 8.13, which is independent of time [Therneau and Gambash 2000].

$$\frac{\lambda_0(t)\exp^{\beta X_1(t)}}{\lambda_0\exp^{\beta X_2(t)}} = \frac{\exp^{\beta X_1}}{\exp^{\beta X_2}} \tag{8.13}$$

Figures 8.12 and 8.13 show that both loans originated as for refinance and cash-out refinance exhibit non-proportionality. If hazard were proportional over time, the loess smooth through the data would

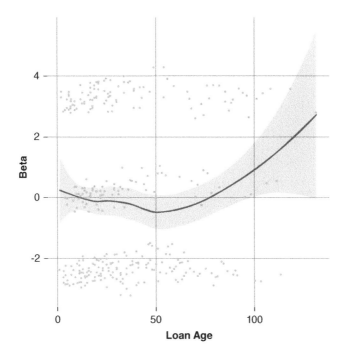

FIGURE 8.12   *Test*—Refinance

have demonstrated a slope of 0—a horizontal line. The interpretation of the test is relatively straight forward:

— Refinance: The beta initially declines and eventually is less than 0, indicating that in the case of a refinance loan, the propensity to prepay declines over time, likely due to the costs associated with refinancing. The propensity to refinance may initially decline as the homeowner recovers the cost of refinancing via a lower monthly mortgage payment.

— Cash-out: Initially the beta is less than 0 indicating that the propensity to repay is less than that of the baseline. However, the beta increases at an earlier loan age relative to refinance before declining again. Given that a cash-out borrower has extracted equity from his home, it is not unreasonable to assume that he may refinance again to extract additional equity from his home. This would result in an increasing and then decreasing beta over time.

■ Finally, decide a modeling strategy. Thus far, the analysis suggests that loan purpose should be included in the model and that its influence may change as a function of loan age. The investor may decide

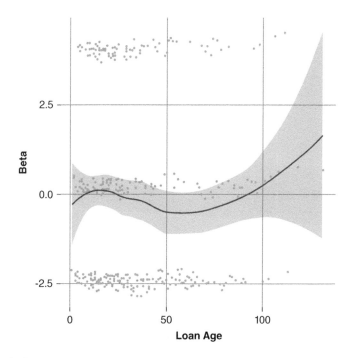

FIGURE 8.13   *Test*—Cash-out

to ignore the non-proportionality or stratify the model along loan purpose. If the model were used strictly for interpretation ignoring the non-proportionality may be an acceptable strategy. However, the investor's goal is to build a predictive model by investigating those variables that influence borrower prepayment rates. Thus, the analyst may approach the model by three three prepayment models based on loan purpose. Further, the analyst may decide to stratify each model over time.

Table 8.9 presents a summary of the results of a stratified model. The stratification of the model along loan age improves the model's fit. For example, the loan age <= 36 model's R-square increases to 0.88. Similarly, the 36 < loan age <= 80 model's R-square increases modestly to 0.83. However, these gains came a modest cost to the R-square of the model loan age > 80. Given the front-loaded nature of MBS cash flows, Table 8.9 suggests a potential modeling strategy that recognizes the non-proportionality of the hazard ratio over time.

TABLE 8.9 Results of Model Stratification on Time

	Loan Age <= 36	36 < Loan Age <= 80	Loan Age > 80
R-square	0.88	0.83	0.75

Before one can endeavor to build any type of predictive model a knowledge of the factors that influence the dependent variable is essential. Both a qualitative and quantitative analysis of the data, the data structure, and the data's functional form of the predictor variables will both lead to a better understanding of the problem and model that will perform as expected. This chapter illustrated the use of Cox's proportional harzards model and residual analysis to explore and identify some the fundamental drivers of mortgage prepayment rates. The model employed is semi-parametric in the following ways:

- First, the model does not assume an underlying distribution of the error terms.
- Second, the model assumes a constant hazard ratio over time.
- Third, in the case presented time dependent predictors are modeled using regression splines.

As a result of the above, the model presented in this chapter will perform as expected so long as the data passed into the model remain within the training space that was used to fit the model. However, for data outside the training space model results are unreliable for the following reasons:

- The Cox model cannot extrapolate beyond the last observation used to fit the model.
- Regression splines linearly interpolate data beyond the end points of the spline—which may not be functionally correct.

This chapter illustrates how the investor can fruitfully employ non-parametric and semi-parametric models to gain a deeper understanding of the mortgage prepayment landscape. A predictive model—like a mortgage prepayment model—is required to perform outside the data training space within which it was fit or "tuned." For this reason the investor must use a parametric model since it will perform reliably outside the data training space.

The Predictive Prepayment Model

Those who have knowledge, don't predict. Those who predict,
don't have knowledge.

Lao Tzu, 6th Century Chinese Poet

Chapter 9 extends the concepts presented in Chapter 8 and presents a framework for the implementation of a predictive residential mortgage voluntary *prepayment model*. Unlike the semi-parametric model outlined in Chapter 8 the predictive model presented in this chapter is parametric. It assumes a structural functional form of $f(x)$ and an underlying error structure. The nature of a *parametric model* allows it to reliably predict outcomes beyond those presented within training data space used to tune "fit" the model.

One may ask, why a parametric model? Indeed, regression splines or piece-wise polynomials may fit the data much better. However, there are two drawbacks to these techniques:

- There is a risk of "overfitting" the model to the data.
- *Predictions* outside the training data space may not be reliable.

On the other hand, a parametric model may not perform as well as a semi-parametric model within the training space. However, this drawback is mitigated by the following qualities:

- A parametric model greatly reduces the risk of overfitting the data.
- The model will perform reliably (extrapolate) outside the training data used to fit its parameters.

From statistical standpoint, a prepayment model, or any predictive model, must be "parsimonious and robust," meaning that the model should use the fewest predictor variables (parsimonious) to explain as much of the variation in the data as possible (robust).

The base Bond Lab® prepayment model is a parametric model. Mortgage prepayment modeling is a time to failure problem that naturally leads to the application survivorship modeling. The base line hazard is:

$$\lambda(t) = [\text{Turnover} \times \text{Loan seasoning} \times \text{Seasonality}]^{\cdot} \qquad (9.1)$$

The influence of borrower incentive is included into the model as an multiplicative term:

$$BI = [\text{Incentive} \times \text{Burnout}] \qquad (9.2)$$

Functionally, the model is:

$$SMM = \lambda(t) + BI \qquad (9.3)$$

9.1 TURNOVER

The investor may choose to model turnover either as a function of predictor variables or simply assume a long-term average turnover rate as presented in section 8.6.2.1. In both cases, it is apparent that the prepayment model takes the form of an exponential survivorship model in that λ, the baseline survival function is housing turnover. For the sake of simplicity, the Bond Lab® prepayment model assumes an average turnover rate of 6%, which translates to an SMM of 0.5143%.

9.2 LOAN SEASONING

The Bond Lab® prepayment model incorporates a three parameter asymptotic function [Crawley 2013]. The function is a multiplier on the estimated turnover rate and given by:

$$\alpha - \beta \times \exp^{-\theta \times LoanAge} \qquad (9.4)$$

Where: α = The function's asymptote
β = The intercept
θ = The point of maximum curvature

9.2.1 Tuning Loan Seasoning Parameters

Given that the seasoning function is multiplicative on the housing turnover rate α (the asymptote) is by definition 1.0. Figure 8.9 suggested the first month prepayment rate begins around 1.0 CPR. Thus, β is calculated as follows:

$$\beta = 1 - \left(\frac{\text{SMM}_{t1}}{\text{SMM}_{t\max}} \right) \tag{9.5}$$

$$= 1 - \frac{1 - (1 - .01)^{(1/12)}}{1 - (1 - .08)^{(1/12)}}$$

$$= 0.879$$

Estimating the parameter for θ is more complex. The point at which the seasoning ramp is rising most steeply (y) is around 3.6% CPR at month 6. Rearranging terms, θ is given by:

$$\theta = -\frac{\log((\alpha - y)/\beta)}{x} \tag{9.6}$$

$$= -\frac{\log((1 - .667)/.879)}{6}$$

$$= 0.192$$

The tuning parameters $\alpha = 1.0$, $\beta = 0.879$, and $\theta = 0.192$ result in the seasoning ramp presented in Figure 9.1.

- The seasoning ramp begins at 1.0% CPR in the first month.
- Prepayments increase over the next 29 months and reach a maximum of 6.0% CPR in month 30.

9.3 SEASONALITY

Mortgage prepayments follow the home selling season in that they increase in the spring and summer months then decline in the fall and winter months. The seasonality function is given by the following equation [Spahr and Sunderman 1992] and shown in Table 9.1.

$$\text{Seasonality} = 1 + \alpha \times \sin \left(\left[\frac{\pi}{2} \right] \times \left[\frac{\text{Month} + \theta - 3}{3 - 1} \right] \right) \tag{9.7}$$

where: α = tuning parameter setting the function's maximum value
θ = tuning parameter setting the point at which the function reaches its maximum value

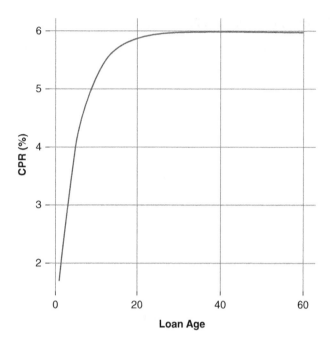

FIGURE 9.1 Loan Seasoning

TABLE 9.1 θ Model Parameter

θ	1	2	3	4	5	6	7	8	9	10	11	12
Mo.	July	June	May	Apr	Mar	Feb	Jan	Dec	Nov	Oct	Sep	Aug

9.3.1 Tuning the Seasonality Parameters

The seasonal factors presented in Table 9.2 are calculated using the National Association of Realtors existing home sales data. The data were obtained from the Federal Reserve of Saint Louis's FRED database and covers the period between January 1999 and April 2014. The seasonal factors are calculated using the R package *decompose*.

- The one-month CPR values presented in Table 9.2 are those of "at-the-money" loans. For this analysis, an *at-the-money loan* is defined as a loan whose note rate is within 20 bps of the prevailing mortgage rate lagged by two months. Constraining the analysis to the "at-the-money" borrower removes the refinancing component and the remaining quantity is housing turnover $(\lambda(t))$.

■ Observations are grouped by calendar month. The reported prepayment rate is the average rate realized in each calendar month across the data set. Simple division of each month's CPR by the average yields a crude estimate of the mortgage prepayment seasonal component.

■ Notice, the average "at-the-money" prepayment rate is 8.2 CPR, which is consistent with the housing turnover analysis presented in Figure 8.7. The pattern of the seasonal factors, although somewhat different, is consistent with the seasonal pattern presented in Figure 8.10.

Based on the analysis presented in Table 9.2, the initial values chosen for the parameters α and θ are 0.15 and 12, respectively. Figure 9.2 compares the function estimate to the seasonal factors calculated using the R package *decompose*. The seasonality model follows the expected seasonal pattern. The model's forecasted prepayment rate increases in the spring and summer months and declines in the fall and winter months.

TABLE 9.2 Seasonals

Month	CPR	Seasonal
Jan	9.8	0.87
Feb	8.5	0.86
Mar	8.0	0.87
Apr	7.4	0.93
May	6.5	1.00
June	8.3	1.08
July	8.6	1.13
Aug	8.4	1.15
Sep	8.9	1.12
Oct	9.6	1.07
Nov	6.9	0.99
Dec	8.0	0.91
Average	8.2	

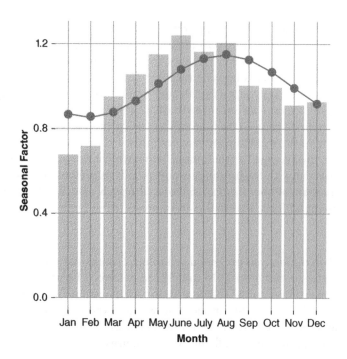

FIGURE 9.2   Model vs. Actual Seasonals

9.4   BORROWER INCENTIVE TO REFINANCE

Chapter 8 illustrated that the homeowner's response to a refinancing incentive is a sigmoid or S-shaped function. Any number of parametric functions representing an S-curve to model the borrower's incentive to refinance may be used. The Bond Lab prepayment model implements an arc tangent function with both a slope and location parameter. Incorporating these two parameters provides a more flexible borrower response function than the basic arc tangent function. The Bond Lab borrower incentive function is given below:

$$\arctan\left([x + \pi] \times \beta \left[\frac{\eta - \arctan(x)}{\pi}\right]\right) \qquad (9.8)$$

where: x = borrower incentive
  β = an integer that defines the slope of the response function
  η = a numeric parameter that defines the location of the response function

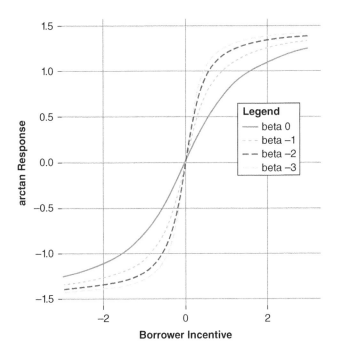

FIGURE 9.3 Slope

- Figure 9.3 shows that decreasing the value of β (i) increases the slope of the function as well as increasing (decreasing) the maximum (minimum) values of the arc tangent response.
- Figure 9.4 shows that negative values of η (n) shift the arc tangent response to the left while positive values shift the arc tangent response to the right.

Together, Figures 9.3 and 9.4 illustrate that equation 9.8 provides sufficient flexibility to model a borrower's response to a given refinance incentive. The complete borrower incentive function is given by equation 9.9:

$$\text{Borrower incentive} = \theta_1 + \theta_2 \arctan \left([x + \pi] \times \beta \left[\frac{\eta - \arctan(x)}{\pi} \right] \right) \quad (9.9)$$

The arc tangent function approaches $-\pi/2$ as $x \to -\infty$ and $\pi/2$ as $x \to \infty$. Thus:

$$\text{minimum SMM} = \theta_1 - \theta_2 \times \frac{\pi}{2}$$

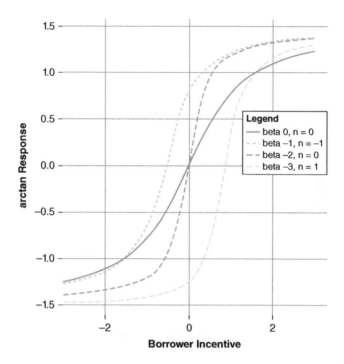

FIGURE 9.4 Inflection

and,

$$\text{maximum SMM} = \theta_1 + \theta_2 \times \frac{\pi}{2}$$

Solving for θ_1 and θ_2 yields the following:

$$\theta_1 = \frac{\max(\text{SMM}) + \min(\text{SMM})}{2} \tag{9.10}$$

and

$$\theta_2 = \frac{\max(\text{SMM}) - \min(\text{SMM})}{\pi} \tag{9.11}$$

Tuning the model to the data presented in Figure 8.5 yields the following initial estimates of θ_1 and θ_2.

$$\theta_1 = \frac{.0292 + .0042}{2} = 0.0167$$

$$\theta_2 = \frac{.0292 - .0042}{\pi} = 0.0080$$

Next, provide an estimate for β as follows:

$$\beta = \tan \left(\frac{SMM_{(\text{Incentive}=0)} - \theta_1}{\theta_2} \right) \qquad (9.12)$$

The estimated slope coefficient is -2.67. Finally, provide a location estimate. Generally, a good starting point is somewhere between 0 and 1.0. To begin, $\eta = 0.50$. The borrower's incentive response model shown in Figure 9.5 fits the "shape" of the data well. However, the model tends to overestimate the "out of the money" prepayment rate while underestimating that of the "in the money" prepayment rate. The results of the initial parameters suggest shifting the incentive curve to the right (increasing η as well as increasing the slope β). Furthermore, increasing both θ_1 and θ_2 should increase the overall predicted borrower response to changes in the prevailing mortgage rate. Figure 9.4 illustrates how changes to *beta* (-6), η (0.75) as well as adjustments to both θ_1 (0.019) and θ_2 (0.01) improved the overall fit of the borrower response function.

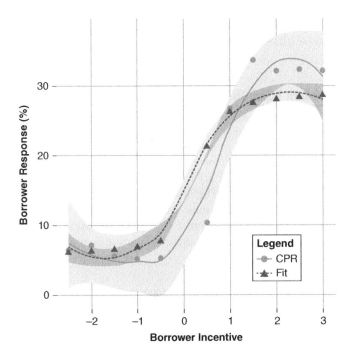

FIGURE 9.5 $\theta_1 = 0.0167, \theta_2 = 0.008$

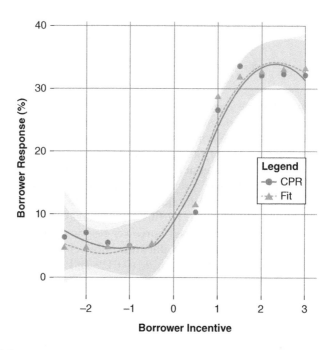

FIGURE 9.6 $\theta_1 = 0.019, \theta_2 = 0.01$

9.5   BORROWER BURNOUT

The term *burnout* refers to the evolution of the composition of borrowers within a pool of securitized mortgage loans. *Burnout* is the attempt to capture the diversity of these borrowers (i.e., the heterogeneity of the pool) and how the pool's borrower diversity influences the investor's realized prepayment rate. In order to capture the diversity of the borrowers within a pool of mortgage loans, the analyst must make assumptions about the characteristics of those borrowers [Stanton 1995] [Hayre 2006]. The two most important and commonly used modeling assumptions center around the following concepts:

- *Refinance velocity*, which is related to a borrower's response to a given refinancing incentive as described in section 9.4. A borrower may be classified as either a *fast payer* or a *slow payer*. A fast payer is a borrower that exercises his option to refinance efficiently while a slow payer is one that does not [Hayre 2006].

- *Adverse selection*, which refers to a borrower's refinancing cost. Typically, those borrowers with a stronger credit profile and consequently a lower cost to refinance exit the mortgage pool sooner, leaving behind those borrowers with a weaker credit profile [Stanton 1995].

It is important to note that the burnout variable does not specify the transition of borrowers from fast payer to slow payer or vice versa, but rather, the change in the composition of the borrowers within the pool as time passes. That is, burnout refers to the migration of borrowers out of the MBS pool rather than the migration of borrowers within the MBS pool. Some have argued that using loan level data to predict prepayment rates eliminates the need to incorporate a burnout variable. This argument is untenable because the analyst does not possess a priori knowledge of borrowers' propensity to prepay; hence, a burnout variable is required. The presence of a burnout variable in the model allows the analyst to observe borrower behavior over time and adjust the composition of the pool or loan level borrower profile with respect to exhibiting either fast or slow payer behavior given the borrowers' response to recurring refinancing incentives. In the case of loan level data, a burnout variable serves to assign a probability to a borrower's tendency to exhibit either fast payer or slow payer behavior for a given economic incentive to refinance.

Figure 9.7 illustrates how borrower response to a given refinancing incentive changes over time. Using FHLMC's loan level data, a loan is classified based on time from origination (*loan age*) as follows:

- New: The loan's age is less than or equal to 36 months. A new borrower exhibits a stronger propensity to refinance given that he has recently closed a loan and may require little preparation in terms of documentation. In addition, he is likely aware of prevailing mortgage rates and as a result more likely to refinance. Furthermore, there is little chance of a negative credit migration due to a life event such as a job loss, divorce, of business failure.
- Moderate: The loan's age is between 37 and 60 months. The moderately seasoned borrower exhibits a weaker propensity to refinance. The borrower may simply be unaware of refinancing opportunities or reluctant to assemble the required paperwork need to document the loan throughout the underwriting process. Given the passage of time, the borrower may have experienced a life event that may have resulted in a negative credit migration, which may increase the cost associated with refinancing.

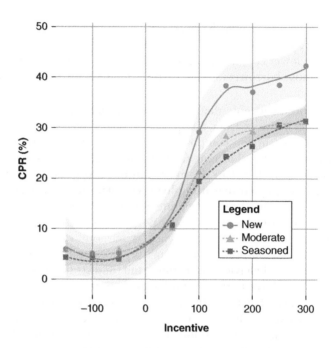

FIGURE 9.7 S-curve by Loan Seasoning

■ Seasoned: The loan's age is greater than 60 months. The seasoned borrower exhibits the weakest propensity to refinance. The longer the borrower maintains his loan, the greater his reluctance to refinance. This is due to potential extension of the term of loan, as well as the cost associated with the refinance relative to the loan's current balance.

In addition to the above:

■ Figure 9.7 suggests that the pool's maximum refinancing response rate declines over time as the loan age increases (*seasons*) as fast payers exit the pool leaving behind the slow payers.
■ Finally, Figure 9.7 illustrates that the "refinancing elbow" or the inflection point of the S-curve shifts to the right, an indication that a greater percentage of slow payers are represented in the MBS pool relative to the fast payers. This is classic definition of MBS pool burnout.

Together, the above suggests that over time the composition of the cohort has shifted as the fast payers exit the pool leaving behind the slow payers. Burnout is also path dependent [Hayre 2006]. The complete path

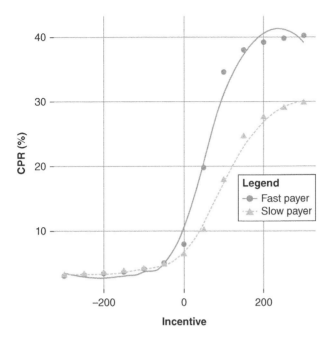

FIGURE 9.8   S-curve Fast and Slow Payer

of rates may also be incorporated into the burnout equation. Typically, the rate path component of the burnout variable measures the maximum incentive forgone by the borrower. Decreasing α increases the baseline rate of burnout while increasing α slows the burnout.

$$\text{burnout} = \exp^{\beta_1 \times \text{Loan Age} + \beta_2 \times \text{Incentive}} \qquad (9.13)$$

where: Incentive = Max[(Note rate − Mtg. rate), Start value]

The burnout function used by Bond Lab recognizes the influence of both the passage of time as well the path of mortgage rates. Figure 9.9 illustrates the behavior of the burnout variable given β_1 tuning coefficients between −0.01 and −0.05 and holding β_2 at 0. The baseline burnout implies that the pool begins with a composition that is 100% fast payers. Higher values of β_1 implies a slower rate of burnout.

Figure 9.10 holds β_1 constant (−0.01) and increases β_2 from −0.05 to −0.01. As the borrowers in the pool forgo successively greater refinancing opportunities, the probability that these borrower's are fast payers declines and the expected borrower response rate converges to that of the slow payer.

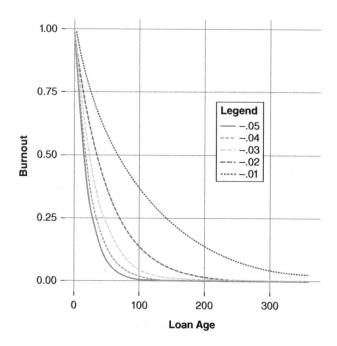

FIGURE 9.9 $\beta 1$ Burnout

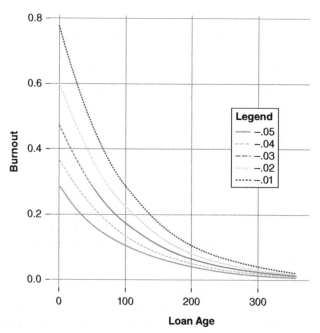

FIGURE 9.10 $\beta 2$ Burnout

Thus, the burnout variable defines the composition of pool of MBS with respect to the relative percentage of fast versus slow payers. In the case of a loan level prepayment model, the burnout variable does not measure the transition of a borrower from that of a fast payer to a slow payer but, rather, revises the posterior probability that the borrower is a fast payer. The burnout variable incorporated into the Bond Lab prepayment model interpolates the composition of pool of mortgages or a borrower's propensity to exhibit either fast or slower payer behavior. The burnout equation extends the borrower incentive equation (9.9) as follows:

$$\text{Borrower incentive} = (BI_{\text{fast payer}} \times \text{Burnout})$$

$$+ (BI_{\text{slow payer}} \times [1 - \text{Burnout}]) \qquad (9.14)$$

where: $BI_{\text{fast payer}}$ = Fast payer S-curve
$BI_{\text{slow payer}}$ = Slow payer S-curve
Burnout = Burnout variable

The modeling challenge is to find the initial tuning parameters such that given a zero incentive the borrower incentive function presented in 9.14 does not add to the baseline turnover assumption. The following steps tune the initial parameter estimates of the Bond Lab model to a 8% CPR turnover assumption, a 0.0069 SMM.

- First, tune the model's baseline seasoning ramp (equation 9.4) such that the seasoning ramp reaches its peak in 30 months. The loan seasoning parameters are $\beta = 0.879$ and $\theta = 0.192$ (section 9.2).
- Second, establish the model's minimum fast and slow payer SMM. The Bond Lab prepayment model is additive on the baseline SMM.
  — Given the data presented in Figure 9.7 the "out of the money" (minimum) CPR is 3%, 0.00254 SMM, subtracting the baseline assumption yields an initial minimum of incentive of −.0043
- Third, tune the model's fast and slow payer "in the money" maximum SMM.
  — The model assumes a fast pay maximum rate of 60% CPR. Deducting the base case turnover rate of 8% CPR yields a maximum fast payer SMM of 0.067%. The astute reader may recall from Figures 9.6 and 9.7 the actual maximum refinance CPR was around 40%. If this is the case, why choose 60% CPR? Recall, we are tuning a fast payer refinance response and the data represent the average refinance response across all payers—that is, burnout is embedded in the data.

— The model assumes a slow pay maximum rate of 25% CPR. Deducting the base case turnover rate of 8% CPR yields a maximum slow payer SMM of 0.017%.
— Using equations 9.9 through 9.11, determine the initial tuning parameters for the fast and slow payer S-curves.
— Table 9.3 summarizes the final tuning parameters for both the fast payer and slow payer S-curves. The tuning parameters set the minimum and maximum incentive SMM of the S-curve net of the model's assumed baseline turnover rate. Additionally, the initial tuning parameters are set such that given a 0-basis-point incentive, the S-curve is neutral on the turnover rate. The fast and slow payer tuning parameters are given in Table 9.3.
— Finally, tune the burnout parameters. The burnout parameters are set initially such that the composition of fast and slow payers are estimated at pool issuance and revised based on the pool's observed prepayment behavior. In the case of a loan, the parameters are set to reflect the investor's belief that the borrower is either a fast or slow payer at loan origination. To begin, the incentive parameter is set at 25 basis points, reflecting the investor's view of the fast payers' refinance threshold, which is the minimum incentive needed to motivate a fast payer to refinance. The initial burnout tuning parameters are given in Table 9.4.

Figures 9.11 through 9.14 illustrate each element of the Bond Lab prepayment model given the initial tuning parameters.

■ The loan seasoning multiplier increases over 30 months to its asymptote (1.0).
■ The seasonality multiplier is representative of the home selling season, reaching a crest of 1.15 in August and its through 0.85 in February.

TABLE 9.3   Fast, Slow Payer Tuning Parameters

	Min SMM	Max SMM	SMM_0	θ_1	θ_2	β	Location
Fast Payer	−0.0043	0.067	0	0.031	0.023	−4.41	1.0
Slow Payer	−0.0043	0.017	0	0.064	0.002	−0.66	0.5

TABLE 9.4   Burnout Tuning Parameters

β_1	β_2	Incentive
−0.01	−0.01	25

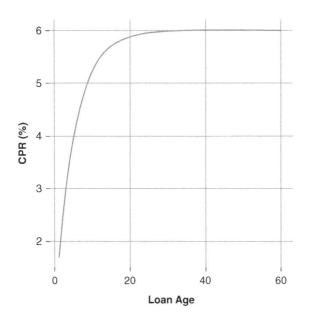

FIGURE 9.11   Loan Seasoning Multiplier

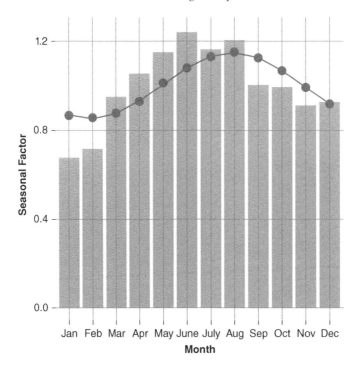

FIGURE 9.12   Seasonality Multiplier

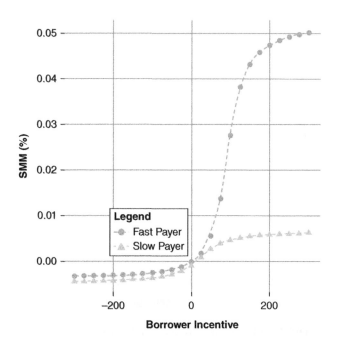

FIGURE 9.13   S-curve Fast/Slow Payer

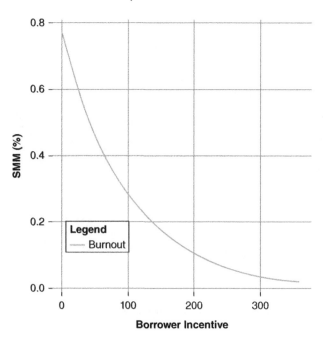

FIGURE 9.14   Burnout

- The borrower incentive function (equation 9.14) reflects the expectations of fast and slow payer behaviors. Both the fast and slow payer functions are tuned such that they are neutral, a 0% SMM, on the turnover component of the model when the borrower's note rate is equal to the prevailing mortgage rate—no incentive to refinance.
- The burnout variable is tuned to reflect the investor's view of the pool's composition of fast and slow payers. In the case of a loan level model, burnout is the probability that the borrower is a fast payer.

The Bond Lab® mortgage prepayment model represents the basic infrastructure used in prepayment modeling and easily extends to include additional variables. The initial tuning parameters result in a model that assumes the percentage of fast-payer borrowers in a pool is around 78%, the model's maximum refinance CPR is 60% and the minimum "out-of-the-money" CPR is 3%.

Figure 9.15 presents the results of the final model assuming the mortgage rate is unchanged (the borrower's incentive is 0). The model

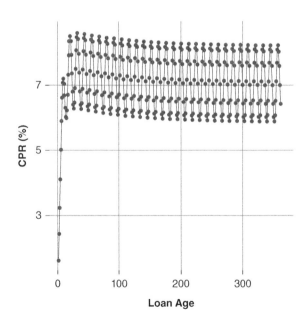

FIGURE 9.15 Bond Lab® Mortgage Prepayment
Model

seasons over 30 months and the expected prepayment range is between 8% and 6% CPR depending on the application of the seasonal factor. The burnout variable controls both the rate, through the age variable, and the extent to which the mortgage pool's composition changes from fast to slow payers via the burnout variable—note in the example burnout is held constant and as a result expected prepayments are a function of loan seasoning and seasonality. Alternatively, in the case of a loan level model, the burnout variable estimates the probability that the borrower is a fast or slow payer.

CONCEPT 9.1

Mortgage prepayment models are "tuned" to the mortgage SMM, not to the mortgage CPR. Tuning to the SMM avoids fitting the model to a CPR assumption greater than 100%. Recall, mortgage prepayment modeling is a binomial in nature. That is, in any given month the borrower may remain current, or terminate his mortgage. Mortgage termination may be voluntary or involuntary. Because prepayment modeling is binomial in nature, the SMM in any given month cannot exceed 1.0.

9.6   APPLICATION OF THE PREPAYMENT MODEL

Recall the following from Chapter 8:

1. Stratification of the Cox model on loan purpose suggested that the survivor function of loans originated for purchase, refinance, or cash-out were significantly different from one another.
2. Stratification of the Cox model on loan age yielded a significant improvement of the model's fit.

The first suggests the investor may tune the Bond Lab prepayment model to each loan purpose, implying three different models each predicting prepayment rates based on loan purpose. The burnout variable includes a time element, which reduces the need to stratify the model over loan age. By tuning three models to loan purpose, the overall predictive ability of the combined models improves by as much as 0.8% CPR.

9.6.1   Additional Variables Influencing Mortgage Prepayment Rates

Adding additional variables that may explain borrower behavior will likely improve the model. For example, some borrower characteristics that may increase the cost (friction) to refinance include:

- Home price inflation/deflation
- Credit score
- Debt-to-income ratio
- Loan-to-value ratio
- Origination channel
- Loan size
- Loan term
- Note rate type—fixed, adjustable, hybrid

Each of these variables can cause greater or less refinancing friction for the borrower. For example, a borrower with a lower credit score, all else equal, will experience a higher refinancing cost in terms of rate, documentation, and mortgage insurance than a borrower with a higher credit score. In addition, the combination of variables may also alter a borrower's propensity to prepay his mortgage. Consider a borrower with a high credit score, low debt-to-income ratio, and high loan-to-value ratio. How would each of these borrower characteristics come together to influence the borrower's expected prepayment rate?

The origination channel (retail, correspondent, or broker) may influence prepayment rates.

- A retail origination is performed directly by the lender. The retail channel is often referred to as a *bricks-and-mortar* because the loan is originated in one of the lender's branch offices. Lenders are often reluctant to solicit retail borrowers to refinance due to the potential impact of higher observed prepayment speeds on their servicing portfolio valuation or, in the case of a lender that relies on securitization for term funding, a higher cost of funds charged by the investor.
- A correspondent is a loan broker with an exclusive arrangement with a lender. The correspondent originates a loan in accordance with the lender's underwriting guidelines. The correspondent's relationship with the lender generally deters the correspondent from soliciting the borrower for a subsequent refinance.
- A broker is independent of an exclusive origination agreement and "sells" closed and funded loans to any number of lenders. As a result, the broker is likely to solicit borrowers to refinance when the borrower

is "in-the-money." Consequently, broker-originated loans tend to exhibit slightly faster prepayment rates than those originated through either the retail or the correspondent channel.

The loan size, or original balance, also influences prepayment rates. The costs associated with refinancing a loan are both fixed and variable. Examples of fixed costs are [Governors of the Federal Reserve System no date]:

1. Attorney and legal fees ($500–$1,000).
2. Title search and insurance fees ($700–$900).
3. Property Inspection fee ($175–$350).
4. Survey fee ($150–$400).

Relative to the original balance of the loan, the fixed fees represent a greater percentage of the cost to refinance increasing the borrower's friction. As a result, a borrower with a lower balance requires a much lower mortgage rate to refinance than does a borrower with a higher mortgage balance.

Table 9.5 illustrates the influence of loan balance on the refinancing decision. A borrower with an original balance of $100,000 refinancing from a 5% mortgage rate to a 4.5% mortgage rate would recover the fixed costs in 66 months. Conversely, a borrower with an original balance of $400,000 refinancing from a 5% mortgage rate to a 4.5% mortgage rate would recover the fixed costs in 16 months.

The loan term and note rate type also influence borrower prepayment rates. Typically, a borrower with stronger credit and greater financial flexibility will choose a 15- over a 30-year amortization term, implying the 15-year borrower may demonstrate a greater propensity to refinance than his 30-year counterpart.

TABLE 9.5   Refinance Analysis by Original Balance

Orig. Bal.	Mtg. Pmt. 5.0%	Mtg. Pmt. 4.5%	Saving	Fixed Cst.	Mos. to Recover
100,000	536.82	506.69	30.14	2,000	66
150,000	805.23	760.03	45.20	2,000	44
200,000	1073.64	1,013.37	60.27	2,000	33
250,000	1342.05	1,266.71	75.34	2,000	26
300,000	1610.46	1,520.06	90.41	2,000	22
350,000	1878.88	1,773.40	105.48	2,000	18
400,000	2147.29	2,026.74	120.55	2,000	16

The type of note rate chosen also indicates the borrower's propensity to refinance. A borrower may choose an adjustable rate or hybrid (a mortgage with an initial fixed rate followed by an adjustable rate) mortgage for its lower relative starting payment versus a standard fixed-rate mortgage. In turn, the borrower might be motivated to refinance when the loan's rate resets depending on the general level of interest rates and the slope of the yield curve.

Together, Chapters 8 and 9 outlines Bond Lab's analysis and predictive model of mortgage prepayment rates. Chapter 9 provides the basic framework for any prepayment model as wells as Bond Lab's base case model tuning parameters for a FHLMC 30-year "generic" loan or pool. The investor's prepayment model plays an important role in the valuation of mortgage-backed securities. There is not a single Bond Lab "prepayment model" but, rather, a library of prepayment models each of which is tuned to reflect the investor's expectation of future borrower behavior. In order to model residential mortgage prepayment rates, the investor employs both semi-parametric and parametric modeling techniques. Based on the insights gleaned from the semi-parametric analysis, the investor must then decide which, if any, borrower and/or loan characteristics upon which to stratify her library of prepayment models.

CONCEPT 9.2

Indeed, modeling mortgage prepayment is central to the valuation of mortgage-backed securities. It forces one to ask the question: build a proprietary model or buy a commonly used model offered by a vendor? The arguments in favor of building proprietary prepayment models are:

- The data are freely available.
- The statistical models needed to understand mortgage prepayments are also freely available.
- Given the wealth of data available and the R packages available for modeling and data mining loan and pool level prepayment modeling is high accessible.

Three

Valuation of Mortgage-Backed Securities

Three

Valuation of Mortgage-Backed Securities

CHAPTER 10

Mortgage Dollar Roll

The future's uncertain but the end is always near.

Jim Morrison

The mortgage *dollar roll* is a financing mechanism used in the agency mortgage-backed securities market. This chapter introduces the reader the mechanics of the dollar roll. Break-even and financing analyses, and the risks associated with implementing a dollar roll program are outlined. The dollar roll provides investors, mortgage originators, and dealers with a flexible means to hedge and finance their respective residential mortgage positions:

- For investors, the dollar roll represents 100% collateralized borrowing at advantageous rates.
- Mortgage originators are able to sell their production forward in the *-to be announced-*, or (TBA), market due to the liquidity of the dollar roll market.
- Dealers are able to hedge or cover their positions efficiently due to the depth and liquidity of the market.

The low cost of funds and flexibility afforded mortgage market participants entails additional risks. Managing these risks is critical to implementing a successful mortgage dollar roll program.

The dollar roll is a specialized type of collateralized borrowing unique to the agency mortgage-backed securities market and allows for a 100% advance rate against a pool of agency MBS. It evolved due to the dealers' need to borrow these securities to cover short positions and mortgage originators' need to hedge their origination pipeline (long positions) by *selling forward*. The dollar roll is named such because dealers are said to either *roll in* collateral (borrowing) or *roll out* collateral (returning).

The mortgage dollar roll is similar in nature to a mortgage repurchase (repo) agreement in that it represents a loan collateralized by mortgage-backed securities and calls for the simultaneous sale and purchase of the MBS at execution. However, it is materially different from a *repurchase agreement* in two ways:

1. The dealer is not required to return the identical securities rolled out by the investor. Instead, the dealer need only return substantially similar securities. Meeting this condition is important from an accounting standpoint as set forth in FAS 140. Failure to meet the FAS 140 standard would result in a dollar roll transaction being accounted for as a sale rather than a financing.[1]
2. Unlike a traditional repurchase agreement, the investor surrenders the right to the bond cash flows. As a result, the forward settlement price is lower than the initial settlement price. The *drop* in price compensates the investor for the forgone interest and principal, which is another feature that differentiates a dollar roll transaction from a traditional repurchase agreement.

Figure 10.1 illustrates the mechanics of the dollar roll and the interaction between MBS pass-through securities and real estate mortgage investment conduits (REMICs). A dealer may roll in MBS securities to deliver against a short position to a REMIC execution—the dealer is short MBS against a long REMIC execution:

- With respect to a REMIC execution, assume a dealer is settling the REMIC in the next month. If the dealer is unable to purchase the collateral required to settle the REMIC, the dealer may roll in collateral. The roll-in is accomplished by *bidding up* the front month roll to the point where it is more favorable for the investor to roll out collateral to the dealer rather than hold it.
- In the case of a short position to an MBS investor, a dealer may simultaneously roll in and roll out collateral.

Through the dollar roll market, dealers are able to obtain the collateral needed to settle REMIC execution while also hedging their MBS pass-through inventory. The MBS investor is able to access favorable advance rates and financing costs.

---

[1]It is incumbent on the reader to familiarize oneself with FAS 140 at http://www.fasb.org/home.

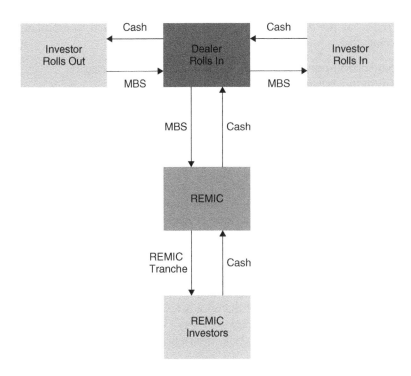

FIGURE 10.1 Mechanics of the Mortgage Dollar Roll

10.1 EVALUATING THE DOLLAR ROLL

Recall from above, unlike a repurchase agreement where the right to the security's cash flows remains with the party that repos (rolls) out the collateral, the dealer or counterparty that repos (rolls) in the collateral retains the coupon interest and any principal paid during the term of the dollar roll. Consequently, the computation of the financing cost of the dollar roll is not as straightforward as that of a typical repurchase agreement.

In a dollar roll transaction, the agreed upon repurchase price is lower than the sale price. At first blush, this pricing may seem counterintuitive; however, since the rights to the mortgage security's cash flows, both principal and interest, are transferred to the party rolling in the collateral, the party rolling out the collateral must make up the difference between the carry on the MBS and the short-term financing rate. As a result, the repurchase price is less than the sale price—this difference is commonly referred to as the *drop*. The following inputs are required to calculate the financing cost:

- Sale or roll-out price and the repurchase or roll-in price
- Coupon payment
- Amounts of both the scheduled and prepaid principal received
- Characteristics of the collateral that is rolled in
- Timing of the settlement dates, i.e., their impact on accrued interest

The dollar roll is a repurchase agreement and reflects an *implied cost of funds* that is calculated from the drop. Thus, by the law of similarity, for a given cost of funds there is also an implied drop. The implied drop is referred to as the *breakeven drop* and is based on the investor's alternative financing cost. The upcoming section reviews the framework for analyzing the breakeven drop.

Consider a 5.5% MBS originated with a first payment date of October 1, 2011. Furthermore, suppose on January 13, 2013, an MBS investor is evaluating a long position in this pass-through security.

- The gross WAC (GWac) of the pool is 6.10%.
- The current weighted-average maturity *(WAM)* is 344 months.
- The recent one-, three-, and six-month prepayment rates (CPR) are: 28, 25, and 21, respectively.
- The current price for January settlement is quoted at $107\,16/32$.
- The investor's alternative financing cost is 0.31%.
- The assumed prepayment rate is 30% CPR.
- The investor roll-out settlement date is January 14, 2013.
- The investor roll-in settlement date is February 12, 2013.

10.1.1 The Breakeven Drop Rate

Given the previous information, the investor must make a decision. She may either finance the position via the dollar roll market or seek an alternative financing source at 0.31%. Table 10.1 illustrates the investor's computation of the breakeven drop rate, which is the drop price at which she will-break even-between financing her position in the dollar roll versus her alternative financing option. The calculation is as follows:

① The investor computes the proceeds on the roll-out date.

- The principal proceeds is the current face amount:

$$\$1,000,000 \times \text{the settlement price } \$107\,16/32.$$

- The accrued interest is calculated on a 30/360 basis:

$$\$1,000,000 \times .055 \times 13/360.$$

- The total market value of the the position is $1,076,986.

TABLE 10.1 Breakven Drop Calculation

Beginning Market Value

Principal Proceeds	$ 1,075,000	$1,000,000 × $107 $^{16}/_{32}$
Accrued Interest	$ 1,986	13 days accrued interest @ 5.50%
① **Market Value**	$ 1,076,986	Total proceeds on the roll-out date

Future Value—*Pmts. Received*

Coupon Income Received	$ 4,583	Interest earned @ 5.50% based on 30/360
Scheduled Principal Received	$ 1,219	Scheduled principal paid
Prepaid Principal Received	$ 29,250	Prepaid principal received @ 30 CPR
Total Payments Received	$ 35,052	Expected payments (remittance date)
② **Disc. Value of the Carry**	$ 35,048	Present value of the payments received assuming the alternate financing rate (0.31%) and using actual day count (13 days)—act/360—on the roll-in date.

Remaining Principal Balance	$ 969,531	Remaining current balance
Principal Proceeds	$ 1,042,246	Remaining balance × $107 $^{16}/_{32}$
Accrued Interest	$ 1,925	13 days of accrued interest
Roll-in Proceeds	$ 1,042,245	Roll-in proceeds
Future Value of Principal and Carry	$ 1,079,220	Total amount financed
Less Financing Cost	$ 268	Actual days between roll-out date and roll-in date based on actual/360 day count
③ **Future Value**	$ 1,078,951	Principal and carry less financing costs

Future Value	$ 1,078,951	
Less Market Value	$ 1,076,989	
Implied Value of the Drop	$ 1,962	
④ **Breakeven Drop** (32_{nds})	6.5	($1,852 ÷ $969,531) × 32

② The investor computes the discounted value of the carry on the roll-in date.

- Calculate the interest paid on the remittance date based on a 30/360 payment date. The MBS pays principal and interest with a 24-day delay. Thus, remittance is the 25th day of the month.

$$\$1,000,000 \times .055 \times 30/360.$$

- Calculate the scheduled principal paid by the borrowers.
- After giving credit to the scheduled principal paid, the investor calculates the expected prepaid principal based her prepayment assumption used to value the dollar roll—in this case, 30 CPR.
- Summing the above items, the investor is able to determine the expected total payments received on the remittance date, which is the carry earned by the investor.
- Finally, the roll-in settlement date occurs on the 12th day of the month, 13 days prior to the remittance date. Thus, the investor must discount the carry by the alternative financing rate using the actual/360 day count convention.

(3) The investor calculates the future value at the roll-in date.
- The principal proceeds at the roll-in date are based on the settlement price.

$$\$969,531 \times \$107^{11}\!/_{32}$$

At first glance, this approach may seem counterintuitive because one might suspect that she should use the roll-out price. She uses the settlement (roll-in) price because she is solving for the *breakeven drop*, which is the compensation for the forgone principal and interest.
- The accrued interest is calculated on a 30/360 basis:

$$\$969,531 \times .055 \times 30/360 \times 13/30.$$

- The roll-in proceeds is the sum of the principal and accrued interest
- The future value of the carry is equal to the sum of the roll-in proceeds plus the discounted value of the carry
- The financing cost represents the cost to finance the future value of the carry between the roll-out date and the roll-in date. The financing cost is based on the actual/360 day count.

(4) Finally, she calculates the implied value of the drop.
- Subtract the future value of the principal and carry at the roll-in date from the market value at roll-out date.
- Divide the above by the remaining balance at the roll-in date $969,531.
- Finally, multiply the quotient by 32—the product is the drop in thirty-seconds. *The breakeven drop is* $^{6.5}\!/_{32}$.

The breakeven drop is $0–$^{6.5}\!/_{32}$. Given that the quoted ($^{0–5}\!/_{32}$) is less than the breakeven drop, the investor would be better off holding her position given alternative financing available (one-month LIBOR) rather than financing her position in the one-month dollar roll market.

10.1.2 The Implied Cost of Funds

The dollar roll, by market convention, is quoted as a drop. However, in practice most investors do not evaluate the dollar roll via the implied drop. Rather, they prefer to evaluate the dollar with respect to its implied financing cost. This section illustrates the analysis by applying the actual drop ($0-5/32$) to compute the implied financing cost. Table 10.2 illustrates that, for the most part, the analysis is the same as that used to calculate the implied drop. The difference is the investor uses the quoted drop, or forward price, to value the remaining principal balance at the roll-in date.

Simply stated, if the implied financing cost is below that of the investor's alternative financing option, in this case 31 basis points, then the dollar

TABLE 10.2 Implied Cost of Funds

Beginning Market Value		
Principal Proceeds	$ 1,075,000	$1,000,000 × $107 16/32
Accrued Interest	$ 1,986	13 days accrued interest @ 5.50%
① **Market Value**	$ 1,076,986	Total proceeds on the roll-out date
Future Value - *Pmts. Received*		
Coupon Income Received	$ 4,583	Interest earned @ 5.50% based on 30/360
Scheduled Principal Received	$ 1,219	Scheduled principal paid
Prepaid Principal Received	$ 29,250	Prepaid Principal Received @ 30 CPR
Total Payments Received	$ 35,052	Expected payments (remittance date)
② **Disc. Value of the Carry**	$ 35,048	Present value of the payments received assuming the alternate financing rate (0.31%) and using actual day count (13 days)—act/360—on the roll-in date.
Remaining Principal Balance	$ 969,531	Remaining current balance
Principal Proceeds	$ 1,040,731	Remaining balance × $107 11/32
Accrued Interest	$ 1,925	13 days of accrued interest
Roll-in Proceeds	$ 1,042,656	Roll-in proceeds
Future Value of Principal and Carry	$ 1,077,709	
Future Value	$ 1,077,709	
Less Market Value	$ 1,076,986	
Implied Cost of Financing	$ 723	
④ **Implied Cost of Funds**	0.81%	($726 ÷ $1,076,986) × 12

roll represents a superior financing choice. In the example presented in Table 10.2, the implied financing cost is 81 basis points.

The implied cost of funds is also referred to as the breakeven financing rate because the investor must invest the borrowed funds for the term of the dollar roll. If her reinvestment rate is equal to the cost of funds, then there is no arbitrage for her and she will break even versus holding the collateral.

10.1.3 Hold-versus-Roll Analysis

The hold-versus-roll analysis presented in Table 10.3 is based on the same inputs as those used in the calculation of the breakeven drop and implied cost of funds. The only additional input to the analysis is the investor's expected reinvestment rate. Building on the previous analysis, the investor's reinvestment rate is 0.31%. For the MBS investor, the hold-versus-roll analysis is straight forward.

- If the reinvestment rate is greater than the dollar roll's implied cost of funds the investor faces a positive economic incentive to *roll* the collateral in the portfolio.
- If the reinvestment rate is equal to the dollar roll's implied cost of funds the investor is indifferent, economically speaking, to holding versus rolling the collateral.
- If the reinvestment rate is below the implied cost of funds, the investor will choose to *hold* the collateral.

The dollar advantage of the hold-versus-roll analysis is often quoted as an annualized basis point advantage. In this case, the advantage to the investor of holding versus rolling the collateral is 0.50% on an annualized basis. The analysis suggests that by holding the collateral the investor gains 0.50% on an annualized basis over rolling the collateral.

TABLE 10.3 Hold-versus-Roll Analysis

Roll			Hold		
Beginning Market Value	$	1,075,000	Future Value of Pmts.	$	35,052
Accrued Interest			Remaining Principal:		
13 days × 5.50%	$	1,986	$969,531 × $107^{11}/$_{32}$	$	1,040,731
Proceeds:	$	1,076,986	Proceeds:	$	1,075,783
Reinvestment Income	$		Accrued Interest		
29 days × 0.31%	$	269	12 days × 5.50%	$	1,777
Future Value:	$	1,077,255	Future Value:	$	1,077,709
Dollar Advantage:				$	454
Basis Points (Annualized)					0.50%

CONCEPT 10.1

The investor, by rolling out collateral, when the analysis suggests it is favorable to roll may add incremental return to her portfolio. Note: The analysis does not apply to specified pools.

10.2 RISK ASSOCIATED WITH THE DOLLAR ROLL

The hold-versus-roll analysis above is predicted on the assumption that both the investor and the dealer return exactly the same notional amount and deliver a substantially identical security that would command the same price. However, there are risks associated with the dollar roll that must be factored into the hold-versus-roll analysis:

- Prepayment risk: the risk that the realized prepayment rate will be significantly different than that used to price the dollar roll.
- Delivery risk: the risk that either party may over- or underdeliver the agreed upon notional amount.
- Adverse selection risk: the risk that neither party is required to return the same securities. Instead, each party is obligated to return substantially similar securities.

10.2.1 Prepayment Risk

The prepayment risk of the dollar roll is attributable to its unique nature. Recall, the party rolling out the collateral does not retain the right to its cash flows. As a result, the party rolling in the collateral accepts the prepayment risk of the roll transaction. The investor's cost of funds is determined by the difference between the actual prepayment rate and the prepayment rate agreed on under the terms of the dollar roll agreement.

- In the case of a premium mortgage, a slower prepayment rate than that agreed increases the borrower's cost of funds because a slower prepayment rate favors the party rolling in the collateral. Conversely, a faster prepayment rate than that agreed reduces the borrower's cost of funds because a faster prepayment rate will favor the party rolling out the collateral.
- In the case of a discount mortgage the opposite holds. A faster prepayment rate than that agreed increases the borrower's cost of funds

because a faster prepayment rate favors the party rolling in the collateral. Conversely, a slower prepayment rate than that agreed reduces the borrower's cost of funds because a slower prepayment rate favors the party rolling out the collateral.

■ Finally, the closer the collateral price to par, the lower the overall sensitivity of the dollar roll's cost of funds to the realized prepayment rate.

10.2.2 Delivery Risk

The dollar roll allows a 1.0% settlement variance, which permits either party to over- or underdeliver the agreed notional amount, creating a delivery option for both parties to the transaction. Essentially, each party owns a put option to the other.

Suppose an investor enters into a roll-in transaction as presented above. The dealer's roll-out price is $107-16/32 to settle on January 14, 2013. Furthermore, assume between the trade date—January 10, 2013—and at the settlement date the price increases $0-5/32 to $107-21/32. The investor will underdeliver to the dealer versus the roll. Conversely, if the price were to decline by a similar amount, the investor would overdeliver to the dealer.

The dealer also owns a delivery option on the roll-out date. The roll-out settlement date is February 12, 2013, and the drop is $0-5/32 for a settlement price of $107-11/32. Assume the price declines to $107-06/32. In this case, the dealer would overdeliver by 1.0% to the investor. Conversely, if the price increases the dealer would underdeliver to the investor.

10.2.3 Adverse Selection Risk

Adverse selection risk arises because neither party to the roll agreement is obligated to return the same securities. Rather, as mentioned above, each party is obligated to return substantially similar securities.

■ For example, in the case of a discount pool, desirable characteristics include such things as a shorter weighted average maturity and faster prepayment rates. Thus, one would deliver to the roll a discount pool with a longer average life and slower prepayments.

■ For a premium pool, desirable characteristics include a longer weighted average maturity and slower prepayment rates. Thus, one would deliver to the roll a premium pool with a shorter average life and faster prepayments.

■ It is in neither party's best interest to deliver pools with better-than-average characteristics. Rather, both parties are motivated to deliver below-average pools into the dollar roll.

Finally, the risk of adverse selection may be managed by the investor via pool stipulations (stips). For example, the investor may stipulate an acceptable range for a weighted-average coupon, weighted average loan age as well as other loan or borrower characteristics. However, stipulations require adjustments to the drop. These stipulations usually result in a lower absolute drop.

This chapter provides a framework for analyzing the mortgage dollar roll. The dollar roll provides a flexible financing mechanism for investors, dealers, and mortgage originator and servicers to manage and finance their positions at a competitive cost of funds. The low cost of funds and flexibility afforded mortgage market participants by the dollar roll comes with additional risks: prepayment, delivery, and adverse selection.

CHAPTER 11

Relative Value Analysis

The ultimate authority must always rest with the individual's own reason and critical analysis.

Dalai Lama

*R*elative value is the desirability of one asset over another based on a given set of metrics. The metrics commonly used are:

- The preceived liquidity of the asset
- Its expected return given an investment horizon
- Its risk or variance of return

11.1 LIQUIDITY

The *liquidity* of an asset may simply be measured by its bid-to-offer spread. A narrow spread implies greater liquidity while a wider spread implies less liquidity. When considering the liquidity of an asset, it is important to note its liquidity is not constant. The factors that may impact the liquidity of mortgage-backed securities are:

- *Cash flow variability*: MBS with greater relative cash flow variability generally trade with a wider bid-to-offer spread than those with lesser relative cash flow variability.
- *Credit risk*: MBS structures that are designed to absorb principal losses due to borrower default often trade with a wider bid-to-offer spread. Generally speaking, the lower the credit rating or greater risk of principal loss due to default, the wider the bid-to-offer spread.

The bid-to-offer spread is a *transaction cost*, and like all costs it must be considered. The time to recover the bid-to-offer spread is measured against the expected "carry" or coupon income earned by the investor.

TABLE 11.1   Bid-to-Offer Recovery Analysis

Bid	Offer	Spread	Duration	Coupon	Breakeven (Mos.)
$100.00	$100.125	$0.125	5.0	1.5%	1.00
$99.00	$101.00	$2.0	5.0	4.0%	5.94

Table 11.1 compares two securities of comparable duration. The first security is liquid, with a low coupon and narrow bid-to-offer spread. The second is a less liquid security with a higher coupon and wider bid-to-offer spread.

- In the first case, the bid-to-offer spread is $0.125 and the coupon is 1.5%. The bid-to-offer spread is 0.124% of the offer price and the investor's time to recovery is one month.
- In the second case, the bid-to-offer spread is $2.0, the coupon is 4.0%. The bid-to-offer spread is 1.98% of the offer price and the investor's time to recovery is 5.94 months.

Assume a six-month investment horizon and the market for each security is unchanged. In the first case, after giving consideration to the bid-to-offer spread, the investor will realize a positive return. In the second case, the investor will incur a modest negative return.

CONCEPT 11.1

When evaluating the cash flow and expected return profile of mortgage-backed securities, the investor should not only consider the security's liquidity but its expected return and its variance of return.

11.2   STATIC CASH FLOW ANALYSIS

Static *cash flow analysis* quantifies how a change in the expected prepayment rate affects the bond's price performance. The analysis is based on a set of interest rate scenarios that alter the prepayment model's predicted SMM vector. No other inputs are used. As a result, the investor is simply considering how a change in the expected prepayment rate influences the bond's valuation metrics of yield to maturity, spread to the curve, weighted average life (WAL), modified duration, and others.

TABLE 11.2 Jan. 10, 2013, Swap Curve

Tenor	1-yr.	2-yr.	3-yr.	5-yr.	10-yr.	30-yr.
	0.31%	0.38%	0.50%	0.91%	1.92%	2.88%

TABLE 11.3 MBS 4.00% Cash-Flow Analysis

Bond ID: bondlabMBS4
Net Coupon: 4.00%
Note Rate: 4.75%
Term: 360 mos.
Loan Age: 0 mos.
WAL: 11.3 yrs.
Price: $ 105.75
Yield to Maturity: 3.31%
Effective Duration: 7.13
Effective Convexity: 201
Spot Spread: 1.22

Scenario bps	DWN 25	No. Chg.	UP 50	UP 100	UP 150	UP 200
Prepayment assumption	MODEL	MODEL	MODEL	MODEL	MODEL	MODEL
Yield to maturity	3.28	3.31	3.34	3.36	3.47	3.38
Spread to curve	1.22	1.16	1.09	1.05	1.02	1.00
WAL	10.78	11.30	11.97	12.35	12.59	12.77
Mod. duration	8.01	8.32	8.71	8.93	9.07	9.16

To illustrate, consider a MBS 4.00% pass-through security priced at $105.75. Based on the Jan. 10, 2013, swap curve presented in Table 11.2 and assuming immediate interest rate changes the Bond Lab prepayment model is used to derive the SMM and cash flow vectors for each scenario. Table 11.3 reports the results of the analysis.

To begin the analysis, consider the first payment date of Jan. 2013 and a prime mortgage lending rate of 4.00%, which implies the pool of loans were originated with an average spread at origination (SATO) of 75 bps, meaning the borrowers in the pool paid a rate 75 bps. above the current "prime" lending rate. A higher SATO suggests a pool of lower credit borrowers. Typically, higher SATO pools tend to exhibit lower relative turnover rates and less responsiveness to refinancing incentives.

- Given the down 25 bps scenario, the prepayment model predicts a weighted average life of 10.78 years, and the yield to maturity goes down 3 bps from 3.31% to 3.28%.

- The spread to the curve widens to 122 bps—an increase of 6 bps from the no-change interest rate scenario. The higher spread to the curve is a result to the shorter WAL—10.78 years—versus the no-change assumption of 11.30 years.
  - The lower yield is attributable to the earlier return of principal at par due to a faster prepayment vector and premium price.
  - The higher spread to the curve is the result of the combination of a shorter average life—caused by the faster prepayment vector—and the upwardly sloping yield curve.
- Given the up 50 bps scenario, the prepayment model predicts a weighted average life of 11.97 years. The yield to maturity goes up 3 bps from 3.31% to 3.34%.
- The spread to the curve falls to 109 bps, a loss of 7 bps. The lower spread to the curve is a result of the longer WAL 11.97 years—versus the no-change assumption of 11.30 years.
  - The higher yield is attributable to the delayed return of principal due to a slower prepayment vector.
  - The lower spread to the curve is result of the combination of a longer average life—caused by a slower prepayment vector—and the upwardly sloping yield curve.
- Given the up 200 bps scenario, the prepayment model predicts a weighted average life of 12.77 years and the yield to maturity goes up 7 bps to 3.38%.
- The spread to the curve falls to 99100 bps, a decline of 16 bps from the no-change scenario. The lower spread to the curve is due to the fact that the MBS 4.00% yield, given a slower prepayment assumption, does not rise one-for-one with the slope of the yield curve.

Cash-flow analysis aids the investor in determining whether a particular security meets her specific investment criteria. For example, her guidelines may require a minimum yield or spread to the curve under certain prepayment scenarios. Similarly, she may require the security to maintain a minimum average life or duration. Singularly, static cash flow analysis may serve as a selection filter on a per security basis.

The investor may also use static cash flow analysis in a comparative framework. Consider a MBS 5.50% originated Jan. 2010 (Table 11.4). The pool's SATO is 25 bps, suggesting a stronger relative borrower profile versus the MBS 4.00% pool. The MBS 5.50% pool's 36 months of seasoning implies a certain degree of borrower burnout (Chapter 9.5).

- The MBS 5.50% pass through price is $107.50, higher than that of the MBS 4.00%, and its yield to maturity is higher by 34 basis points.

TABLE 11.4 MBS 5.50% Cash Flow Analysis

Bond ID: bondlabMBS55
Net Coupon: 5.50%
Note Rate: 6.10%
Term: 360 mos.
Loan Age: 36 mos
WAL: 4.55 yrs.
Price: $ 107.50
Yield to Maturity: 3.55%
Effective Duration: 3.91
Effective Convexity: 19.3
Spot Spread: 2.24

Scenario bps	DWN 25	No. Chg.	UP 50	UP 100	UP 150	UP 200
Prepayment assumption	MODEL	MODEL	MODEL	MODEL	MODEL	MODEL
Yield to maturity	3.50	3.55	3.75	4.02	4.30	4.47
Spread to curve	2.74	2.76	2.79	2.75	2.63	2.48
WAL	4.35	4.54	5.30	6.66	8.65	10.31
Mod. duration	3.76	3.87	4.34	5.14	6.28	7.22

In this case, the investor would "pay-up" $1.75 and pick-up 24 basis points. Generally, when dealing with contingent cash flows, the investor will demand a higher yield as the pay-up increases due to the following reasons:

— The premium exposes a greater amount of principal at risk to an earlier than expected return of principal at ($100), which reduces the investors realized yield.
— A premium price indicates that the borrower's option to call (prepay) may be "at" or "in-the-money," which increases the likelihood of the early return of principal.

■ The MBS 5.50% WAL is shorter 4.54 years versus 11.30 years, respectively. Due to the steepness of the curve its spread to the curve is higher (2.76 versus 1.16). In this case, the MBS 5.50% is said to offer a curve plus 160 bps spread pick-up.
■ Given the down 25 basis point interest rate scenario, the prepayment model predicts the MBS 5.50% weighted average life is 4.35 years and a yield to maturity of 3.50%, a decline of 15 basis points. Relative to the MBS 4.00%, the MBS 5.50% demonstrates a modestly higher of degree of call risk both in its relative average life change and its overall all yield decline.
■ Given the up 200-basis-point interest rate scenario, the MBS 5.50% exhibits a greater amount of extension risk; its average life extends from

4.54 to 10.31 years. Alternatively, the MBS 4.00% extends modestly from 11.30 to 12.77 years.

— The yield to maturity of the MBS 5.50% increases from 3.75% given the no-change interest scenario to 4.47% given the up 200-basis-point interest rate scenario. The higher relative yield of the MBS 5.50% versus MBS 4.00% is due to the delayed return of principal and its higher price.

— The MBS 5.50% average life extension along the steep yield curve causes its spread to the curve to fall by 28 basis points. Furthermore, relative to the MBS 4.00%, its spread to the curve declines by a greater margin (28 bps versus 16 bps).

The analysis presented thus far suggests that the MBS 5.50% is a defensive investment relative to the MBS 4.00% in that it benefits from a rising interest rate environment more so than the MBS 4.00%. Static cash flow analysis provides the investor with a tool that may be used to:

- Filter structured securities and ensure each falls within her investment guidelines or fit her particular investment strategy.
- Perform comparative analysis to assess how a change in the interest rate environment impacts valuation metrics like yield, average life, and spread to the curve.

11.3   RETURN ANALYSIS

Return analysis is used to further augment the static cash flow analysis. Return analysis enables the investor to quantify how a change in the valuation metrics presented translate into a change in her expected return. Recall from Chapter 5, the components of a fixed income investor's realized return are:

- Coupon income, the income received by the investor over the investor's holding period.
- Reinvestment income, the income received by the investor from the reinvestment of coupon and/or principal returned to the investor over her holding period.
- Price change, the change in the value of the bond on the horizon date caused by a change of the yield used to price the bond. The horizon price may be determined by the following:

— Assume a horizon yield curve.
— Assume a spread to the pricing point along the yield curve, typically the MBS average life, and price the bond accordingly. The investor assigns a static cash flow spread to the curve under each scenario. This pricing method applies a linear term structure assumption.
— Alternatively the investor may assume a spread to the spot rate curve which is derived from the horizon yield curve and used to price the bond. This method applies a non-linear term structure assumption.

Recall from Chapter 4, the proper pricing of a fixed-income security treats a bond's cash flows as a bundle of zero coupon bonds that are discounted along the spot rate curve. To determine the forward price of a bond, the investor must make two assumptions:

CONCEPT 11.2

Relative value analysis is the application of both the valuation framework discussed in Chapter 4 and return analysis discussed in Chapter 5 across multiple investment choices.

▪ A horizon yield curve assumption [Jones 1999]. Given a yield curve at horizon, the investor can derive the appropriate spot and forward rates required for determining the forward price of the bond.
— The investor may assume an immediate shift of the yield curve by a specified amount. Thereafter, the evolution of interest rates is unchanged. Thus, the horizon yield curve is equal to the settlement yield curve plus the interest rate shift specified by the investor. The reinvestment assumption is flat and equals the short-term rate plus the assumed interest rate shift.
— The investor may assume that interest rates follow the evolution of the forward rate curve—the rational expectations hypothesis. This approach assumes a strong form of the rational expectations hypothesis producing an arbitrage-free total return because the calculation is based on the market's expectations of both the reinvestment rate and the horizon yield curve.
▪ A spread assumption. In the case of non-benchmark securities, like MBS, a spread assumption is required to properly determine the forward price.

The analyst may apply any number of assumptions. When performing return analysis, the question is not whether the assumptions will prove correct; rather, it is dependent on the following:

- Understanding the inherent bias of the method chosen
- Consistent application and interpretation of that method

11.3.1 Return Analysis Case Study

The return analysis that follows compares the above MBS 4.00% and 5.50% pass-through securities and assumes the following:

- As shown in Figure 11.1, interest rates are assumed to follow the evolution implied by the forward rate curve.
- The assumed changes in the yield curve are parallel shifts.

The return analysis is biased as follows:

- When the yield curve is positively sloped the implied forward curve is both higher and steeper (increased slope), which will bias the

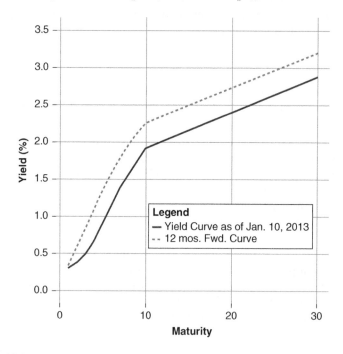

FIGURE 11.1 Forward Yield Curve

analysis to favor less convex bonds like higher coupon pass-through mortgage-backed securities.

— The bias to both a higher and steeper yield curve results in a steeper forward rate curve, and by extension slower expected prepayment rates. As a result, premium pass-through MBS whose return is dependent on the delayed return of principal will benefit from the expectation of slower projected prepayment rates.

▪ At the same time, the assumption of a steeper horizon yield curve also causes the analysis to favor securities structured with a principal lock-out. Typically, bonds with this structural feature are often positively convex.

— Securities with a principal lock-out are said to "roll-down-the-curve" because their average life declines one-for-one with time so long as the return of principal is "locked-out" from the investor. As a result, these securities benefit from greater relative price appreciation at the horizon date than those absent a principal lock-out. At the horizon date, principal locked-out securities are priced to a shorter tenor and in the case of a positively sloped yield curve, a lower yielding pricing benchmark resulting in greater relative price appreciation versus pass-through securities.

At first blush, the above statements seem to contradict one another, which is not the case. Rather, they illustrate the complexity of choices presented to the structured securities investor. Given a no-change interest rate scenario, the investor must choose between securities structured with a principal lock-out offering the benefit of rolling-down-the-curve versus less structured securities that often offer a higher yield.

▪ When the yield curve is negatively sloped, the implied forward curve is both lower and flatter (declining slope) and may in fact become inverted. This scenario will bias the analysis to favor bonds that are more convex, such as lower coupon pass-through MBS.

— The bias to a lower and flatter yield curve results in an inverted forward rate curve and, by extension, faster expected prepayment rates. As a result, discount pass-through MBS whose return is dependent on the early return of principal will benefit.

▪ Concurrently, the assumption of a flat to inverted yield curve biases the analysis against securities structured with a principal lock-out. When the yield curve is inverted, these securities will roll up the curve to a shorter tenor and higher yielding pricing benchmark.

These points illustrate the complexity of choices faced by the investor across the structured securities markets. The interaction between the expected level and slope of the yield curve, expected prepayment rates, and structural choices creates a wide array of return possibilities. Return analysis allows the investor to investigate and quantify how these factors come together to influence the expected return of structured securities.

Figure 11.2 graphically compares the return profile of the 4.00% versus the 5.50% MBS pass-through securities. Under the no-change scenario, the 5.50% MBS outperforms the 4.00% MBS by 37 basis points, largely attributable to the fact that the 5.50% offers a higher yield (an additional 24 basis points) to compensate the investor for assuming greater relative prepayment risk. Illustrated by the down 25-basis-point scenario, the 4.00% coupon outperforms the 5.50% coupon by 50 basis points due to its longer effective duration, higher effective convexity, and lower prepayment risk.

A rising interest rate scenario favors the 5.50% MBS for the following reasons:

- A rising interest rate environment implies slower mortgage prepayment rates. Slower prepayment rates favor in-the-money premium MBS.

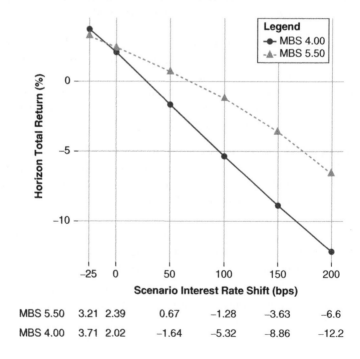

MBS 5.50	3.21	2.39	0.67	−1.28	−3.63	−6.6
MBS 4.00	3.71	2.02	−1.64	−5.32	−8.86	−12.2

FIGURE 11.2 Return Analysis

As prepayment rates slow, the return of principal is delayed and the investor earns more interest—a higher interest rate environment is said to increase the interest only (IO) price component of premium MBS.

■ Shorter duration and negative convexity. The combination of shorter duration and negative convexity act to mute the influence of rising interest rate on the price of a fixed-income security.

Given an up 50-basis-point scenario (Figure 11.2), the 5.50% MBS maintains a positive return and outperforms the 4.00% MBS by 231 basis points. Under the up 100-basis-point scenario the 5.50% MBS reports a negative expected return but non-etheless outperforms the 4.00% MBS by 404 basis points.

The 5.50% MBS is said to offer the investor a defensive return profile versus the 4.00% MBS because its relative performance is superior in a rising interest rate environment. Return analysis quantifies the expected return of securities given the investor's interest rate outlook. In combination, static cash flow and return analysis may be used to filter and select those securities that provide the investor superior relative value.

CHAPTER 12

Option-Adjusted Spread Analysis

If you can't explain it simply, you don't understand it well enough.
Albert Einstein

*O*ption-adjusted spread *(OAS)* analysis simulates interest rate paths (the economy) to value the embedded option in a mortgage-backed security. The option embedded in a mortgage-backed security arises from the following:

- The borrower's option to prepay his mortgage. The borrower holds two options:
  - Voluntary repayment: The voluntary repayment option is exercised via refinancing to obtain a favorable funding term over the existing mortgage note rate or by the sale of the home due to turnover related reasons.
  - Involuntary repayment: The involuntary repayment option is exercised when the borrower experiences a negative life event such as illness or job loss which ultimately triggers a default.
    * Related to the above is strategic default: The strategic default option may be exercised when the value of the home significantly falls below the value of the borrower's loan balance (liability). In this case, the borrower simply walks away from the liability exercising his "put" option to the lender.
- Residential loans are often structured with embedded options. In particular, adjustable rate and interest only mortgages carry note rate reset options.
  - Adjustable rate mortgages are structured with period caps, which limit the extent to which the borrower's payment may change from one reset period to the next.
  - An adjustable rate mortgage is also structured with both a life cap and floor. The life cap and floor limits the extent to which

the borrower's minimum or maximum mortgage rate may decline or increase.

- Structured securities like REMICs, discussed in the upcoming section, also contain embedded options. For example, prepayment protected classes like a planned amortization class (PAC) bond represent a long barrier prepayment option sold by the companion bond investor to the PAC bond investor.
- Often, securities are structured in such a way that the investor may express an opinion regarding the forward rate curve. For example, interest only structures allow the investor to follow (go long) the forward curve while an inverse interest only structure allows the investor to fade (go short) the forward curve.

Each of the above are options and the MBS investor may be long or short several or all the above options given the underlying collateral and, in the case of a REMIC, structural allocation of principal and interest. The base Bond Lab option-adjusted spread (OAS) model implements the Cox, Ingersoll, Ross interest rate model, hereafter referred to as the *CIR* model. Before presenting the CIR model and OAS methodology, some background regarding numerical methods of modern financial theory is required.

12.1 NUMERICAL METHODS OF MODERN FINANCIAL THEORY

The price of an asset is denoted by 12.1. The function defines the price of an asset at time t given $t >= 0$.

$$(P(t), t >= 0) \tag{12.1}$$

where: $(P(t), t >= 0)$ is the price of the asset at t, for $t >= 0$

Next, we envisage t as a small interval of time. The interval of time is denoted (Δt) and the change in the price of the asset across the interval of time $(t, t + \Delta t)$ is given by equation 12.2. This is the trajectory of the price of the asset across time.

$$\Delta P(t) = P(t + \Delta t) - P(t) \tag{12.2}$$

where: $P(t)$ = price of the asset at time t
$P(t + \Delta t)$ = the price of the asset at $(t + \Delta t)$

Thus, the asset return can be written as follows:

$$\text{Asset return} = \frac{\Delta P(t)}{P(t)} \qquad (12.3)$$

Equation 12.3 states the return of the asset across the interval of time $(t, t + \Delta t)$ is equal to the change in the price $\Delta P(t)$ of the asset across the time interval $(t, t + \Delta t)$ divided by the starting price of the asset $P(t)$.

Further equation 12.3 can be decomposed into either a systematic (non random) or a stochastic (random) component [Iacus 2011]. The systematic component of the above asset return model is the risk-free rate and represents the risk-free trend of the model. It is often referred to as the model's *drift*. The stochastic component of the asset return model represents external random price shocks that influence an asset's price. Typically, the price shocks applied in the model are assumed to follow a Gaussian distribution with a mean of zero and standard deviation of one (normal distribution).

12.1.1   Systematic Return—*Drift*

Following [Iacus 2011], if one assumes a constant return denoted as μ across the interval $(t, t + \Delta t)$ the *systematic return* is given by equation 12.4, which defines the average asset return over time.

$$\text{Systematic return} = \mu \Delta t \qquad (12.4)$$

where: μ = risk-free return
Δt = the time interval $(t, t + \Delta t)$

12.1.2   Stochastic Return—*Randomness*

The *stochastic* component of the return model is the product of two variables: σ representing the *natural volatility* of the asset price, and $dW(t)$ (a Weiner process) denoted W, and representing the "randomness" around the asset's natural price voatility.

$$\text{Stochastic return} = \sigma \Delta W(t) \qquad (12.5)$$

where: σ = natural volatility
$\Delta W(t) = W(t + \Delta t) - Wt$ (a Weiner process)

Equation 12.3 can be rewritten as follows:

$$\text{Asset return} = \text{Systematic return} + \text{Stochastic return} \qquad (12.6)$$

where: systematic return $= \mu\Delta t$
stochastic return $= \sigma\Delta Wt$

Substituting equations 12.4 and 12.5 into equation 12.3:

$$\frac{\Delta P(t)}{P(t)} = \mu\Delta t + \sigma\Delta W(t) \qquad (12.7)$$

which can be reduced to the equation below:

$$\Delta P(t) = \mu P(t)\Delta t + \sigma P(t)\Delta W(t) \qquad (12.8)$$

12.2   COX, INGERSOLL, ROSS THEORY OF THE TERM STRUCTURE

The model introduced by Cox, Ingersoll, and Ross (CIR model) for modeling the spot interest rate (r) is defined by the following stochastic differential equation [John C. Cox 1985].

$$\Delta r = \kappa(\theta - r(t)) \times \Delta t + \sigma\sqrt{r(t)} \times \Delta W(t) \qquad (12.9)$$

where: $\kappa =$ the speed at which spot rate is pulled to its long-term value
$\theta =$ the long-term (central) value of the interest rate
$\sigma =$ the variance of the interest rate

According to Cox et al., when $\kappa, \theta > 0$ the model is a continuous time first-order autoregressive process. The randomly moving interest rate r is pulled to θ and the parameter κ determines the speed at which r is pulled to its long-term value. The boundary conditions are such that if $\sigma^2 > 2\kappa\theta$, the short-term rate can reach zero. If $2\kappa\theta \geq \sigma^2$, the upward drift is sufficiently large enough to make zero inaccessible by the model. Additionally, the diffusion coefficient at zero implies that an initially non-negative interest rate cannot evolve to a negative value [John C. Cox 1985]. According to John C. Cox the interest rate behavior implied by equation 12.9 has the following relevant properties:

- Negative interest rates cannot occur.
- If the short-term interest rate reaches the lower zero bound (LZB) it can subsequently become positive.

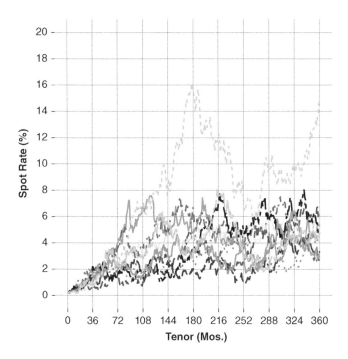

FIGURE 12.1   CIR Simulated Interest Rate Paths

- The absolute variance of the interest rate increases when the short-term rate increases.
- There is a steady state distribution for the short-term interest rate.

Figure 12.1 illustrates the results of simulating ten interest rate paths assuming short-term rate $r = 0.0016$, $\kappa = 0.1$, $\theta = 0.052$, and $\sigma = 0.015$. Each path represents the evolution of the short-term rate from $(t, t + \Delta t)$. Each path follows the behavior listed above. The simulated short-term rate is always positive and the absolute variance of the simulated short-term rate increases as the short-term interest rate itself increases.

12.2.1   Model Response to Changes in κ (Mean Reversion)

As mentioned above κ determines the speed at which r is pulled to its long-term value θ. Setting the random seed to 10,000 ensures that each simulation will result in the same path. In addition, volatility σ is also held at a constant value of 0.015. With both the random seed and σ held constant, κ is set to the values of 0.1 (Figure 12.2) and 0.7 (Figure 12.3).

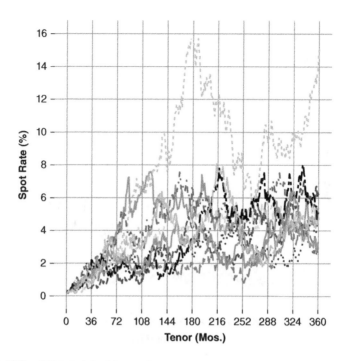

FIGURE 12.2 CIR Model with $\kappa = 0.1$

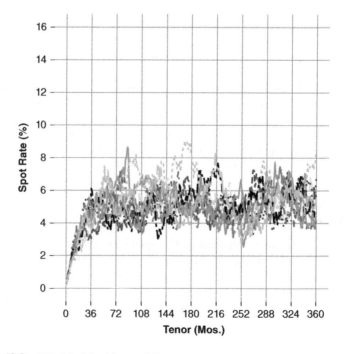

FIGURE 12.3 CIR Model with $\kappa = 0.7$

Figures 12.2 and 12.3 illustrate the effect of changing κ on the simulated spot rate path. Figure 12.2 shows that the lower κ value results in a slower rate of *mean reversion*. That is, it takes longer for the simulated spot rate to pull to its long-term value θ. Conversely, a higher value as shown in Figure 12.3 illustrates that the short-term rate is pulled to the θ value sooner. Furthermore, together Figures 12.2 and 12.3 show that higher values of κ also lower the dispersion of the simulated short-term rate around its long-term value. This relationship is due to the fact that higher values of κ strongly pull the simulated short-term rate to its long-term value, thus reducing drift. It is important to note that higher levels of κ do not reduce the volatility, σ, of the spot rate. Rather, since the absolute variance of the short-term rate changes directionally with its value variance, not volatility, changes inversely with κ.

12.2.2 CIR Model Response to Changes in θ (Long-Term Forward Rate)

Consider Figures 12.4 and 12.5. Holding κ (0.70), σ (0.015), and the random seed constant, the value of θ is lowered to 0.02 (2.0%) and raised

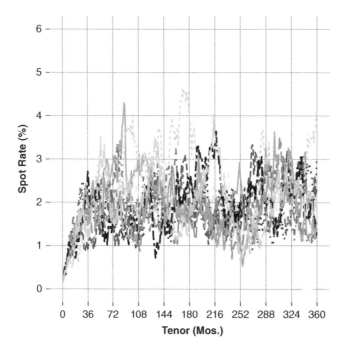

FIGURE 12.4   CIR Model with $\theta = 0.02$

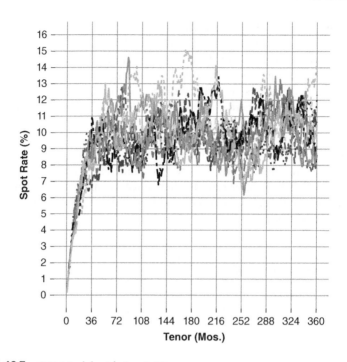

FIGURE 12.5 CIR Model with $\theta = 0.10$

to 0.10 (10.0%). The lower θ value results in lower overall variance. For example, with θ set to 0.02, the simulated forward spot rate approaches a maximum value around 4.5% and a minimum value near 0.5%, a 4.0% range. Conversely, Figure 12.5 shows that a higher θ value (10.0%) results in greater variance. Figure 12.5 shows the maximum value of the forward spot rate nears 15.0% and its minimum value nears 6.0%, a 9.0% range. This is consistent with the model assumptions outlined at the beginning of this section.

12.2.3 CIR Model Response to Changes in σ (Volatility)

Sigma σ is the volatility of the short-term rate. Note, the volatility parameter 1.5% is the standard deviation of the short-term rate. Most OAS models require an annualized volatility assumption. If one assumes 240 trading days, 1.5% is equivalent to a 23.2% annualized volatility assumption ($.015 \times \sqrt{240}$). Once again, holding the random seed at 10,000 ensures that each simulation presented in Figures 12.6 and 12.7 will result in the same path trajectory. However, in this case κ is held constant at 0.10 and θ

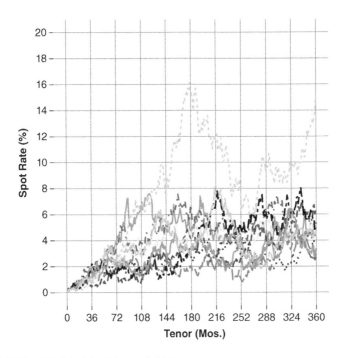

FIGURE 12.6 CIR Model with $\sigma = 0.015$

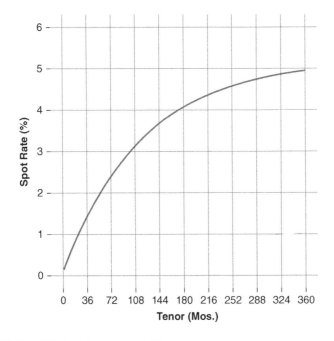

FIGURE 12.7 CIR Model with $\sigma = 0.00$

is held constant at 0.052 (5.2%). Figure 12.6 shows that assuming a *sigma* value of 0.015, the simulated interest rate paths may drift as high as 16.0% and as low as 1.0%. At this point, both Figures 12.2 and 12.6 are the same in terms of parameter settings. Notice the dispersion (15.0%), given *sigma* and θ values of 0.015 and 0.052, respectively, is greater than the variance (9.0%) presented in Figure 12.5 given κ and θ values of 0.7 and 0.10, respectively.

Dispersion declines as σ declines. Indeed, Figure 12.7 shows that given a σ value of zero all forward short-term rate trajectories converge to the same value. The projected rate path given a σ value of zero is the forward rate curve. This is the origin of the term *zero volatility (ZV) spread* and the foundation of the framework for the valuation of structured securities presented earlier in Chapter 4.

12.3 CALIBRATING THE MODEL

Recall from Chapter 2, parametric *term structure* models employ an indirect method to derive the required discount rates by fitting the theoretical forward rate curve. That is, the CIR model described fits the term structure indirectly and the model projects, given a zero volatility assumption, the forward rate curve. The CIR model belongs to a class of interest rate models referred to as affine term structure models, meaning that it relates zero coupon bond prices to a spot rate model. The variables of the model, like the indirect methods discussed in Chapter 2, have economic meaning which were already discussed. The model also provides a closed form solution for the price of a zero coupon bond as shown below in equation 12.10 [John C. Cox 1985].

$$P(r, t, T) = A(t, T)e^{-\beta(t,T)r} \tag{12.10}$$

where: $A(t, T) = \left[\dfrac{2\gamma e^{[(\kappa+\lambda+\gamma)(T-t)]/2}}{(\gamma+\kappa+\lambda)(e^{\gamma(T-t)}-1)+2\gamma} \right]^{\frac{2\kappa\theta}{\sigma^2}}$

$\qquad\quad B(t - T) = \dfrac{2(e^{\gamma(T-t)}-1)}{(\gamma+\kappa+\lambda)(e^{\gamma(T-t)}-1)+2\gamma}$

$\qquad\quad \gamma = ((\kappa + \lambda)^2 + 2\sigma^2)^{\frac{1}{2}}$

The dynamics of prices are given by the stochastic differential equation presented below:

$$dP = r[1 - \lambda B(t, T)]P\Delta t - B(t, T)P\sigma\sqrt{r}W(t) \tag{12.11}$$

Finally, bond prices are generally quoted as a yield to maturity. The yield to maturity is given by the equation below:

$$R(r, t, T) = [rB(t, T) - \log A(t, T)]/(T - t) \qquad (12.12)$$

The CIR model, because it provides a closed-form solution to bond prices, reduces the computational time and complexity needed to fit the model to market prices. Typically, interest rate models are fitted to the prices of options on swaps. This procedure is referred to as fitting the volatility surface; however, the approach suffers from the following limitations:

- First and most important, market data (prices) related to options on swaps (swaptions), caps, and floors and their implied volatilities are not readily available because these securities are traded over the counter. Recall the point of Bond Lab: The investor can create a workable structured securities valuation model with open source software and readily available data.
- Second, due to the lack of transparency, the depth and liquidity of these markets are subject to question. That is, there is a difference between a quoted price and trade executions at the quoted price. Consequently, one risks fitting her model to indicative prices rather than to market clearing prices.

Swap rates, on the other hand, are readily available from the Federal Reserve's website and most likely represent market clearing levels. Using quoted swaps rate the investor can construct both the cash flow and maturity matrices required to fit the interest rate model. Thus, the method used calibrates the CIR model to the swap rate curve. The optimization routine (R package optimx) [John C. Nash 2011] [Nash 2014] fits the parameters; κ, λ, and θ as outlined in equation 12.10. The parameter σ is specified by the investor, and in this case is set to 0.015 (23.2% volatility). Fitting equation 12.10 to the Jan. 10, 2013, swap curve yields the following parameters: $\kappa = 0.109$, $\lambda = 0.001$, $\theta = 0.0442$. Typically, κ is also set to a fixed value giving rise to only λ (the risk premium) and θ (the long-term forward rate) within the optimization routine.

Figure 12.8 shows the difference between the actual and fitted prices. The model fits the 1-, 3-, and 6- month eurodollar prices well. Additionally, the model also fits the 1-, 5-, and 30-year swap rates reasonably well. In the single-factor CIR model, all bond prices depend on a single predictor variable—the spot rate. Although the term structures given by the model can assume alternative shapes, the model requires that price changes in bonds of all maturities are perfectly correlated. As a result, a single factor model can

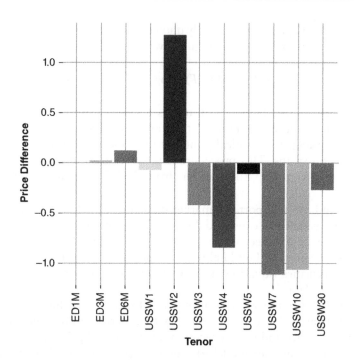

FIGURE 12.8 CIR Model Fit: Actual Swap Prices less Fit Swap Prices

only achieve a certain "goodness of fit." Cox, Ingersoll, and Ross also out-line a framework for a multifactor model. However, they state the following: "The resulting multifactor term structures will have more flexibility than the single factor model, but they will inevitably also be more cumbersome and more difficult to analyze" [John C. Cox 1985]. This statement crystallizes the *investor's dilemma*: Either accept models that are tractable and clearly inter-preted or pursue models of increasing complexity whose interpretation may be opaque. Irrespective of the choice made, understanding the single-factor interest rate model is the gateway to understanding more complex interest rate models like multifactor models.

Furthermore, due to the CIR single-factor model's tractability, under-standing the broader implementation of the mortgage OAS model is eased due to the following:

■ The single-factor model is easily understood. So, rather than facing the distraction of more complex interest rate models, the investor is freed to focus her attention on the finer aspects of the option-adjusted spread model.

- The closed-form solution to bond prices (equation 12.10) and the term structures implied by the simulated short-term rate allow for easier simulation and understanding of the additional required inputs derived from the model, like the 2- and 10-year swap rates that are used to motivate the model prepayment.
- She is able to plainly trace the link between the interest rate model simulations and the mortgage *prepayment model*.

Overall, given the model's fit, particularly with respect to short-term rates, one expects reasonable simulation of the short-term rate process. A multifactor model may provide a better fit to market prices; however, as mentioned above, translation of the model's parameters to the market and overall economy is less clear.

12.4 BUILDING THE OPTION-ADJUSTED SPREAD (OAS) MODEL

Once the interest rate model is fit to market prices, the next step is to build a *simulation cube*. The simulation cube is a multidimensional array that holds the following:

- The short-term interest rate trajectory (CIR model output)
- CIR model inputs to the Bond Lab prepayment model (2- and 10-year swap rates)
- The discount rate paths used to value the expected cash flows along each simulation trajectory

12.4.1 Short-Term Interest Rate Trajectory

Before building the simulation cube, an understanding of the use and implementation of the short-term interest rate trajectory (path) is required.

- Each interest rate along a path's trajectory represents a forward short-term spot rate.
- Recall, within the CIR model the spot rates associated with other maturities are a function of the forward short-term interest rate. Indeed, in the case of the CIR single factor model, bond returns are perfectly negatively correlated with changes in the short-term rate.
- By equation 12.10, the investor can derive required discount rates to solve for the term structure implied by each simulated short-term rate. Further, equation 12.12 solves for the yield rather than the discount

rate. With equations 12.10 and 12.12, the investor can derive the term structure and yield curve associated with each simulated short-term rate.
- Plainly said, each simulated short-term rate implies a term structure. From these rates and by employing equation 12.12, the investor can derive the required inputs along each trajectory to motivate the prepayment model, namely the required 2- and 10-year swap rates.

Consider a single trajectory of the short-term spot rate presented in Figure 12.9. The simulated path uses the parameter settings outlined above and the random seed is set at 10,000. Figure 12.10 illustrates the yield curve associated with select points along the short rate path.

- At t = 10 the simulated short-term rate is 0.375%. The short-term spot rate at $t = 10$ is below the long-term spot rate θ; therefore, the yield curve is upward sloping.
- Conversely, at $t = 120$ the short-term rate is 6.96%. The short-term rate is above the long-term spot rate θ; therefore, the yield curve is downward sloping (inverted).

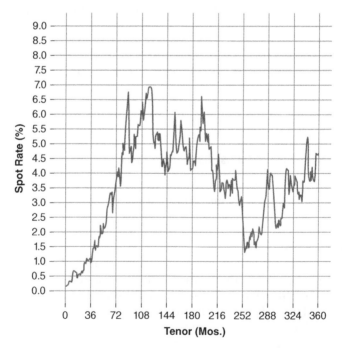

FIGURE 12.9 CIR Model—Single Path

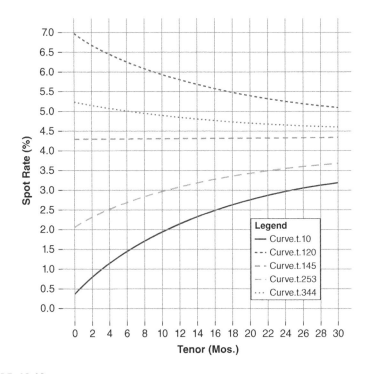

FIGURE 12.10 CIR Model Yield Curve

- Finally, notice that when $t = 145$, the short-term rate (4.29%) is near θ and the yield curve is flat.

    Figures 12.9 and 12.10 illustrate the CIR model is capable of producing a number of yield curve shapes. Recall from Chapter 4, the level, steepness, and curvature of the yield curve influence the valuation of structured securities. The analysis presented above shows the single-factor CIR model is capable of simulating the yield curve shapes and changes thereto that most effect the valuation of structured securities.

12.4.2 Motivating the Prepayment Model

Building the simulation cube requires the investor to extract the interest rates along the trajectory required to motivate the prepayment model. Figure 12.11 depicts the relationship between the simulated short-term rate and the 2- and 10-year swap rates which are used to motivate the prepayment model and are derived using equation 12.12 along a single trajectory.

- Again, notice when the simulated short-term rate is below θ the bias of the short-term rate is upward and the yield curve is positively sloped. The 2-year swap rate is less than the 10-year swap.
- As the short-term rate rises above θ the yield curve becomes inverted and the 2-year swap rate is higher than the 10-year swap rate.
- Finally, when the short-term rate is close or equal to θ, the 2-year and the 10-year swap rates are close to one another—the yield curve is flat.

Figure 12.11 suggests the simulation of the short-term rate also produces unique mortgage prepayment paths given the shapes of the yield curve shown above. Recall from Chapter 4, the influence of changes in the level, steepness, and curvature of the yield curve on valuation. The simulation model chosen should be such that it reproduces the yield curve outcomes required for the proper valuation of the security presented for analysis. The single-factor CIR meets this criteria.

The next step in building the simulation cube is to apply the prepayment model and build a vector of SMM forecasts which will be used to estimate mortgage cash flows along each trajectory. Recall, the Bond Lab prepayment model uses both the 2- and 10-year swap rates to predict the mortgage rate.

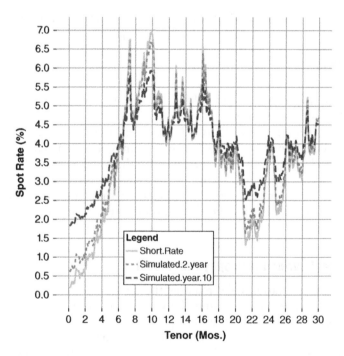

FIGURE 12.11 CIR Model, Simulated Short-Term Rate, 2- and 10-Year Swap Rates

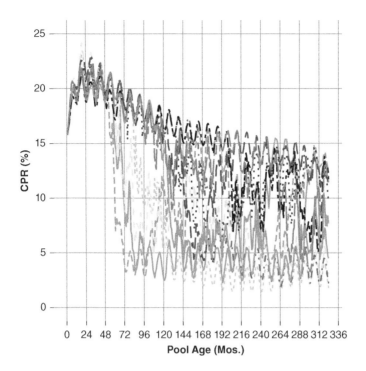

FIGURE 12.12   CIR Model, MBS 5.50 Predicted SMM Vector

Using equation 12.12, both the 2- and 10-year swap rates associated with the simulated short-term rate for each period along the simulation trajectory are calculated and passed to the Bond Lab prepayment model.

In turn, the prepayment model produces an SMM estimate for each month along the simulation trajectory. Figure 12.12 illustrates the MBS 5.50 pass-through SMM simulation trajectories over ten interest rate paths. Notice, the simulated SMM tracjectories project relatively high prepayment rates over the next 48 months. Figure 12.2 illustrates the importance of understanding both the implications of the prepayment model assumptions (tunings) and the parameters of the interest rate model. Together, both the prepayment and interest rate model assumptions determine the valuation of an MBS within the framework of the OAS model. Once derived, the SMM vectors are passed to the MBS cash flow model and the expected value of the MBS security along each simulation trajectory is calculated.

12.4.3   Discounting Cash Flows

Once the investor derives the cash flows along each simulation trajectory, her next step is to discount those cash flows and determine the spread along each path such that the discounted present value is equal to the current price of the security. Recall from Chapter 2, "Theories of the Term Structure of Interest Rates", long-term bond returns are the product of short-term bond returns (equation 2.1). Combining the lessons learned in Chapters 1 and 2, she can derive the discount curve from the simulated short-term trajectory as follows:

$$\text{Discount rate} = \prod_{t=n}^{j} [(1 + i_t)]^{(1/t)} \qquad (12.13)$$

where: i = the simulated short rate
  n = starting period
  j = ending period

The discount rates are translated into spot interest rates using the following:

$$\text{Spot rate} = \left[\left[(\text{Discount rate})^{(1/t)} \right]^{(1/12)} \right] - 1 \qquad (12.14)$$

Finally, the investor solves for the following:

- Option-adjusted spread (OAS), the constant spread over all the spot rate curve that equates the average price across all trajectories to the market price.
- Zero volatility spread (ZV spread), the average of the spread across each trajectory, that equates its price to the market price. This can also be accomplished by setting the model volatility to zero and solving for OAS.

$$\text{Present value} = \sum_{t=n1}^{n2} \left[\frac{1}{(1 + (\text{Spot rate} + \text{Spread}))^n} \right] \times [\text{Cash flow}_n] \qquad (12.15)$$

The constant spread across all simulated trajectories of the spot rate which equates the average price to the market price is option-adjusted spread.

$$\text{Option-adjusted spread (OAS)} = \sum_{t=n_i}^{nj} \frac{1}{n} \times [\text{price}_n] \qquad (12.16)$$

where: Price = the price given a constant spread over all the
  simulated spot rate curves
  n = the simulation path

12.4.4 How Many Trajectories?

Figures 12.13 through 12.16 provide a distributional analysis of the MBS 4.00% pass-through security. Together, the figures show that as the number of paths (trajectories) of the short-term rate increase, the model begins to converge to the actual distribution of the option-adjusted spread. Given 125 paths, the model provides a poor approximation of the OAS distribution. However, given 250 simulations, the model begins to provide a better representation of the underlying distribution. Figure 12.15 suggests the model begins converging to the actual distribution around 500 paths and Figure 12.16 shows the model converges to the OAS distribution at 5,000 paths.

Computationally, evaluating structured securities over 5,000 simulations is unrealistic—it takes too long. Thus, the investor must strike a compromise between the time required to perform the analysis and its convergence to the actual underlying distribution. Mindful, the goal of the analysis is to estimate the value of the short option position to the home owner to prepay his mortgage as well as any embedded options structured in the mortgage loan contract or REMIC security. Overall, the figures

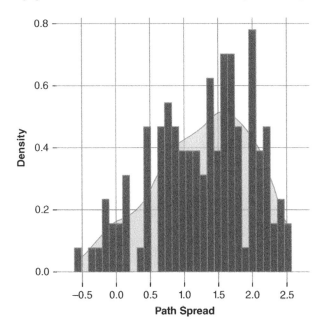

FIGURE 12.13 Short Rate Paths = 125

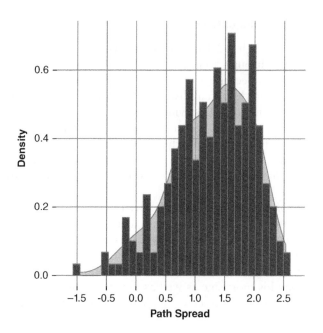

FIGURE 12.14 Short Rate Paths = 250

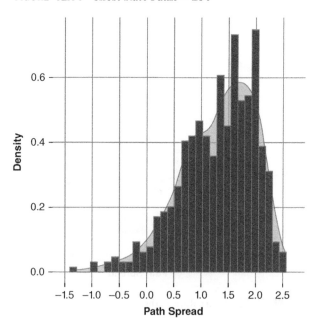

FIGURE 12.15 Short Rate Paths = 500

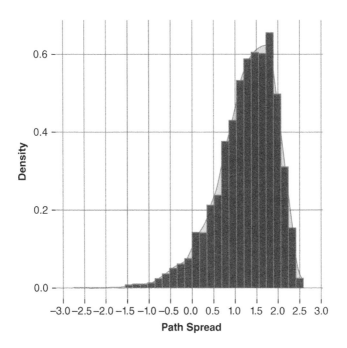

FIGURE 12.16 Short Rate Paths = 5,000

suggest that in the case of a pass-through security, 500 paths reasonably approximate the distribution.

12.5 OAS ANALYSIS AS A DECISION-MAKING TOOL

Recall from Chapter 4 the valuation framework for structured securities presented again in Figure 12.17.

- If the zero volatility spread is less than the nominal spread, the "rich" cash flows outweigh the "cheap" cash flows.
- If the zero volatility spread is greater than the nominal spread, the "cheap" cash flows outweigh the "rich" cash flows.

The summary statistics of interest given by the OAS model are:

- Spread to the curve measures the yield and average life based on the SMM and cash-flow vector, assuming a zero volatility input. The measure is simply the yield to maturity less the yield of the weighted average life along the pricing benchmark curve.

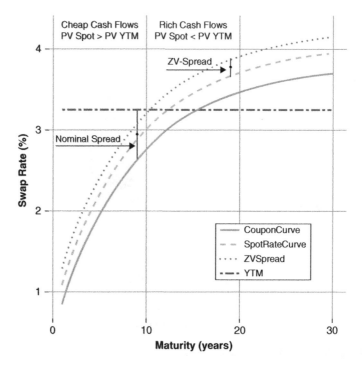

FIGURE 12.17   The Valuation Framework for Fixed-Income Securities

- Zero volatility spread measures the spread over the spot curve assuming a zero volatility input to the interest rate model.
- Option-adjusted spread, the average spread across all simulated trajectories, which equates the average of each price along the simulated trajectories to the current price.

Table 12.1 summarizes the results of the option-adjusted spread model simulating 5,000 paths for the MBS 4.00% and 5.50% pass-through securities. The astute reader will notice differences between the ZV spread reported Table 12.1 and the spot spread presented in Chapter 11. The difference between the two is the result of the interest rate model chosen by the investor. For the analysis presented in Chapter 11, the Nelson-Siegel, a parametric term structure model, was used to motivate the analysis whereas the Cox, Ingersoll, Ross model motivates the OAS analysis presented in this chapter. Neither analysis is incorrect with respect to the prepayment model, yield to maturity, average life, spread to the curve, and zero volatility spread. Rather, each model fits the term structure differently and as a result produces changes

TABLE 12.1 Option-Adjusted Spread Analysis

	MBS 4.00%	MBS 5.50%	Difference
Net Coupon	4.00%	5.50%	
Note Rate	4.75%	6.10%	
Term	360 mos.	360 mos.	
Loan Age	0 mos.	36 mos.	
Model WAL	11.9	5.36	−6.54
Price:	$105.75	$107.50	+$1.75
Yield to Maturity	3.33%	3.71%	+0.39%
Spread to Curve	1.46%	2.78%	−1.31%
Zero Volatility Spread	1.22%	2.09%	−0.83%
Option-Adjusted Spread	0.49%	0.19%	−0.32%

in the prepayment model's projected SMM vector and consequently changes the reported valuation metrics.

CONCEPT 12.1

The above example illustrates the differences between modeling applications. The model itself does not produce superior investment results. Rather, a disciplined investment approach, a clear understanding of the model, and consistent application produces superior investment results.

Consider the metrics yielded by the OAS model:

- The ZV spread of the MBS 4.00% is 122 basis points and the ZV spread of the MBS 5.50% is 209 basis points. Recall, the difference between the ZV spread and the spread to the curve indicates the relative richness or cheapness of the cash flows. Said another way, the difference between the two quantifies the *cost of the curve* or the cost associated with amortizing cash flows along a non-linear term structure.
  - In the case of the MBS 4.00%, the cost of the curve is 24 basis points.
  - In the case of the MBS 5.50%, the cost of the curve is 69 basis points.
  - Further, according to the valuation framework presented in Figure 12.17, when the ZV spread is less than the spread to the curve, the rich cash flows outweigh the cheap cash flows. Thus, it

stands to reason that the higher the cost of the curve, the rich flows are greater relative to the cheap cash flows.

■ The difference between the zero volatility spread and the option-adjusted spread indicates the value of the investor's *short option* position—the MBS option cost.

— In the case of the MBS 4.00%, the option cost is 0.73% (1.22% − 0.49%).

— In the case of the MBS 5.50%, the short option value is 1.90% (2.09% − 0.19%).

The OAS model suggests the short prepayment option embedded in the MBS 5.50% is 117 basis points greater than that of the MBS 4.00%; hence, the 5.50% MBS's higher yield to maturity.

The MBS 4.00% OAS is 0.49%, 30 basis points more than that of the MBS 5.50% of 0.19%. The option-adjusted spread analysis suggests that after considering the short option position to the home owner, the MBS 4.00% offers a higher relative spread compared to the MBS 5.50% pass through.

12.6 OAS DISTRIBUTION ANALYSIS

In the Bond Lab model, the metrics calculated by the MBS cash flow engine are available to the OAS model. Thus, the investor can evaluate the distribution of price given OAS, path spread, as well as weighted average life, yield to maturity, or modified duration along each interest rate trajectory.

Each short-term rate trajectory represents a possible realization of the future. The simulated price distribution is derived by discounting a constant OAS along each short-term rate trajectory. The OAS spread (basis), like any other spread will change with the level, steepness, curvature of the yield curve, and volatility. Similarly, the analyst may calculate a price distribution by assigning an OAS other than that realized along each path of the simulation—*OAS to price*—much like one calculates price given yield to maturity.

12.6.1 OAS Price Distribution Analysis

Figures 12.18 and 12.19 illustrate the price distribution from the option-adjusted spread model. The range of the distribution of the MBS 4.00% is wider than that of the MBS 5.50%. The MBS 4.00% price distributions is negatively skewed (Table 12.2), meaning there are more price observations to the right of each distribution, while that of the MBS 5.50% is modestly

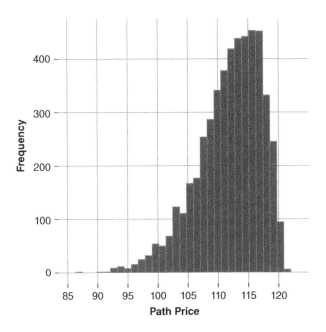

FIGURE 12.18 Price Dist. MBS 4.00%

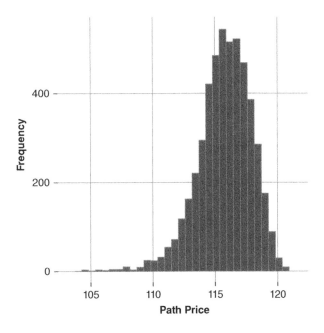

FIGURE 12.19 Price Dist. MBS 5.50%

TABLE 12.2 Price Distribution Summary Statistics

	MBS 4.00%	MBS 5.50%
Mean	111.97	115.75
Mode	115.21	115.53
Standard Deviation	5.29	2.17
Pearson's Second Coefficient	−1.83	0.30

positively skewed. One can quantify the degree of skewness using Pearson's second coefficient given in equation 12.17.

$$\text{Pearson's second coefficient} = \frac{3(\text{mean} - \text{mode})}{\text{Standard deviation}} \quad (12.17)$$

The negative skewness of the MBS 4.00% implies more downside price risk than that of the MBS 5.50%. Further, the MBS 5.50% price distribution exhibits a lower standard deviation. Together, the skewness and standard deviation highlight the lower predicted price volatility of the MBS 5.50% and explain its lower OAS relative to that of the MBS 4.00%.

12.6.2 Spot Spread Distribution Analysis

Figures 12.20 and 12.21 present the spot spread distribution. As mentioned earlier, the zero volatility (ZV) spread represents the average of the spot spread across each short-term rate trajectory that equates the present value along each trajectory to the of the present value of the security (Price + Accrued interest). The ZV spread distribution exhibits a negative skew. To compare securities based on the ZV spread distribution, one normalizes the ZV spread by its standard deviation. Normalizing in this manner produces a ZV spread statistic that is conceptually equivalent to the Sharp ratio. Table 12.3 summarizes the technique. The MBS 4.00% ZV spread standard deviation is 6 basis points, which results in a normalized ZV spread of 20 basis points: 0.208 = 1.25/.06. The MBS 5.50% standard deviation is 5 basis points, which results in a normalized ZV spread of 41 basis points:

TABLE 12.3 Spot Spread-Adjusted Spread Analysis

	Mean	Standard Deviation	Adjusted Spot Spread
MBS 4.00%	1.25	0.06	20.8
MBS 5.50%	2.08	0.05	41.6

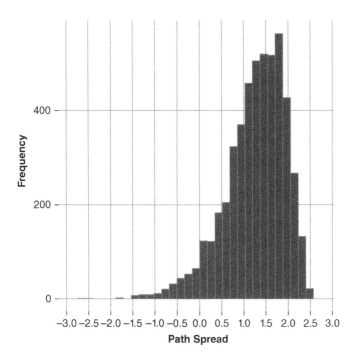

FIGURE 12.20 ZV Spd. MBS 4.00%

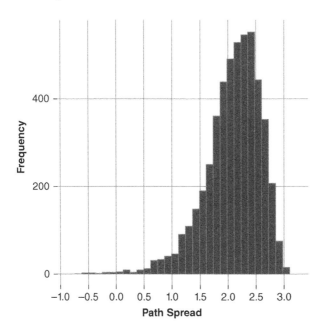

FIGURE 12.21 ZV Spd. MBS 5.50%

0.416 = 2.08/.05. The analysis suggests the MBS 5.50% MBS offers a superior risk adjusted ZV spread.

- The MBS 5.50% offers the investor a higher risk-adjusted ZV spread.
- The range of MBS 5.50% ZV spread distribution is narrower than that of the MBS 4.00%, indicating greater cash flow certainty.
- In all, the analysis shows the MBS 5.50% offers a higher average ZV spread and fewer potential adverse outcomes.

12.6.3 Weighted Average Life Distribution Analysis

Figures 12.22 and 12.23 present the weighted average life (WAL) distribution of each security. Recall from Table 12.1 the prepayment model average life of the MBS 4.00% is significantly longer than that of the MBS 5.50%. The WAL distribution analysis further illustrates the differences between the two securities.

- MBS 4.00% pass-through:
  - The OAS WAL is 10.0 years, modestly shorter than the prepayment model average life presented in Table 12.1 (11.9 years).

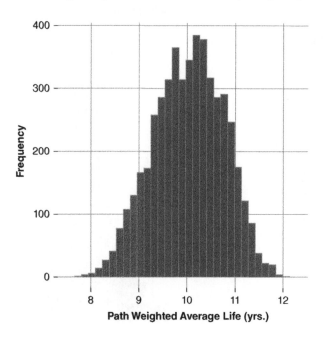

FIGURE 12.22 WAL Dist. MBS 4.00%

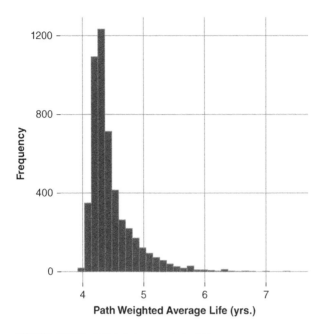

FIGURE 12.23 WAL Dist. MBS 5.50%

— The OAS WAL ranges between a minimum of 7.7 years and maximum of 12.0 years. The range of average life is shorter than that presented under the scenario-based analysis in the previous chapter. The scenario-based return analysis suggested the average life ranges between a minimum of 11.09 years and a maximum of 13.04 years.

■ MBS 5.50% pass-through:
— The OAS WAL is 4.47 years. Once again, this is modestly longer than the average life presented Table 12.1.
— The OAS WAL ranges between a minimum of 3.9 years and a maximum of 7.3 years. Again, shorter than the range of the average life presented under the scenario-based analysis. The scenario-based return analysis suggested the average life ranges between a minimum 4.43 years and maximum of 10.31 years.

12.6.4 OAS Yield to Maturity Distribution

Finally, consider the distribution of the yield to maturity presented in Figures 12.24 and 12.25. Again, each simulated trajectory represents a potential realization of the future short-term rate path. It follows that each

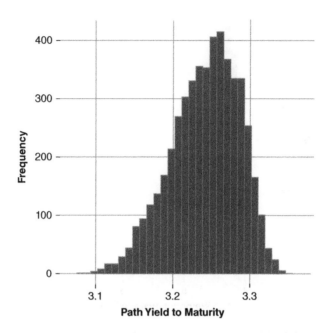

FIGURE 12.24 YTM Dist. MBS 4.00%

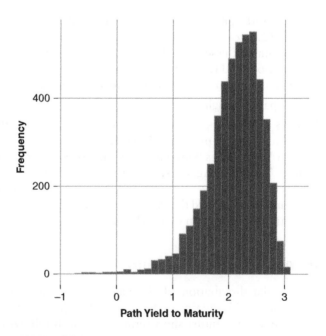

FIGURE 12.25 YTM Dist. MBS 5.50%

short-term rate trajectory represents a potential prepayment realization given by the relationship between the interest rate model and the prepayment model resulting in a potential yield to maturity realization along each short-term rate trajectory. The yield to maturity analysis is summarized below:

- The MBS 4.00% pass-through yield to maturity exhibits greater variability than the MBS 5.50%.
  - The average yield to maturity is 3.24%, which is less than that of the no-change scenario analysis (3.31%) presented in Table 11.3.
  - Similarly, the OAS scenario's maximum and minimum yields to maturity (3.34% and 3.07%) are lower than than their respective yields reported under the scenario-based return analysis.
- The MBS 5.50% pass-through yield to maturity exhibits less variability than the MBS 4.00%.
  - The average yield to maturity is 3.53%. Again, this yield to maturity is lower than that reported under the no-change scenario analysis (3.55%) presented in Table 11.4.
  - The OAS scenario's yield to maturity ranges from a low of 3.34% and a high of 4.12%, each lower than their respective yields reported under the scenario-based return analysis.

Based on OAS alone the investor may be tempted to simply assume the MBS 4.00% pass-through is priced cheaper than the MBS 5.50% pass-through given its higher OAS. However, a detailed inspection of the OAS output sheds some light on the valuation MBS 5.50% cash flows. As mentioned in Chapter 11, the MBS 5.50% offers investors a defensive return profile, which is further illustrated by the OAS analysis. Thus, the questions facing the investor are:

- Is the average life and return profile of the MBS 4.00% acceptable within her investment policy?
- Will her overall portfolio return benefit by including the defensive MBS 5.50%?
- If so, does the MBS 5.50%, given its lower OAS, represent good relative value or should she look to other fixed-income sectors or MBS structures to achieve her investment goals?

12.7 OAS ANALYSIS STRENGTHS AND LIMITATIONS

Any analytic framework has both strengths and limitations. The more clearly the investor understands them, the better she is able to apply the model.

- OAS analysis strengths:
  - — Clearer representation of the price of the modeled securities versus static cash-flow analysis.
  - — Incorporates the effect of different yield curve shapes and recognizes the potential alternative realization of future interest-rate trajectories.
  - — Allows for the explicit measurement and representation, through distribution analysis, of the risks associated with each investment choice.
- OAS analysis limitations:
  - — Dependent on the quality of both the interest rate and prepayment models.
  - — May only be used to compare OAS between similar securities with similar embedded options. That is, one cannot compare the OAS of a callable corporate bond versus that of mortgage-backed security.

This chapter illustrates the construction and use of an option-adjusted spread model as an input to the investment decision making process. OAS analysis provides a richer understanding of the possible realizations of future outcomes based on simulation and provides a framework to further understand the risk/reward profile of structured securities beyond that of a cash flow or scenario-based analysis.

Recall from Chapter 5 the measures that define the price of a security and those that define the risk of a security. OAS analysis provides the measures that define both the price and risk of a security. Individually, neither the valuation nor the risk measures fully define the potential return of a security. Consequently, return analysis should also be incorporated into the investment decision-making process. By exploiting the relative strengths of both OAS and return analysis the investor builds a robust decision making framework allowing her to identify relative value within the structured securities markets.

Four

Structuring Mortgage-Backed Securities

CHAPTER 13

Introduction to REMICs

*...then something went BUMP! How that BUMP made us
jump ... we looked! ... then we saw him! ... the cat in the hat!*
Dr. Seuss, *The Cat in the Hat*

The investor should understand the legal structure that governs both the creation and the administration of the trust which holds the assets and their cash flows and remittance payments. The trustee oversees the trust for the benefit of the investor. The servicer services the loans in accordance with the servicing agreement and remits payments to the trust. The trustee advances the funds to the investor in accordance with the trust document and cash allocation waterfall outlined in the prospectus. In combination, the legal structure of the trust, the trustee's obligations, and the servicing agreement, constitute a structured security.

The creation of a *real estate mortgage investment conduit (REMIC)* is achieved through the division of principal and interest. This section covers a brief history of REMICs, taking the reader through the legal evolution of the REMIC, structuring a REMIC beginning with the collateral cash flows through the creation of tranches that offer the investor a unique risk/reward profile based on the allocation of principal and interest.

13.1 BACKGROUND AND LEGAL STRUCTURE

The legal and structural innovations found in the residential mortgage-backed securities market are the foundation upon which the full spectrum of the structured securities markets rest. Prior to the adoption of the REMIC and the tax reform act of 1986, securitization of mortgage cash flows was achieved through the use of a grantor trust. Perhaps the most significant innovation in the mortgage-backed securities market was the 1984 formation of an investment trust (grantor trust) by the Sears Mortgage Securities Corporation SMS 1984-1. The SMS 1984-1 transaction, by issuing multiple classes of time-tranched mortgage pass-through securities, was the first example of the division of principal [Arnholz and Gainor 2006]. Prior to the division of principal, mortgage pass-through certificates entitled each certificate holder to a proportionate or pro-rata share of the principal cash flow of the underlying mortgage loans used to collateralize the transaction. The SMS 1984-1 cash waterfall principal payment priority allocated both scheduled and prepaid principal to the first—fast pay—class until its principal balance was reduced to zero. The following sequential classes would receive principal only once each higher priority class was paid down to zero. The Sears structure prompted both the Internal Revenue Service and the Treasury Department to issue a regulatory amendment denying trust classification to any trust like the SMS 1984-1 that issued more than one class of beneficial ownership interest. The "bright line" approach taken by the IRS and the Treasury addressed two concerns arising from the new structure.[1]

- First, as a result of time tranching, the investor's ownership share can no longer be considered a direct investment in the trust because the investor's share in the trust will change each month as principal payments are allocated to each class on a priority rather than on a pro-rate basis.
- Second, time tranching results in a deferral of income that both the IRS and Treasury Department deemed unacceptable.

The grantor trust's limitation against issuing multiple classes of securities led to the development of the owner trust structure. An owner trust structure issues two types of securities:

1. Certificates that represent beneficial interest in the trust
2. Notes issued in accordance with an indenture and secured by the trust's assets

Figure 13.1 outlines the mechanics of a REMIC transaction, which is executed in the following order:

- The sponsor of the REMIC transfers the mortgage loans to the depositor and the loans are "deposited" into a trust.
- The issuing entity (issuer) exchanges notes with the depositor for the mortgage loans.

[1]Ibid, pp. 8–10

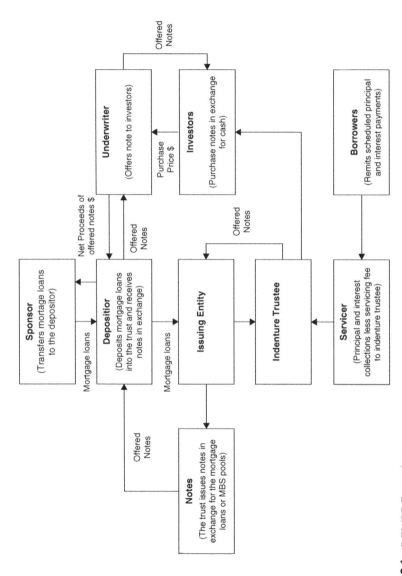

FIGURE 18.1 REMIC Execution

217

- The underwriter offers the notes to investors and receives cash, which is remitted to the issuer.
- The issuer remits the cash to the depositor, who in turn remits the cash to the sponsor in exchange for the mortgage loans.
- Once the transaction is closed, the underlying borrowers remit scheduled principal and interest payments to the servicer.
- The servicer remits the borrower's payments to the indenture trustee, who in turn remits the appropriate scheduled principal and interest to the investors (note holders).

The owner trust structure can issue multiple classes of notes in a "fast pay" or "slow pay" structure like that of the SMS 1984-1 transaction. This is because the grantor trust prohibition against issuing multiple classes of securities applies to the beneficial ownership interests in the trust, not to the debt securities—notes—issued by the trust. Thus, so long as the notes are treated as debt for tax purposes, the issuance of multiple notes does not result in the same income allocation concern that arises when a grantor trust issues multiple classes of beneficial interests. Ultimately, the bright-line approach of the IRS and the Treasury Department was abandoned in the final regulations addressing the issuance of multiple classes in a fast-pay or slow-pay structure. Because the regulations governing these structures were adopted in response to the SMS 1984-1 Sears transaction, they are sometimes referred to as the "Sears Regulations."

As part of the tax reform act of 1986, Congress added REMIC provisions to the tax code:

- A REMIC is generally not subject to tax at the entity level. However, the REMIC must compute taxable income or loss in the same manner as would an individual taxpayer.
- A REMIC must issue a residual interest, and any holder of the residual must include the REMIC's reported income or loss as part of its taxable income.

A REMIC is any qualified legal entity that chooses to elect REMIC status and satisfies the following three statutory tests: an asset test, an interest test, and an arrangement test.[2]

- Asset test, substantially all of a REMIC's assets must at all times consist of qualified mortgages and other permitted assets. A qualified mortgage is an obligation principally secured by an interest in real property that is

---

[2] Ibid, pp. 8–33

either transferred to the REMIC on its start-up date or purchased within a three-month period subject to a fixed price contract on the start-up day. A mortgage is considered principally secured if it meets either a loan-to-value test or an alternative proceeds test [Service 2012a].

— Under the loan-to-value test, a mortgage loan is considered to be principally secured by an interest in real property if the mortgage loan has an original LTV of at least 80% either at the time it was contributed to the REMIC by the sponsor or at loan origination.

— Under the alternative proceeds test, a mortgage loan is considered to be principally secured by an interest in real property if substantially all the proceeds of the loan were used to acquire, improve, or protect an interest in real property, that at the origination date, is the only security for the loan.

▪ Interest test, a REMIC must have one class, and only one class, of residual interest (stake) and may issue one or more classes of regular interests (notes) [Service 2012b].

▪ Arrangement test, a REMIC must adopt reasonable arrangements designed to ensure that disqualified entities do not hold residual interests in a REMIC. A disqualified entities include the following:

— The United States government or political subdivisions thereof

— A foreign government, a political subdivision thereof, or an international organization

— A foreign central bank of issue or the Bank of International Settlements (BIS)

13.2 TWO-TIERED REMICS

…but we can have fun, lots of good fun that is funny…
−Dr. Seuss, The Cat in the Hat

Two-tiered REMICs facilitate the creation of interest only classes. A REMIC interest-only class must meet the specified portion test under the tax code [Service 2012a]. Under this test the interest only class must be expressed as a fixed percentage of the interest payable on some or all of the qualified mortgages. Further, under U.S. Code 860G, a qualified mortgage is defined as, but not limited to:

▪ Any obligation principally secured by an interest in real property, and which

▪ Is transferred to a REMIC on start-up day in exchange for regular or residual interest (stake).

▪ Any regular interest (stake) in a REMIC or another REMIC transferred to the REMIC on the start-up day in exchange for regular or residual interest in the REMIC.

For the most part, investors use the terms *Collateralized Mortgage Obligation* (CMO) and REMIC interchangeably to describe a residential MBS transaction in which interests in a pool of mortgage loans are issued. However, there is a subtle, yet important, distinction between the two.

The term CMO generally describes a grantor trust structure issuing multiple beneficial classes, while the term REMIC describes an owners trust issuing multiple notes and making a REMIC election for tax purposes.

A REMIC may be structured with either agency (FNMA, FHLMC, GNMA) collateral pools or whole loans—residential or commercial. Whole loans require credit enhancement—either internal or external—due to the absence of a government guarantee. A CMO almost always elects REMIC treatment in order to avoid double taxation, and as a result, the terms CMO and REMIC have become interchangeable.

The ability to issue multiple beneficial interests in a pool of mortgage loans using a fast-pay or slow-pay structure was a significant step forward in the securitization of mortgage loans. REMICs enable issuers to create securities that are tailored to meet investors' specific risk/reward objectives and to take advantage of the various term structure theories discussed in Chapter 2.

13.3   REMIC ARBITRAGE

A REMIC structure exploits the market segmentation theory through time tranching by creating bonds of different maturities using the fast-pay or slow-pay structure. Examples of REMIC structures that exploit the market segmentation theory include sequential bonds and time-tranched planned amortization class (PAC) bonds.

Other REMIC structures allow the investor to express her view with respect to the forward rate curve. These structures seek to exploit either the rational expectations or pure expectations hypothesis. Examples are tiered index bonds, inverse floaters, interest-only stripped bonds, and accrual bonds.

To address the investor's liquidity and maturity preferences, a REMIC transaction alters the nature and timing of the cash flow derived from the underlying mortgage loans. In turn, the valuation of these cash flows is changed because the investor may be willing to pay a premium for those cash flows that have been segregated from the underlying mortgage pools or loans and that offer a specific risk/reward profile, average life profile, prepayment protection, or allow the investor to express a particular view with respect to the forward rate curve.

REMIC execution (*arbitrage*) exploits the valuation framework presented in Chapter 4 by creating front-loaded cash flows that are priced relative to the short end of the coupon curve. These cash flows are priced "rich" or expensive relative to either the longer-dated REMIC or collateral cash flows. The pricing of front-loaded cash flows to a lower yielding short-dated Treasury or interest rate swap benchmark increases the value of the REMIC cash flows vis-à-vis the MBS pass-through cash flows. In turn, REMIC creation is profitable, and this relationship explains why REMIC issuance tends to go up when the yield curve is steep. In addition to the slope of the coupon curve, the REMIC basis relative to the MBS pass-through basis also influences the profitability of the REMIC arbitrage.

For example, as the MBS pass-through basis tightens relative to the REMIC:

- The profitability of the REMIC arbitrage declines.
- Astute investors may take advantage of the dislocation in the MBS/REMIC pricing spread by selling the MBS collateral and buying the REMIC as a "cheaper" collateral substitute.
- At the same time, a lower arbitrage profit results in a decline in REMIC issuance, which, when combined with selling pressure against the MBS pass-through market, may, over time, cause a widening of the MBS/REMIC pricing spread.
- The above dynamic increases the profitability of REMIC execution and dealers "buy" collateral placing technical downward pressure on the MBS/REMIC pricing spread, while greater REMIC issuance places supply pressure (wider) on the MBS/REMIC pricing spread.

In the opposite case, as the MBS pass-through pricing spread widens relative to the REMIC:

- The profitability of the REMIC arbitrage increases.
- Astute investors may take advantage of the dislocation in the MBS/REMIC basis and buy collateral while selling REMICs as a "rich" collateral substitute.
- At the same time, an increase in REMIC issuance when combined with buying pressure against the MBS pass-through market may, over time, cause a tightening of the MBS/REMIC basis.
- Taken together, the above dynamic decreases the profitability of REMIC execution and dealers "sell" collateral, placing upward pressure on the MBS/REMIC basis, while less REMIC issuance places demand pressure (tighter spread) on the MBS/REMIC pricing spread.

CONCEPT 13.1

REMICs seek to exploit the term structure theories to attain a profitable arbitrage. The legal structure of the REMIC facilitates the division of principal and interest, allowing a dealer to create tranches meeting specific maturity and risk/reward preferences.

13.4   BOND LAB MBS STRUCTURING MODEL

Before further considering the allocation of interest and principal, a brief overview of the Bond Lab REMIC structure model is required. Understanding the structure of the model provides greater overall insight into the techniques used to create REMICs and their valuations. The investor must be cognizant of three crucial information blocks when evaluating structured securities:

- The REMIC structuring information at issuance. Structuring information includes the REMIC tranche detail and the final data statements, which enumerate both the details of the tranches (notes) and the underlying collateral and the group(s) to which to the collateral belongs.
- REMIC monthly update information tracking both collateral and tranche factors, as well as updating coupon rates in the case of variable step-up, floating, or inverse floating rate securities.
- The investor must understand the bond payment rules, often referred to as the cash waterfall that prescribes the payment of interest and principal to the tranches (notes).

The Bond Lab structuring model is based on five objects representing the information blocks outlined above:

- The REMIC At Issuance Disclosure class (RAID). This class contains the deal information at issuance.
- The Tranches class. This class contains the tranche issuance information like tranche coupon, first and last payment dates, the relationship to the collateral groups, etc.
- The Groups class. This class contains the collateral group information. Generally, pool numbers, a reference to a representative aggregation of the underlying collateral, or loan level detail.

- The REMIC Disclosure At Month End class (RDME). This class contains the updated bond information and reports tranche factors, payment dates, coupon rates.
- The Schedule class. This class contains additional structuring information such as PAC or TAC bond sinking fund schedules.
- The REMIC waterfall script. The REMIC waterfall defines the allocation of principal and interest across the REMIC classes.

Together, the above elements constitute the data structure required to model, update, and analyze REMICs collateralized by either residential or commercial mortgage loans or pools.

CHAPTER 14

Stripped Mortgage-Backed Securities

The previous chapter outlined the evolution of REMICs from a *grantor trust* to the owner trust structure. As mentioned in Chapter 12, the creation of a REMIC is achieved through the division of principal and interest. Thus, although structured as a grantor trust and not a *REMIC* through its legal formation, the first structure presented is a simple two-tranche interest and principal stripped mortgage-backed security (SMBS). In the forthcoming example, the transaction is collateralized by an MBS 4.00% pass-through. Tranche 1 is allocated the interest and tranche 2 is allocated all principal payments, scheduled and prepaid, that are received from the underlying pass-through security.

Key rate duration analysis provides the insight needed to understand how the division of principal and interest influence the parametric measures that define both the valuation and risk of REMIC tranches. Table 14.1 outlines the valuation metrics of the underlying collateral, the *interest only* tranche, and the *principal only* tranche. For the comparative analysis presented the following assumptions are used:

- Arbitrage free pricing, the value of the IO + PO is equal to the value of the underlying collateral from which they were structured.
  - Zero transaction costs. A dealer structuring and bringing an MBS transaction to market incurs costs, including registration and legal fees.
  - The investor is indifferent between holding the collateral, the interest only or principal only tranche.

In the cash waterfall, allocation is first to interest than to principal. In the case of the *bondlabSMBS* transaction the cash allocation rules may be expressed as follows:

- { Pay 100% of available interest to tranche 1 }
- { Pay 100% of available principal to tranche 2 }

TABLE 14.1 REMIC IO-PO Analysis

	MBS 4.00%	Tranche 1 (IO)	Tranche 2 (PO)
Net Coupon	4.00%	4.00%	0.00%
Note Rate	4.75%	4.75%	4.75%
Term	360 mos.	360 mos.	360 mos.
Loan Age	0 mos.	0 mos.	0 mos.
Price:	$105.75	$24.00	$81.75
Yield to Maturity	3.31%	8.31%	1.95%
Spot Spread	1.22%	6.64%	−0.31%
Model WAL	11.3	15.9	13.4
Modified Duration	8.32	5.75	9.58
Convexity	61.3	28.3	80.0
Effective Duration	7.13	−7.55	12.3
Effective Convexity	201	16752	1065

Table 14.1 provides a comparative analysis between the collateral and the IO and PO tranches based on the January 10, 2013, swap curve and assuming an 8.0% CPR pricing speed. The IO is priced at $24.00. Its price may be quoted by the dealer at 6 times. That is, the IO price is 6 × its coupon (4.0). The PO is priced at $81.75.

Of the metrics presented below, perhaps the most important to notice are both the modified duration and the effective duration. Notice, the IO reports a negative effective duration of 7.55 years, 14.7 years shorter than the underlying collateral, while the PO reports a positive duration of 12.3 years, 5.2 years longer than the underlying collateral. Recall from Chapter 3, effective duration is the sum of each key weight duration. Further, key rate duration is computed by "shocking" each key rate along the curve by (+/−) 25 basis points. Thus, the difference between the measures of modified duration and convexity and those of effective duration and convexity is one of a static (unchanged yield curve) versus a dynamic (key rate shock) cash flow analysis.

The negative duration of the IO tranche implies that as interest rates rise the price of the IO increases. Why negative duration? The IO represents interest cash flow that is stripped from the MBS. Recall, higher interest rates and/or a steeper yield curve result in slower borrower prepayment rates. Consequently, a greater share of principal is outstanding for a longer period of time which increases the value of the interest only tranche. Conversely, the PO duration is almost two times greater than that of the underlying collateral, implying the PO exhibits greater price sensitivity to changes in interest rates than the collateral.

The analysis summarized in Table 14.1 highlights an important point. Namely, adding or subtracting interest only (IO) to a tranche through the division of interest payment rules will reduce or increase the effective duration of the tranche to which the interest is redirected—often referred to as "coupon stripping." Similarly, one may add or subtract principal to a tranche through division of principal payment rules—the net effect is the same. Recall the relationship between a bond's coupon, maturity, and duration. Specifically, as the bond's coupon increases its duration declines.

A REMIC, even one as simple as the IO-PO execution, seems complex given the degree to which it alters cash flows and their associated value and risk metrics. However, once given deeper consideration one will see it is not the case. In fact, REMIC cash flows follow the basic fixed-income fundamentals outlined in Chapter 3.

Consider the IO tranche. We know from Chapter 3, Figure 3.2, duration declines as the bond's coupon increases. Thus, in the absence of principal (an interest only security)—representing an infinite coupon—and given the contingent nature of MBS cash flows due to prepayment risk, a negative effective duration follows. With respect to the PO tranche, Figure 3.3, shows duration increases with maturity. In fact, a zero coupon bond's effective duration is equal to its time to maturity, thus irrespective of the contingent nature of MBS cash flows a positive effective duration follows. Understanding the influence of the division of interest and principal on the fundamental metric of bond risk—effective duration—provides the foundation for understanding the analysis and valuation of all possible REMIC cash flow combinations that can be created though the division of interest and principal.

CONCEPT 14.1

At first blush, one may be tempted to say that the IO tranche is trading to a *discount*—a price below par—which is not the case. Indeed, given that the IO tranche represents a return of interest only and no principal the IO trades at an infinite premium, which is why IO prices are often quoted using a multiplier. The PO tranche on the other hand is priced at a discount.

Table 14.1 illustrates two important points:

- The IO-PO example illustrates how the division of principal and interest may create securities with extreme risk metrics as measured by effective duration and convexity.

- Irrespective of the division of principal and interest, REMICs follow the basic fixed-income principles outlined in Chapter 3.

14.1 KEY RATE DURATION ANALYSIS

Key rate duration analysis provides insight into how the division of principal and interest influences the return profile a REMIC tranche by altering the nature and timing of its cash flows. Key rate duration also reveals those points along the key rate tenors that most influence a REMIC tranche's expected return profile.

14.1.1 Interest Only

Figures 14.1 and 14.2 illustrate the key rate durations of both the underlying collateral and the interest only tranche. The collateral exhibits positive key rate durations across all tenors. However, the IO tranche exhibits positive key rate durations across the earlier tenors up to seven years and negative key rate durations thereafter. Recall the valuation framework for

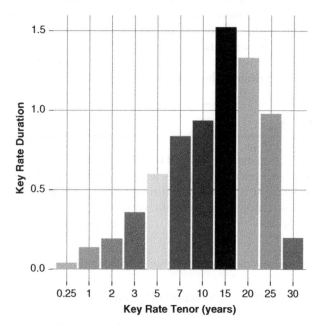

FIGURE 14.1 Key Rate Duration MBS 4.00% Pass-Through

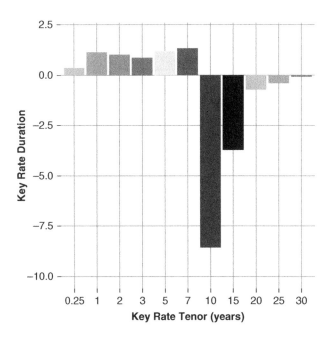

FIGURE 14.2 Key Rate Duration MBS 4.00% Tranche 1 (IO)

structured securities presented in Chapter 4. The IO's key rate duration profile suggests that it will perform better under the following interest rate scenarios:

- A parallel shift up, under this scenario the expected prepayment rate slows down and cash flows extend along the curve. The benefit of the negative key rate durations at the longer tenors more than offsets the detriment of the positive key rate durations at the shorter tenors as interest rates rise.
- Twist steepen, under this scenario the IO benefits from both lower short-term rates and higher long-term rates. The steeper yield curve and higher long-term rates imply a slower expected prepayment rate.
- Bear steepen, under this scenario the IO benefits from higher long-term rates and the steeper yield curve implies an expected slower prepayment rate.

14.1.2 Principal Only

Figures 14.3 and 14.4 illustrate the key rate duration of both the underlying collateral and the principal only tranche. Again, the collateral exhibits

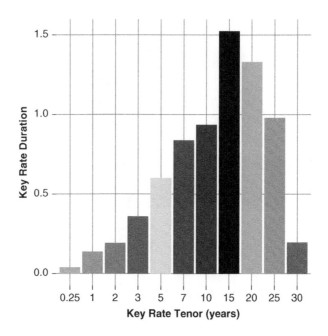

FIGURE 14.3 Key Rate Duration MBS 4.00%

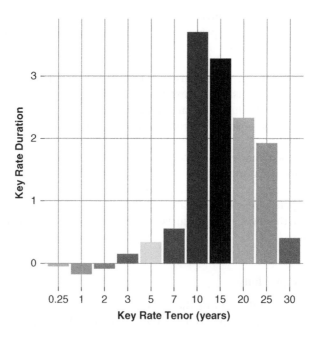

FIGURE 14.4 Key Rate Duration MBS 4.00% Tranche 2 (PO)

positive key rate durations across all tenors. However, the PO tranche exhibits negative duration across the earlier key rate tenors up to two-years and positive key rate durations thereafter. Notice, the PO key rate durations exhibit relationships opposite to those of the IO. The PO tranche benefits from the following interest rate scenarios:

- A parallel shift down, under this scenario the expected prepayment rate speeds up and cash flows shorten along the curve. The benefit of the positive key rate durations at the longer tenors more than offset the detriment of the negative key rate durations at the shorter tenors as interest rates fall.
- Twist flatten, under this scenario the PO benefits from both higher short-term rates and lower long-term rates. The flatter curve and lower long-term rates imply a faster expected prepayment rate.
- Bear flatten, under this scenario the PO benefits from lower long-term rates and the flatter yield curve implies an expected faster prepayment rate.

14.2   OPTION-ADJUSTED SPREAD ANALYSIS

Option-adjusted spread analysis may also be used to value MBS derivative cash flows. Table 14.2 compares the collateral's OAS and ZV-spread to those of the IO and PO. Notice the difference across OAS valuations. The IO tranche OAS is 542 basis points while that of the PO is 17 basis points. The division of interest and principal fundamentally altered the valuation of the IO and PO relative to its underlying collateral. Further, the OAS valuation reflects the tuning of the prepayment model. For example, a model tuned to

TABLE 14.2   REMIC IO-PO OAS Analysis

	MBS 4.00%	Tranche 1 (IO)	Tranche 2 (PO)
Net Coupon	4.00%	4.00%	0.00%
Note Rate	4.75%	4.75%	4.75%
Term	360 mos.	360 mos.	360 mos.
Loan Age	0 mos.	0 mos.	0 mos.
Price	$105.75	$24.00	$81.75
OAS	0.52%	5.42%	0.17%
ZV-Spread	1.28%	4.97%	0.16%

faster "out-of-the-money" turnover will result in lower IO OAS and higher PO OAS valuations.

14.2.1 Weighted Average Life Analysis

Figures 14.5 and 14.6 compare the average life distribution of the underlying collateral versus the IO tranche. The analysis is based on 200 simulated interest rate trajectories. Generally, the IO weighted average life distribution follows that of the underlying collateral. Similarly, Figures 14.7 and 14.8 compare the average life distribution of the PO tranche versus the underlying collateral. As in the case of the IO, the PO's average life distribution reflects that of the underlying collateral.

Both tranche's weighted average life distribution reflects that of the underlying collateral because the cash water fall allocates 100% of the interest to Tranche 1 and 100% principal to Tranche 2. The analysis suggests that the simplest division of principal and interest does not alter the weighted average life profile of either security. Creating a fast pay/slow pay structure as discussed earlier in Chapter 13, which alters the average life profile, requires a more sophisticated principal allocation scheme than that of an IO-PO structure.

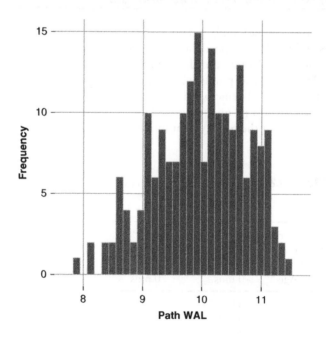

FIGURE 14.5 WAL Dist. MBS 4.00%

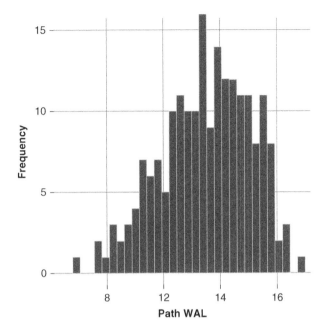

FIGURE 14.6   WAL Dist. Tranche 1 (IO)

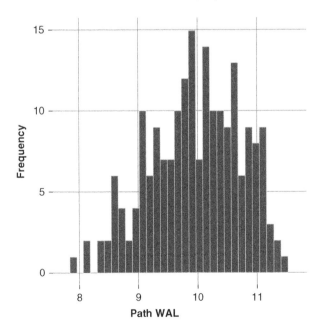

FIGURE 14.7   WAL Dist. MBS 4.00%

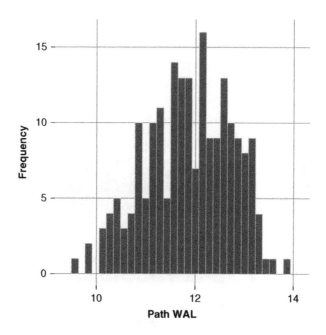

FIGURE 14.8 WAL Dist. Tranche 2 (PO)

14.2.2 Yield to Maturity Analysis

Figures 14.9 and 14.10 compare the yield to maturity distribution of the underlying collateral to the IO tranche and highlight the following:

- The average yield to maturity of the MBS 4.00% pass-through is lower than that of the IO, 3.23% versus 6.71%, respectively.
- The IO yield to maturity also exhibits a greater degree of dispersion, ranging from 4.00% to 8.75%.

Figures 14.11 and 14.12 compare the yield to maturity distributions of the underlying collateral to the PO tranche and highlight the following:

- The PO average yield (2.24%) is lower than that of the collateral (3.28%). The PO tranche, unlike the IO tranche, offers lower expected yield to maturity relative to that of the collateral.
- The PO yield to maturity distribution, like its IO counterpart, exhibits a greater degree of dispersion than that of the collateral.
- Finally, notice the PO yield to maturity distribution exhibits right skew while the pass-through yield to maturity distribution, like that of the IO, exhibits a modest degree of left skew.

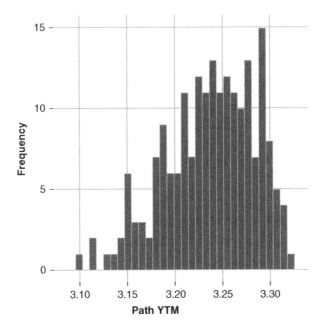

FIGURE 14.9 YTM Dist. MBS 4.00%

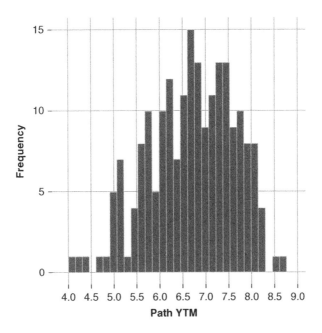

FIGURE 14.10 YTM Dist. Tranche 1 (IO)

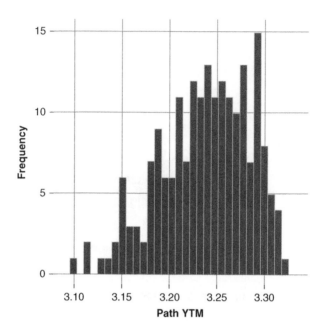

FIGURE 14.11 YTM Dist. MBS 4.00%

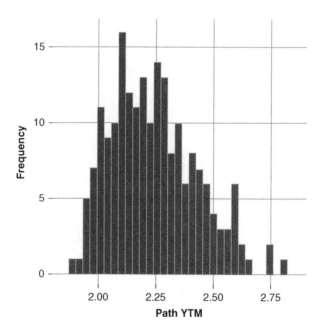

FIGURE 14.12 YTM Dist. Tranche 2 (PO)

The analysis of the yield to maturity distribution of each tranche indicates that the division of interest and principal fundamentally alter the valuation of MBS cash flows. Further, the changing valuations also alter the investor's risk/reward profile by creating IO and PO tranches that exhibit yield to maturity distributions that exceed the "tails" of the MBS pass-through's yield to maturity distribution.

14.3 THE INFORMATION CONTENT OF THE IO-PO MARKET

REMICs exist due to the presence of arbitrage. As discussed in Chapter 13, REMIC execution seeks to exploit the various term structure theories. Arbitrage must exist for profitable REMIC execution, however the relationship between the price of underlying collateral and REMIC tranches cannot stray too far out of line. The relationship between the value of the underlying collateral and the IO-PO REMIC arbitrage is apparent. Consequently, the IO-PO market provides an excellent pricing benchmark for the following:

- Relative value across both the pass-through and REMIC sectors
- Measuring investor prepayment expectations
- Calibrating both interest rate and prepayment models to IO and PO market prices

14.3.1 Relative Value Analysis Using IO and PO Prices

The relationship between the IO tranche, PO tranche, and collateral is straightforward and unencumbered by additional structuring vagaries. Consequently, the IO-PO market provides an excellent benchmark for relative value comparisons. Although some IO-PO REMICs are structured as simple two-tranche transactions, in reality most are structured with a range of coupon combinations. That is, the IO and PO tranches may be combined into alternative classes, each with a different coupon. How may one price each coupon available within the transaction? The investor may impute the price of any given coupon by using coupon stripping ratios:

$$\text{Coupon strip ratio} = \frac{TC}{CC} \qquad (14.1)$$

where: TC = Tranche target coupon
CC = Collateral coupon

The price of any coupon combination given the comparable underlying collateral is given by the following equation:

$$\text{Coupon price} = \left[\frac{TC}{CC} \times FS\right] + PO \qquad (14.2)$$

where: TC = Tranche target coupon
CC = Collateral coupon
FS = Full strip price
PO = PO price

Table 14.3 illustrates the use of coupon strip ratios. Consider Tranche 1 (IO) a 4.00% IO stripped from a 2013 origination, 4.00% MBS pass-through priced at $24.00, and Tranche 2 (PO) priced at $81.75. Given the prices of each, Table 14.3 provides prices for representative coupon combinations. For example, the price of a 1.0% coupon stripped from a 4.00% MBS pass-through is $87.75. The price is calculated as follows:

$$1.00\% \text{ price} = \left[\frac{1}{4} \times \$24\right] + \$81.75$$

TABLE 14.3 REMIC IO-PO OAS Analysis

	MBS 4.00%	Tranche 1 (IO)	Tranche 2 (PO)
Net Coupon	4.00%	4.00%	0.00%
Note Rate	4.75%	4.75%	4.75%
Term	360 mos.	360 mos.	360 mos.
Loan Age	0 mos.	0 mos.	0 mos.
Price	$105.75	$24.00	$81.75
Yield to Maturity	3.31%	8.31%	1.95%
OAS	0.55%	5.42%	0.17%
ZV-Spread	1.28%	4.97%	0.16%
IO Price	$24.00		
PO Price	$81.75		
1.0%	$87.75		
2.0%	$93.75		
3.0%	$99.75		
4.0%	$105.75		
5.0%	$111.75		
6.0%	$117.75		
7.0%	$123.75		
8.0%	$129.75		

$$1.00\% \text{ price} = \$87.75$$

The price of a 1.00% pass-through stripped from a 4.00% pass-through, given the pricing outlined in Table 14.3, is $87.75. Adding incremental IO strip increases the price. Notice, the coupon strip ratio yields the correct price for the 4.00% coupon stripped from a 4.00% pass-through security—a reconstitution of the MBS 4.00% pass-through security.

The coupon stripping equation only works for a given underlying MBS. For example, one cannot determine the price of a 1.00% coupon stripped from a 5.00% pass-through given the prices of an IO and PO collateralized by a 4.00% MBS pass-through. For the investor to determine the price of a 1.00% coupon stripped from a 5.00% pass-through, she requires comparable 5.00% MBS IO and PO prices. The coupon stripping example presented in Table 14.3 illustrates the importance of following the derivative market as a guide to determine relative value across the broader structured MBS sectors.

14.3.2 IO Prices as a Measure of Prepayment Sentiment

The IO market can also provide investors with a measure of prepayment sentiment across the market. Consider the 4.00% IO priced at $24. The market sentiment regarding forward prepayment outlook can be determined using simple static cash-flow analysis presented earlier in Chapter 11.

Table 14.4 illustrates the use of IO prices and static cash-flow analysis as a tool to gauge the market's prepayment sentiment. At the current price of $24, prepayment speeds as measured by CPR cannot exceed 12.0 before the IO yield turns negative. Often, a trader may say something to the effect, "4.00% IOs are priced such that prepayments cannot exceed 12.0 CPR." Of course, this is not to say a 4.00% MBS cannot prepay faster than 12.0% CPR—rather, the trader is referring to the fact that the IO yield turns negative when the prepayment speed is at or above 12.0 CPR.

TABLE 14.4 IO Prepayment Sentiment

CPR/Price	$20	$24	$30	$35	$40
4	13.77	10.63	8.48	6.29	4.06
6	10.27	7.13	4.99	2.80	5.74
8	6.63	3.49	1.35	−0.82	−3.05
10	4.44	1.31	−0.8	−3.00	−5.23
12	2.72	−0.4	−2.53	−4.715	−6.93

Notice as the IO price declines the prepayment threshold increases. For example, given a price of $30, the prepayment speeds cannot exceed 10.0 CPR before the IO yield turns negative. Given a price of $25, the prepayment speed cannot exceed 12.0 CPR before the IO yield will begin to turn negative. Indeed, if the investor believed that the long-term prepayment rate of the 4.00% MBS pass-through used to collateralize the IO/PO REMIC was 12.0 CPR, then the highest price she should be willing to pay is around $25.

14.3.3 Calibrating Interest Rate and Prepayment Models

The *OAS* IO and PO price distributions presented in Figures 14.13 and 14.14 suggest greater upside price potential of the IO tranche and greater downside price potential of the PO tranche. The price distributions suggest the following:

- The paths given by the interest rate model are likely biased to higher rates, which is not surprising given the low interest rate environment under which the simulation begins.

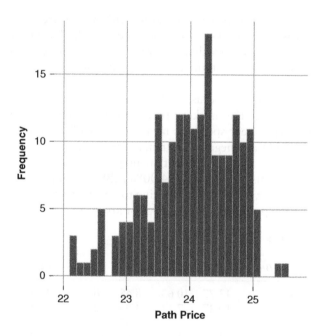

FIGURE 14.13 Price Dist. Tranche 1 (IO)

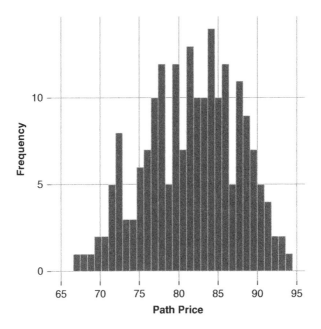

Frequency

Path Price

FIGURE 14.14 Price Dist. Tranche 2 (PO)

- The prepayment model's SMM vectors across the simulation imply a long-term average prepayment rate of 6.4% CPR. Recall, the model is calibrated to an "at-the-money" prepayment rate of 8.0% CPR.

Given both the yield table presented in Table 14.4 and the OAS price distribution presented in Figures 14.13 and 14.14, the investor may choose one of the following:

- Accept the analysis and subsequent valuations.
- Change either or both the drift *theta* (θ) and volatility *sigma* (σ) of the interest rate model to reduce the upward rate bias of the spot rate trajectories given by the model. Changing these parameters to reduce either the variance and/or volatility of the short-term interest rate reflects a belief on the part of the investor that interest rates may remain low for a prolonged period of time thereby increasing the predicted SMM vectors given by the prepayment model.
- Recalibrate the prepayment model to reflect higher out-of-the money and at-the-money prepayment speeds. Altering the prepayment model to report a faster prepayment speed when the collateral is "out of" or

"in the" money reflects a belief on the part of the investor that housing turnover rates will be higher than those to which the model is currently calibrated.

The IO-PO structure outlined in this chapter illustrates how the division of principal and interest changes the valuation of MBS cash flows. MBS investors, particularly those investing beyond the standard pass-through MBS markets, monitor the IO-PO market as a guide to pricing REMIC structures, a gauge of the market's prepayment sentiment, and a means to calibrate prepayment models to market prices. Although relatively simple in execution, the IO-PO market serves as a keystone to understanding the creation and pricing of increasingly complex REMIC structures.

CHAPTER 15

Sequentially Structured REMIC

Sequentially structured REMICs are based on the *division of principal* and seek to exploit both the market segmentation and liquidity preference theories of the term structure of interest rates.

- Recall, the market segmentation theory asserts that the markets of different maturity bonds are segmented. As a result, the interest rate for each bond is determined by the supply and demand for bonds without consideration given to the expected returns on bonds with different maturities. Under this theory, investors are thought to prefer short-term over long-term bonds. Thus, there is greater demand for short-term bonds and as a result, the price of short-term bonds is higher, resulting in lower yields than those offered by long-term bonds.
- The liquidity preference theory asserts that bonds are perfect substitutes for one another. However, because the investor may be required to sell her bond prior to maturity, thereby assuming interest rate risk, a greater premium is offered to the investor to hold longer-term bonds via higher implied forward rates.

The sequential REMIC waterfall *bondlabSEQ* cash allocation rules may be expressed as follows:

- { Pay 100% of available interest to each class on a pro-rata basis, based on each class's respective accrued interest }
- { Pay 100% of available principal in the following order: }
  - { Tranche 1 until the outstanding balance is reduced to zero, }
  - { Tranche 2 until the outstanding balance is reduced to zero, }
  - { Tranche 3 until the outstanding balance reduced to zero, }

The deal pricing speed is 125 PSA. Table 15.1 provides a comparative analysis between the collateral, Tranche A, Tranche B, and Tranche C. The astute reader will notice the following:

- The sum of the coupon interest paid to the bond holders is less than that derived from the underlying collateral.

TABLE 15.1   REMIC Sequential Analysis

	MBS 4.00%	Tranche A	Tranche B	Tranche C
Net Coupon	4.00%	0.63%	1.41%	2.72%
Note Rate	4.75%	4.75%	4.75%	4.74%
Term	360 mos.	360 mos.	360 mos.	360 mos.
Loan Age	0 mos.	0 mos.	0 mos.	0 mos.
Orig. Bal.		$50mm	$75mm	$75mm
Price	$105.75	$100.00	$100.00	$100.00
Yield to Maturity	3.26%	0.63%	1.41%	2.71%
Spot Spread	1.33%	0.18%	0.07%	0.24%
Pricing WAL	9.81	2.19	6.91	17.40
First Principal Pmt	1-2013	01-2013	11-2016	08-2023
Last Principal Pmt	1-2043	11-2016	08-2023	11-2042
Modified Duration	7.72	2.17	6.56	13.7
Convexity	49.9	3.91	26.50	110.00
Effective Duration	7.13	1.78	8.97	13.7
Effective Convexity	−15065	1377	−18941	−49830

- The proceeds, as shown in Table 15.1, are less than the cost required to accumulate the collateral.

In order to improve deal execution, the dealer may create an additional "IOette" class that represents the excess of the underlying collateral's interest payments over those paid to that of tranches A, B, and C. For purposes of this discussion, assume the existence of an additional IOette class whose valuation is sufficient to create a profitable arbitrage. Later, in Chapter 17, we will review the structuring and valuation of the IOette class.

The sequential structure alters the timing of the principal cash flow to the investor. Namely, Figure 15.1 and Table 15.1 show that Tranche A receives cash flows from Jan 2013 to Nov 2016, while Tranches B and C are said to be *locked out*. That is, principal is paid to these tranches only after the preceding tranche's principal balance is reduced to zero. For example, Tranche B's payment window, given a 125 PSA pricing speed, begins in Nov 2016 and ends Aug 2023. Tranche C's payment window begins in Aug 2023 and ends in Dec 2042 (recall section 7.2.2).

Time tranching is parsing the timing of the return of principal to the tranches. It changes the average life profile of each tranche relative to the underlying collateral. As shown in Table 15.1, both Tranche A and Tranche B report a shorter average life than the underlying collateral, which is 9.81 years. Tranche C reports a longer average life than the underlying collateral at 17.4 years. The dealer, by structuring tranches with

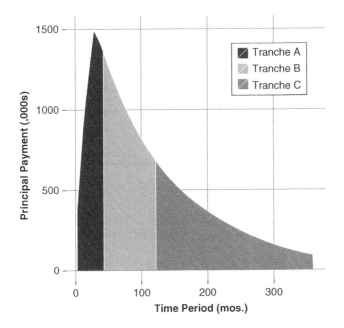

FIGURE 15.1 Sequential Principal Cash Flow Diagram

a shorter average life than the collateral, is exploiting both the *market segmentation* and liquidity preference theories of the term structure of interest rates, discussed earlier in sections 2.2 and 2.3, thereby creating a positive arbitrage.

A sequential transaction relies on the division of principal to create each tranche. As a result, both *call risk* and *extension risk* are asymmetrically distributed across the transaction's capital structure. The fast-pay tranches bear greater call risk relative to either the underlying collateral or the last cash flow tranche. Conversely, the penultimate and last cash flow tranches bear greater extension risk relative to either the underlying collateral or the fast-pay tranche.

At first blush, one may view the fast-pay tranche (Tranche A) as the tranche bearing the brunt of prepayment risk. However, it is not the case that the fast-pay tranche is subject to greater call risk. Rather, it is the last cash flow tranche that bears the greater prepayment risk relative to either the underlying collateral or the fast-pay tranche. Stated differently, the risk that the realized prepayment rate will deviate over time from the assumed pricing speed has a higher probability of occurring in the tranches that have a longer average life compared to those with shorter average life. As a result, the last cash flow tranche exhibits greater average life variability than the first or fast-pay tranche.

> ## CONCEPT 15.1
>
> The division of principal across a sequential structure asymmetrically distributes both call and extension risk across each tranche.

15.1 KEY RATE DURATION ANALYSIS

Key rate duration analysis illustrates how the allocation of principal across time (*time tranching*) impacts each security, further reinforcing the points above. Figures 15.2 and 15.3 provide a side-by-side comparison of both the collateral and Tranche A's key rate duration. Notice the following:

- The collateral's key rate durations are heavily concentrated along the longer key rate tenors, whereas Tranche A's key rate durations are heavily concentrated along the shorter key rate duration tenors. Thus, Tranche A has greater price risk relative to the shorter tenors of the curve than that of the underlying collateral.

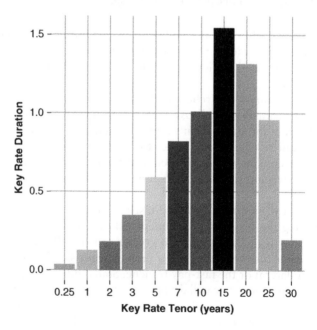

FIGURE 15.2 Key Rate Duration MBS 4.00%

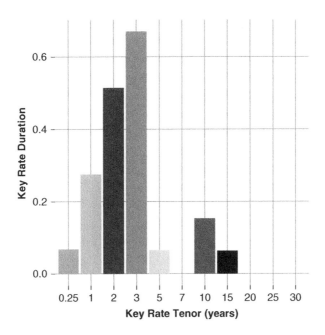

FIGURE 15.3   Key Rate Duration Tranche A

- Tranche A's 10-year key rate duration is less than half that of the collateral's 10-year key rate duration. Recall the forward mortgage rate, which determines borrower prepayment rates, is a function of the forward 2- and 10-year swap rates. Thus, Tranche A's lower 10-year key rate duration reflects not only its shorter average life but also its lower sensitivity to mortgage prepayment rates. Furthermore, the key rate duration analysis clearly shows Tranche A's price sensitivity to shorter key rate durations is greater than that of the underlying collateral, suggesting a greater overall price sensitivity to the shorter end of the term structure.

Figures 15.4 and 15.5 provide key rate duration analysis for both Tranche B and Tranche C. Figure 15.4 shows Tranche B's 10-year key rate duration is four times that of the underlying collateral, whereas tranche C's 10-year key rate duration is less than one-quarter that of the underlying collateral. The key rate duration analysis highlights the following:

- Tranche B is highly leveraged against the 10-year swap rate relative to either the underlying collateral or Tranches A or C. As such, Tranche B represents the fulcrum of the transaction.

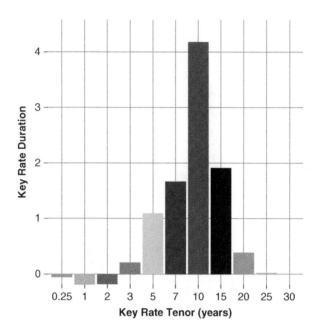

FIGURE 15.4 Key Rate Duration Tranche B

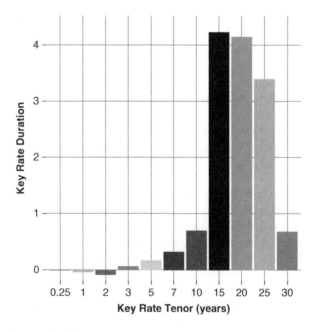

FIGURE 15.5 Key Rate Duration Tranche C

- Tranche C's 10-year key rate duration is less than that of the underlying collateral or Tranche B. However, the longer key rate durations are significantly higher, suggesting Tranche C is most sensitive to the longer tenors of the term structure and prepayment expectations. Consider the following, the term structure flattens between the 10- and 30-year maturities (a bull flattening of the yield curve), which, in turn, leads to a lower forward mortgage rate and higher forward prepayment expectations. Conversely, a steepening between the 10- and 30-year maturities (a bear steepening of the yield curve) leads to a higher forward mortgage rate and lower forward prepayment expectations.

Taken together, Table 15.1 and Figures 15.2 though 15.4 indicate, all else equal, Tranche C, after giving consideration to effective duration, is more negatively convex than both the underlying collateral and Tranches A or B.

15.2 OPTION-ADJUSTED SPREAD ANALYSIS

The OAS analysis presented in Table 15.2 further illustrates the impact of time tranching on the valuation of MBS cash flows. Notice, Tranche C, the last cash flow tranche, OAS is higher than that of either Tranche A or B, indicating the investor receives addition compensation, in the form of a higher OAS, for accepting the greater negative convexity of Tranche C—further reinforcing the notion that the last cash flow tranche bears greater relative prepayment risk.

TABLE 15.2 REMIC Sequential OAS Analysis

	MBS 4.00%	Tranche A	Tranche B	Tranche C
Net Coupon	4.00%	0.63%	1.41%	2.72%
Note Rate	4.75%	4.75%	4.75%	4.75%
Term	360 mos.	360 mos.	360 mos.	360 mos.
Loan Age	0 mos.	0 mos.	0 mos.	0 mos.
Price:	$105.75	$100.00	$100.00	$100.00
Yield to Maturity	3.26%	0.63%	1.41%	2.70
OAS	0.52%	0.00%	0.05%	0.31%
ZV-Spread	1.28%	0.00%	0.00%	0.27%
Spread to the Curve	1.52%	0.26%	0.11%	0.35%
Effective Duration	7.13	1.78	8.97	13.7
Effective Convexity	−15065	1377	−18941	−41132

The degree to which each tranche is leveraged against the underlying collateral prepayment rate will determine its convexity and valuation. Those tranches most leveraged against the underlying collateral's prepayment rate will typically exhibit greater relative negative convexity, and naturally trade to a higher yield and OAS than those with less relative leverage and more positive convexity. Option-adjusted spread analysis aids the investor in estimating the value of the embedded prepayment option across structures.

15.3 WEIGHTED AVERAGE LIFE AND SPOT SPREAD ANALYSIS

The investor may gain additional insight by examining the results of the short-rate simulation. In particular, the weighted average life distribution allows the investor to visually examine how the allocation of principal influences each tranche's average life profile. Further, examining the spot spread distribution yields additional insights relating to the allocation of principal and its impact on cash flow valuation.

15.3.1 Tranche A—WAL and Spot Spread Distribution Analysis

Figures 15.6 and 15.7 compare the weighted average life distribution of the underlying collateral to that of Tranche A. Notice, across all short-rate trajectories the WAL of Tranche A is shorter than that of the underlying collateral. Furthermore, the WAL is also less than that reported using the transaction pricing speed of 125 PSA, indicating the prepayment model is forecasting a faster near-term prepayment rate than the prepayment assumption used to price the transaction.

As a result of the model's faster prepayment forecast and consequently shorter WAL the spread to the curve declines. Additionally, the ZV-spread is less than both the spread-to-the curve using the prepayment model (0.26%) and the nominal pricing spread (0.25% over the 2-year swap rate). Thus, by the valuation framework outlined in Chapter 4, Tranche A's rich-priced cash flows outweigh the cheap-priced cash flows. The low ZV- and OA- spreads in Table 15.2 result from a loss of coupon income due to faster prepayment expectations relative to the transaction's pricing speed.

Figure 15.8 provides additional insight. Recall, the ZV-spread is calculated as the average of the spot spread realized along each short-rate trajectory. The distribution of the spot spread along each path illustrates how the cash flow valuation changes given the short-rate trajectory and its impact on the estimated borrower prepayment vector given by the prepayment model.

The spot spread distribution ranges from a low of −1.09% to a high of 0.49% while the average, ZV-spread, is 0.00%. Short-rate trajectories

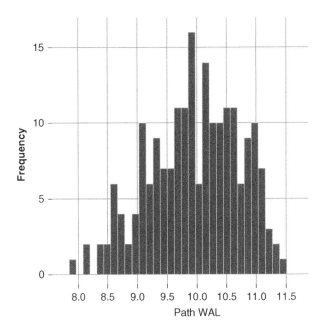

FIGURE 15.6 WAL Dist. MBS 4.00%

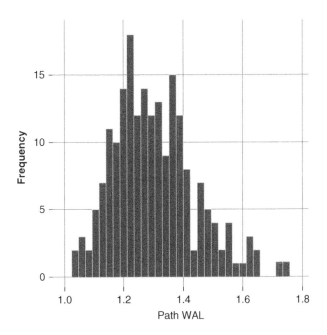

FIGURE 15.7 WAL Dist. Tranche A

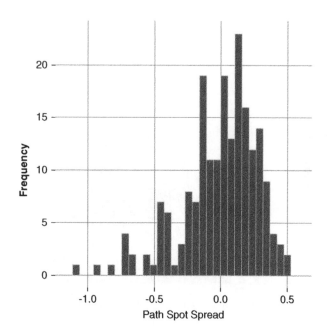

FIGURE 15.8 Tranche A—Spot Spread Distribution

resulting in faster prepayment vectors will act to shorten Tranche A's average life and reduce the coupon income received by the investor. In turn, a lower path spot spread results. Conversely, those trajectories resulting in slower prepayment vectors extend Tranche A's average life and increase the coupon income received by the investor. These paths result in a higher path spot spread. The left skew of Tranche A's spot spread distribution illustrates the extent to which the tranche is callable (negative spot spreads). Analysis of the spot spread distribution aids the investor in quantifying the extent to which Tranche A's call risk influences the overall valuation of its cash flows.

15.3.2 Tranche B—WAL and Spot Spread Distribution Analysis

Given a 125 PSA pricing speed the average life of the underlying collateral is 9.81 years and the average life of Tranche B is 6.91 years (Table 15.1). Tranche B's weighted average life distribution, as shown in Figure 15.9, reports less relative extension risk than the underlying collateral (Figure 15.6). Specifically, the maximum weighted average life of Tranche B is 7.95 years while that of the collateral is 11.49 years. Similarly, Tranche B exhibits greater relative call risk than the underlying collateral. Its minimum average life is 4.70 years versus the underling collateral minimum average

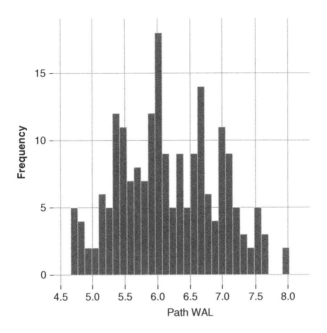

FIGURE 15.9 WAL Dist. Tranche B

life of 7.93 years. The average life distribution analysis confirms the finding in Table 15.2, which indicates Tranche B is more negatively convex than the underlying collateral.

Figure 15.10 presents Tranche B's spot spread distribution. Again, the distribution is negatively skewed and reports an average of 0.00%. Notice, the extreme value in the left tail of the distribution. The minimum spot spread is −2.21%, which accounts for the zero average ZV-spread and indicates that Tranche B also has embedded call risk. The maximum spot spread is 1.01%.

Tranche B reports a greater relative negative convexity than that of the underlying collateral and that of Tranche A. However, Tranche B's extension risk is minimized by the presence of Tranche C; the last cash flow Tranche. The allocation of principal to the last cash flow tranche minimizes, in absolute terms, the extension risk of Tranche B.

15.3.3 Tranche C—WAL and Spot Spread Distribution Analysis

Figures 15.11 and 15.12 illustrate the weighted average life and spot spread distributions for Tranche C. Notice, the WAL and spot spread distributions exhibit less skewness than those of either Tranche A or B. Overall,

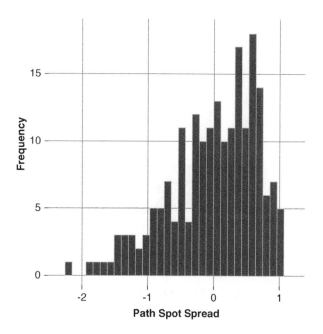

FIGURE 15.10 Spot Spd. Dist. Tranche B

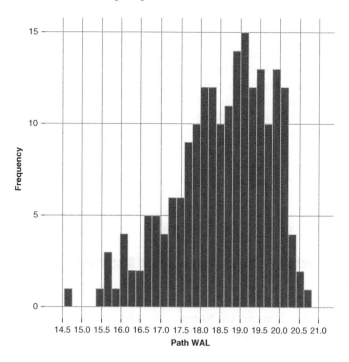

FIGURE 15.11 WAL Dist. Tranche C

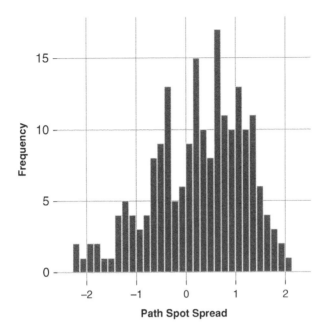

FIGURE 15.12   Spot Spd. Dist. Tranche C

Tranche C's weighted average life profile exhibits greater relative stability as does its spot spread distribution. Recall Figure 15.5, key rate duration analysis, C exhibited a much lower key rate duration at the 10-year tenor than either A or B. However C exhibits greater key rate duration exposure beyond the 10-year tenor. Hence, one would expect C to exhibit greater sensitivity to both longer tenor interest rates as well as expected borrower prepayment rates.

15.4   STATIC CASH FLOW ANALYSIS

Often the investor employs static cash flow analysis as a simple yet effective filter for eligible securities. Investment guidelines may specify a maximum allowable maturity. For example, a bank's portfolio investment guidelines may state the average life or maturity of any investment cannot exceed seven years. In this case, as part of the screening process the portfolio manager may employ static cash flow analysis such as that shown in Figure 15.13 to test the eligibility of each tranche based on its average life profile. The static cash flow analysis in Figure 15.13 presents the average life of each sequential

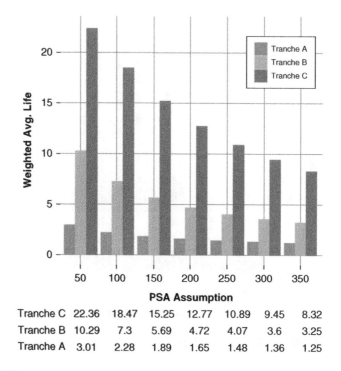

PSA Assumption	50	100	150	200	250	300	350
Tranche C	22.36	18.47	15.25	12.77	10.89	9.45	8.32
Tranche B	10.29	7.3	5.69	4.72	4.07	3.6	3.25
Tranche A	3.01	2.28	1.89	1.65	1.48	1.36	1.25

FIGURE 15.13 Average Life Analysis

tranche given PSA assumptions ranging from a low of 50 PSA to a high of 350 PSA. Given the bank's investment guidelines:

- Tranche C is considered an ineligible investment since under all PSA assumptions its average life is beyond the seven-year limit.
- Trance B is also ineligible since is average life extends beyond the seven year limit under both the 50 and 100 PSA scenarios.
- Tranche A is an eligible investment since its average life is under seven years across all PSA scenarios and the portfolio manager may conduct further analysis against competing investment alternatives.

Alternatively, a life insurance company's investment guidelines may set a eight-year minimum maturity or average life in order to fund longer dated liabilities—such as a pension buyout. Given the insurance company's guidelines:

- Tranche C is an eligible security and the investor may conduct further analysis on the relative value merits of Tranche C versus competing investment alternatives.

- Both tranches B and C are ineligible securities since their average lives are less than eight years under most PSA scenarios.

Both examples presented above suggest there is a degree of market segmentation (section 2.2) on the part of institutional investors. In each case, market segmentation is primarily motivated by each institution's unique liability stream. Dealers are able to create securities that meet each institution's portfolio guidelines by time tranching cash flows through the allocation of principal.

CHAPTER 16

Planned Amortization Class (PAC) and Companion REMICs

A *planned amortization class*, or *PAC bond*, is a REMIC class structured with a sinking fund schedule. A PAC bond provides protection against both faster and slower prepayment rates as long as they remain within the PAC bond's structuring bands. A PAC bond is said to provide both call and extension protection. The prepayment protection and subsequent cash flow certainty of the PAC bond is provided by the companion bond. The *companion bond*, also referred to as a support bond, absorbs the PAC bond's prepayment risk.

The reallocation of prepayment risk between the PAC and companion bonds is achieved via the division of principal. However, rather than parsing principal across time like a sequential structure, the PAC-Companion structure asymmetrically distributes prepayment risk across the transaction; irrespective of time, the companion bond assumes the prepayment risk—the early return of principal—shunned by the PAC bond.

16.1   THE PAC BOND SINKING FUND SCHEDULE

The PAC bond's principal repayment schedule is determined as follows:

- Calculate the projected principal cash flows, scheduled and unscheduled (prepaid), of the underlying collateral at both the lower and upper PSA bands used to structure the PAC bond. The structuring rule used to determine the PAC projected principal cash flow is as follows:

$$\text{PAC cash flow} = \text{Min}(\text{MP}_{\text{Lower PSA}}, \text{MP}_{\text{Upper PSA}}) \qquad (16.1)$$

where:

MP = Monthly principal (scheduled and unscheduled)

- Once the PAC principal repayment schedule is determined, the original balance of the PAC bond at deal inception is equal to the summation of the expected PAC principal cash flows:

$$\text{PAC orig. bal.} = \sum_{n=i}^{j} \text{PAC cash flow}_{(i,j)} \qquad (16.2)$$

- Finally, to complete the structure, compute the companion balance. By extension of equation 16.2, the companion bond original balance is the remaining balance of the structure's underlying collateral.

$$\text{Companion orig. bal.} = \text{REMIC pool balance} - \text{PAC orig. balance} \qquad (16.3)$$

Figure 16.1 illustrates the determination of the PAC bond's principal repayment schedule. In the earlier months the principal repayment schedule is determined by the lower structuring band. During this time a slower prepayment assumption results in a lower return of principal. In the later months, the schedule is determined by the upper structuring band. The intuition is relatively straightforward: Given the upper structuring assumption and the passage of time eventually the collateral balance outstanding declines to a point such that despite its faster prepayment rate the upper limit principal repayment is not sufficient to continue yielding principal repayments

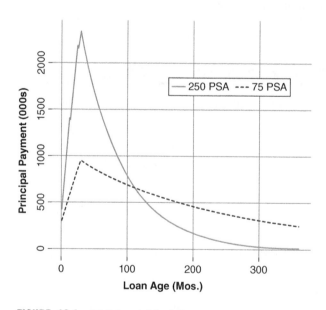

FIGURE 16.1 PAC Bond Schedule

exceeding those given by the lower structuring assumption. Once this inflection point is reached, the PAC principal repayment schedule is determined by the upper structuring band.

Using the PAC bond structuring technique outlined above, a dealer is able to structure REMIC classes that offer a certain degree of both call and extension protection. Notice, the PAC bond's allocation of principal is independent of time meaning that prepayment risk is allocated across the capital structure between the PAC and its companion class.

Figure 16.2 graphically illustrates the expected principal cash flows of a PAC bond collateralized by a 4.00% 30-year MBS. Initially, principal prepayments exhibit a monthly increase due to both scheduled principal and seasoning (section 9.2). Once the collateral balance declines to the point at which the upper band principal repayment (16.1) is less than that of the lower band the PAC schedule takes on a markedly steeper slope.

Initially, based on the above discussion one may conclude the PAC principal payment schedule represents a fixed amount that must be paid to the PAC bond each month. Although this conclusion is conceptually appealing it is not the case. In fact, there may be times when the collateral's prepayment rate is so slow it does not cover the PAC bond's scheduled principal payment.

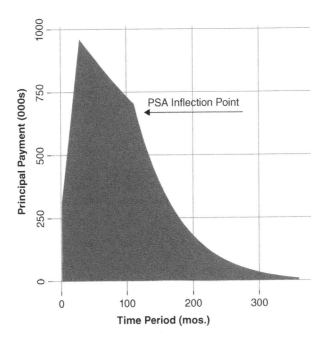

FIGURE 16.2 PAC Bond Schedule

With the former in mind, it becomes evident that the PAC principal payment schedule represents a cumulative amortization target, which, in turn, requires the establishment of the PAC bond's targeted principal balance. The targeted principal balance is used in the REMIC's waterfall payment rules to allocate the principal payments to the PAC and its companion bond.

Table 16.1 illustrates the point based on the cash flow profile presented in Figure 16.2. In the first period, the original balance of the PAC is $148,769,215 and the PAC's scheduled principal payment is $301,663, resulting in a target balance of $148,467,552.

- Assume the underlying collateral reported a prepayment in period one that is less than the lower band PSA target amount, returning $201,663 instead of $301,663. As a result, the PAC bond outstanding balance is $148,567,552—greater than the targeted balance.
- In the second period, the principal returned by the underlying collateral is also less than scheduled PAC principal, again due to a slower prepayment rate than the lower PSA structuring band. In all, the PAC bond is now $200,000 behind schedule ($148,140,045 − $148,340,045).
- In the third period, the underlying collateral returns $400,000, which is more than the amount scheduled in the period. The PAC bond receives the scheduled amount plus any shortfall from the targeted amount—in this case the PAC bond is paid the full $400,000, which is more than the scheduled amount of $353,298. Thus far, the PAC bond is $153,298 behind schedule.
- In the fourth period, the underlying collateral returns $550,000. The PAC bond receives a $532,295 principal payment and is brought to its scheduled balance while the companion bond is paid the remaining principal amount $17,705.

The PAC's target balance is established using equation 16.1. In turn, the target balance is used to determine the principal payment needed to bring the PAC's ending balance equal to its target balance, in the same period. As illustrated in Table 16.1, the principal paid in any period is equal to

TABLE 16.1 PAC Bond Cash Flow Example

Period	PAC Bond Target Bal.	PAC Bond Sched. Pmt.	Actual Principal Pmt.	Actual PAC Bond Ending Bal.
1	$148,769,215	$301,663	$201,663	$148,567,552
2	$148,467,552	$327,507	$227,507	$148,340,045
3	$148,140,045	$353,298	$400,000	$147,940,045
4	$147,786,747	$378,997	$550,000	$148,467,581

the beginning balance less the target balance in the period. With the above example in mind, the bondlabPAC waterfall cash allocation rules may be expressed as follows:

- {Pay 100% of available interest to each class pro-rata, based on each class's respective accrued interest}
- {Pay 100% of the available principal in the following order:}
    1. Pay principal to Tranche 1, the PAC bond, the minimum of:
       (a) The amount required to bring its period outstanding balance equal to the period PAC target balance.
       (b) The PAC bond beginning balance.
    2. Pay the remaining principal received in each period to tranche 2, the companion bond, until its balance is reduced to zero.
    3. Once the companion bond balance is reduced to zero, pay to the PAC bond the minimum of:
       (a) The PAC bond period beginning balance.
       (b) The PAC bond beginning balance less the principal paid in (1) above,
       until the PAC bond balance is reduced to zero.

Together the PAC sinking fund schedule and the waterfall payment rules highlight the structural support provided to the PAC bond by the companion bond. Indeed, a companion bond is often referred to as a *support bond* reflecting the market's recognition of the additional cash flow support provided to the PAC bond by the companion bond.

Notice, the first payment priority in the principal waterfall 1.(a). The payment rule maintains the PAC bond's targeted balance schedule thereby regulating its average life profile. For example, should the prepayment rate slow-down and there is insufficient principal to maintain the PAC's scheduled balance, then the entire principal amount is paid to the PAC bond and none to the companion bond.

- Payment priority 1.(a) limits the PAC bond's extension risk while increasing that of the companion bond.

Payment priority 2 directs the excess principal to the companion bond. Thus, should the prepayment rate speed-up resulting in more than sufficient principal to maintain the PAC's scheduled balance, then principal exceeding that required to bring the PAC to its scheduled balance is directed to the companion bond.

- Payment priority 2 limits the PAC bond's call risk while increasing that of the companion bond.

Payment priority 3 indicates that the structural relationship between the PAC and companion bond exists so long as the companion bond's outstanding principal balance is greater than zero. Once the companion bond is paid-down to zero, the PAC bond's outstanding principal balance is equal to the collateral's outstanding balance and the PAC bond's structuring bands are extinguished—that is, they no longer apply to the principal payment rules. Once the companion bond is paid to zero the transaction's structural enhancements are exhausted and the PAC bond is referred to as a *broken PAC*.

Figure 16.3 illustrates the point. Assuming the underlying collateral repays at 350 PSA, above the PAC bond's upper structuring band, the PAC bond breaks at month 36, the point at which the companion bond's outstanding balance is retired. The companion bond is retired early because the prepayment speed applied over the life of the transaction is above the upper structuring band. Consequently, principal repayments, both scheduled and prepaid, exceeding the PAC's scheduled payments are directed to the companion bond. Once the companion bond's balance reaches zero the PAC's structuring bands are extinguished the PAC bond begins to pay-down at a faster rate than that set by its scheduled balance.

The allocation of principal via the application of a scheduled payment (along the capital structure) alters both the magnitude and timing of the

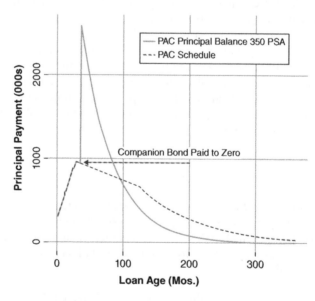

FIGURE 16.3 Broken PAC Bond Principal Repayment vs. Scheduled

principal cash flow to the investor. The magnitude of principal returned is managed by the structural element of the transaction, namely, the PAC bond's sinking fund schedule. In the event the realized prepayment rate is either below or above the PAC's structuring bands, the timing of the principal cash flow to the investor is also changed.

Table 16.2 summarizes key metrics of the PAC-Companion transaction. Notice, the longer average life of the companion bond relative to that of either the underlying collateral or the PAC bond. The longer average life is the result of the transaction's structuring rule (equation 16.1), which results in the companion bond receiving a greater relative share of the backloaded cash flows. Another point of interest is that the companion bond, despite its longer average life, reports a lower effective duration relative to the PAC bond, an indication of its callable nature. Finally in the example presented, both the PAC and companion bonds are priced at a premium.

Dealers typically create newly issued bonds at par to meet investor preference. The need to create par-priced bonds illustrated in both this chapter and the previous chapters highlights the importance of derivative execution in a successful REMIC issuance, which is dependent on both the allocation of principal and interest. Interest allocation strategies will be presented in later chapters.

TABLE 16.2 REMIC PAC-Companion Analysis

	MBS 4.00%	Tranche 1 (PAC)	Tranche 2 (Companion)
Net Coupon:	4.00%	3.00%	6.33%
Note Rate:	4.75%	4.75%	4.75%
Term:	360 mos.	360 mos.	360 mos.
Loan Age:	0 mos.	0 mos.	0 mos.
PAC Band (PSA)		75–250 PSA	
Orig. Bal.		$148.7mm	$51.3mm
Price:	$105.75	$105.00	$110.00
Yield to Maturity	3.26%	2.38%	5.67%
Spot Spread	1.33%	0.40%	3.32%
Pricing WAL:	9.81	8.97	13.5
First Principal Pmt:	01-2013	01-2013	01-2016
Last Principal Pmt:	12-2042	11-2042	11-2042
Modified Duration	7.72	7.96	8.43
Convexity	49.9	51.2	71.2
Effective Duration	7.13	7.19	2.60
Effective Convexity	−15065	307	6236

CONCEPT 16.1

The PAC-Companion structure reallocates prepayment risk via the division of principal. Unlike a sequential bond principal it is not divided by time. Rather, principal is divided based on the PAC bond's sinking fund schedule and both the PAC and companion bond receive principal on a scheduled basis. Conceptually, the PAC bond transfers, via the sinking fund schedule, call, and extension risk to the companion bond.

16.2 KEY RATE DURATION ANALYSIS

Figures 16.4 and 16.5 illustrate how the allocation of principal via a sinking fund schedule alters the key rate duration profile of the PAC bond relative to that of the underlying collateral. The PAC bond's short-dated key rate tenors are, in the aggregate, modestly longer than those of the underlying collateral while the long-dated key rate tenors are less than those of the underlying collateral. The key rate duration analysis implies the PAC bond is more sensitive to the shorter tenors of the curve than is the underlying collateral. Further,

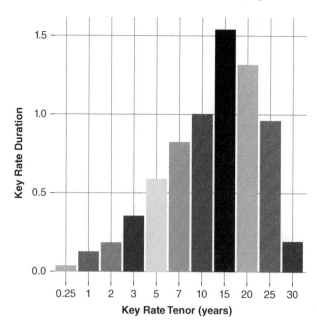

FIGURE 16.4 Key Rate Duration MBS 4.00%

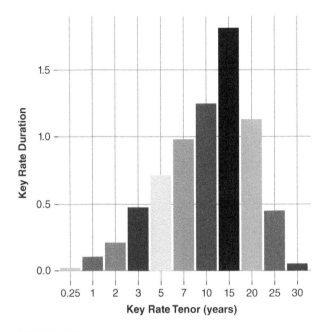

FIGURE 16.5   Key Rate Duration Tranche 1 (PAC)

notice the PAC bond's higher 10-year key rate duration relative to the collateral, implying greater sensitivity to prepayment expectations. The PAC bond's greater sensitivity to the 10-year, and by extension mortgage prepayment expectations, is a direct result of the structural elements employed in the transaction—the PAC sinking fund schedule.

Figures 16.6 and 16.7 illustrate the companion bond's key rate duration profile relative to that of the underlying collateral. The companion bond exhibits greater exposure to the short tenor key rates than does either the underlying collateral or the PAC bond. Furthermore, the companion bond reports a negative 10-year key rate exposure, which in absolute terms is greater than those of either the collateral or PAC bond, which indicates it is more leveraged against mortgage prepayment rates than is either the underlying collateral or the PAC bond.

- The companion bond's negative 10-year key rate duration is a reflection of its callable nature (equation 3.8). Indeed, the key rate duration analysis presented in Figures 16.5 and 16.7 suggests the PAC bond investor has "purchased" prepayment protection from the companion bond investor which is evident in the relative yield to maturity difference between the two: the companion bond offers a higher yield to maturity.

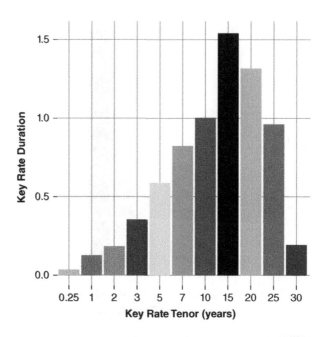

FIGURE 16.6 KRD MBS 4.00%

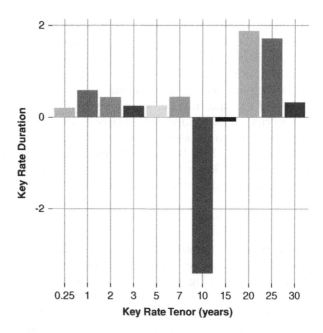

FIGURE 16.7 KRD Tranche 2 (Comp.)

16.3 OPTION-ADJUSTED SPREAD ANALYSIS

The option-adjusted spread analysis presented in Table 16.3 further illustrates how the division of principal along the capital structure alters the valuation of MBS cash flows. The PAC bond's OAS is negative indicating the tranche is priced "rich" relative to either the collateral or the companion bond. The PAC bond's ZV spread is less than its spread to the curve indicating the cost of amortizing cash flows along the curve is 22 basis points. Notice the curve cost is greater for the companion bond, due to the fact that its cash flows are heavily back loaded.

The PAC bond OAS is negative and its option cost (58 bps) is less than that of either the underlying collateral (76 bps) or the companion bond (157 bps). The lower option cost of the PAC bond is due to the structural element employed—the sinking fund schedule—and reflects the prepayment protection afforded by the *PAC schedule*. The higher option cost of the companion bond reflects the transfer of prepayment risk from the PAC bond to the companion bond. Indeed, the companion bond's option cost is greater than that of the underlying collateral. The option-adjusted spread presented in Table 16.3 further reinforces the notion that the PAC bond investor has effectively transferred prepayment risk to the companion bond investor in exchange for a lower yield.

16.4 OAS DISTRIBUTION ANALYSIS

Additional insight may be gleaned by examining the output of the short-term rate simulation. Examination of the weighted average life distribution allows

TABLE 16.3 REMIC PAC-Companion OAS Analysis

	MBS 4.00%	Tranche 1 (PAC)	Tranche 2 (Companion)
Net Coupon:	4.00%	3.00%	6.30%
Note Rate:	4.75%	4.75%	4.75%
Term:	360 mos.	360 mos.	360 mos.
Loan Age:	0 mos.	0 mos.	0 mos.
Price:	$105.75	$105.00	$110.00
Yield to Maturity	3.33%	2.39%	5.67%
OAS	0.52%	−0.14%	1.34%
ZV-Spread	1.28%	0.44%	2.91%
Spread to the Curve	1.52%	0.66%	3.29%
Effective Duration	7.13	7.19	2.60
Effective Convexity	−15065	307	6236

the investor to examine the degree to which prepayment risk was transferred between the PAC and companion bonds. The spot spread distribution helps to quantify the degree to which the presence of the structural element—the PAC bond sinking fund schedule—alters the valuation of the MBS cash flows across the capital structure.

16.4.1 PAC WAL and Spot Spread Distribution Analysis

Figures 16.8 and 16.9 illustrate the average life profiles of the underlying collateral and that of the PAC bond. The PAC bond exhibits a weighted average life distribution that lies within that of its underlying collateral.

- The minimum average life of the PAC bond's distribution is 8.6 years while that of its collateral is 7.9 years.
- Similarly, the maximum average life of the PAC bond's distribution is 10.4 years while that of its collateral is 11.49 years.

Overall, the OAS weighted average life analysis indicates the PAC bond does offer somewhat more certainty in terms of weighted average

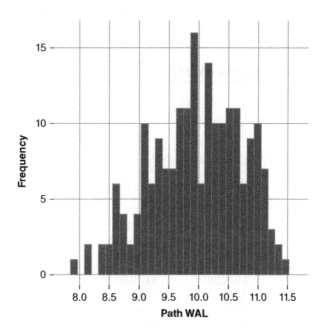

FIGURE 16.8 WAL Dist. MBS 4.00%

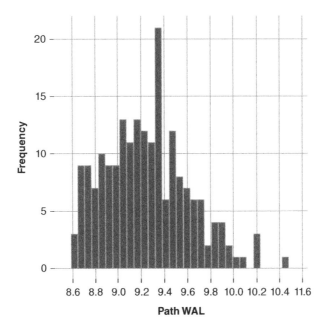

FIGURE 16.9 WAL Dist. PAC

life vis-a-vis the collateral. However, the distribution analysis suggests that over time the PAC bond's underlying structural element degrades and as a consequence the PAC bond's average life profile slowly begins to resemble that of its underlying collateral.

Figures 16.10 and 16.11 illustrate the spot spread distribution of the PAC bond and its underlying collateral. Notice the downside tail risk—potential negative spot spread—of the PAC bond relative to its collateral which contributes to the PAC bond's negative OAS. The negative tail risk is a function of the PAC bond's call risk. That is, given a strong downward trajectory of the short-term spot rate prepayments are expected to increase. Recall, a prepayment rate consistently above the upper *PAC band* will ultimately result in a broken PAC or loss of prepayment protection as the companion bond's outstanding balance is paid down faster relative to that of the PAC bond. Table 16.3 clearly shows that the PAC bond investor accepts both a lower yield and option adjusted spread in exchange for the prepayment protection afforded by the PAC schedule. However, once the PAC's bands are exhausted the PAC bond is as equally callable as its underlying collateral. In turn, the faster prepayment rates result in a lower spot spread.

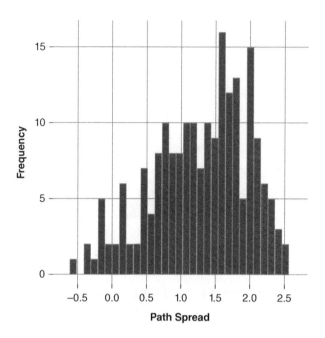

FIGURE 16.10 Spot Spd. MBS 4.00%

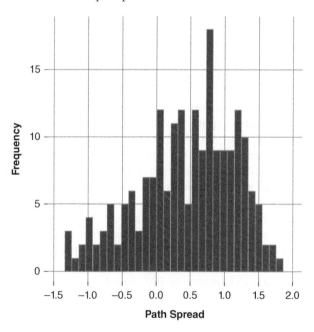

FIGURE 16.11 Spot Spd. Dist. PAC

16.4.2 Companion WAL and Spot Spread Distribution Analysis

An examination of the companion bond's weighted average life and spot spread distributions highlight the extent to which prepayment risk is transferred from the PAC bond to the companion bond. In addition, the distribution analysis aids the investor in quantifying the influence of the companion bond's sharply negative 10-year key rate duration.

Figures 16.12 and 16.13 illustrate the average life profile of the companion bond and that of its underlying collateral. The companion bond's underlying WAL distribution lies outside that of its underlying collateral.

- The companion bond's minimum weighted average life is 1.8 years while the underlying collateral's weighted average life is 7.9 years.
- The companion bond's maximum weighted average life is 14.5 years while the underlying collateral's weighted average life 11.49 years.

Overall, the OAS weighted average life analysis indicates the companion bond has less cash flow certainty than the underlying collateral.

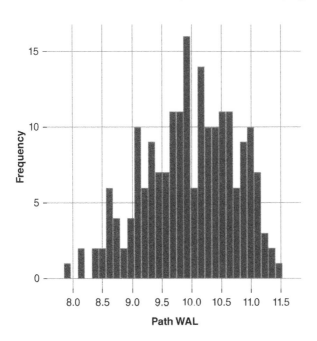

FIGURE 16.12 WAL Dist. MBS 4.00%

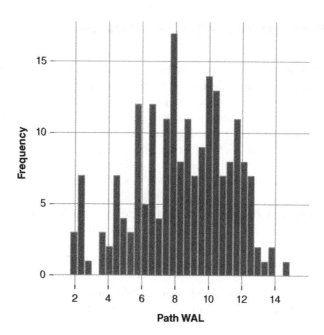

FIGURE 16.13   WAL Dist. Companion

The companion bond exhibits both greater call and extension risk than does the underlying collateral, which reflects its strongly negative 10-year key rate duration and by extension its leverage against borrower prepayment.

Figures 16.14 and 16.15 show the spot spread distributions. The companion bond, unlike either the PAC bond or the underlying collateral does not report a negative spot spread. Furthermore, the companion bond's spot spread distribution exhibits both more dispersion, suggesting a greater range of possible outcomes relative to the underlying collateral, and its distribution is shifted to the right, which improves its overall tail risk relative to its underlying collateral.

Together, the option-adjusted spread analysis (Table 16.3) and the distribution analysis suggest the PAC bond pricing is rich relative to the underlying collateral, while the companion bond is priced cheap relative to the underlying collateral. Naturally, one would expect such a finding since REMIC arbitrage is dependent on creating a greater relative share of "rich" cash flows (PAC bond) based on investor preferences, than "cheap" cash flows (companion bond). However, the spot spread distribution analysis suggests that the companion bond, given its pricing, may offer better relative value than the underlying collateral.

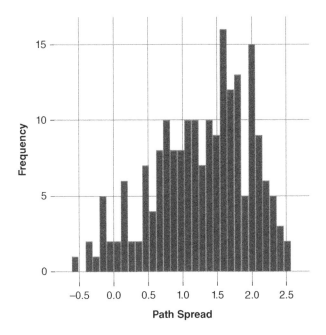

FIGURE 16.14 Spot Spread MBS 4.00%

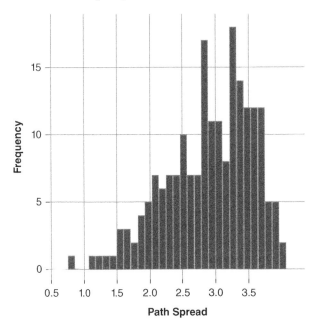

FIGURE 16.15 Spot Spread Dist. Comp.

16.5   A FINAL WORD REGARDING PAC BANDS

A PAC bond may be created such that it provides more or less prepayment protection. For example, a PAC bond structured with wider bands will provide more prepayment protection than a PAC bond structured with narrower bands. The PAC scheduled principal rule (equation 16.1) dictates a declining PAC bond original balance as the PAC bands widen. Thus, by extension, the ratio of PAC bond principal to companion principal declines as the PAC bands widen:

- A wider PAC band results in stable PAC and companion bonds. The intuition is as follows:
  - The wider PAC band provides more prepayment protection to the PAC investor.
  - As the PAC band range increases the ratio of the PAC principal to the companion principal falls.
  - As the PAC to companion principal ratio falls the inverse increases—contributing to the average life stability of the companion bond.
- As the ratio of the companion bond to underlying collateral increases, the companion bond's average life profile will begin to mirror that of the underlying collateral. Thus, it is reasonable that as the outstanding balance of the companion bond converges to that of the underlying collateral its average life profile will become more stable, the extent to which is limited by the underlying collateral.

16.5.1   PAC Band Drift

The discussion above clearly illustrates PAC bands are not constant over time. Indeed, PAC bands tend to drift with the ebb and flow of mortgage prepayment rates, a phenomenon known as *PAC band drift*. Following the previous intuition we can formulate general rules describing the expected PAC band drift:

- In the event the collateral's prepayment rate remains consistently below the lower end of the PAC's PSA band the ratio of the PAC bond's principal balance outstanding to that of the companion declines. Recall from the above, when structuring a PAC-Companion transaction wider bands are associated with a lower PAC:Companion ratio.
  - Under the slower prepayment scenario, the lower band falls and the upper band goes up; the PAC band widens.

- Should the collateral's prepayment rate remain consistently above the upper end of the PAC's PSA band the ratio of the PAC principal balance outstanding to that of the companion increases. Again, when structuring a PAC-Companion transaction narrow bands are associated with a higher PAC:Companion ratio.

  — Under the faster prepayment scenario, the lower band goes up and the upper band falls; the PAC band narrows.

16.6   STATIC CASH FLOW ANALYSIS

Static cash flow analysis further illustrates the points above. Figure 16.16 presents the average life analysis of the PAC and companion bonds across seven prepayment scenarios ranging from 50 to 350 PSA.

- Notice, within the 100 to 150 PSA PAC bands, the PAC bond's average life is stable at 9.02 years, while the companion bond reports a more

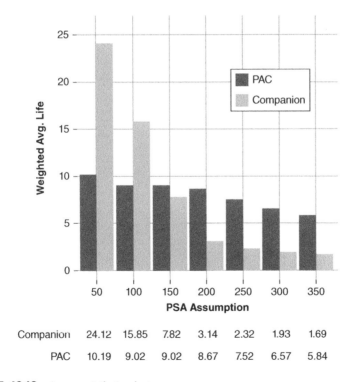

	50	100	150	200	250	300	350
Companion	24.12	15.85	7.82	3.14	2.32	1.93	1.69
PAC	10.19	9.02	9.02	8.67	7.52	6.57	5.84

FIGURE 16.16   Average Life Analysis

volatile average life between 15.8 year to 7.8 years. Specifically, given a faster PSA assumption the companion bond must absorb greater principal repayment, reducing its average life. Conversely, under a slower PSA assumption, principal repayment is directed to the PAC bond and away from the companion bond extending its average life.

- Both the PAC and companion average lives shorten under faster PSA assumptions—the PAC to a lesser degree.
- Both the PAC and companion bond average lives extend under a slower PSA assumption—the companion bond to a greater degree. The PAC bond average life extends modestly to 10.19 years while that of the companion bond extends to 24.12 years.

CHAPTER 17

Sequential IO REMIC

As mentioned in Chapter 16, most investors prefer to purchase par-priced ($100) bonds in the new issue market. As a consequence, dealers prefer to structure REMICs with the goal of creating par bonds. Thus the MBS pass-though security (asset) priced closest to par is the most desirable security for REMIC arbitrage because it is the lowest coupon with which to execute a REMIC transaction. However, since the profitability of a REMIC execution is largely dependent on the slope of the yield curve, the dealer is often unable to fully monetize the interest component of the MBS pass-thorough via the liability coupons (transaction notes) when creating par bonds. In order to fully monetize the interest, the dealer often relies on a derivative execution. Profitable REMIC arbitrage is often accomplished via the allocation of interest.

Recall, Chapter 15 made reference to a tranche IOette whose value resulted in a profitable arbitrage. The IOette tranche represents the unsecuritized interest portion of the underlying MBS. It is the excess interest of the MBS pass-through (asset) not paid via the REMIC's bond coupons (liabilities). The REMIC interest only class, as opposed to the grantor trust IO-PO combination, is made possible by the two-tiered REMIC structure discussed earlier in Section 13.2. The IO class, in REMIC form, must meet the specified portions test under the tax code [Service 2012a].

- Conceptually, the IO represents three interest only strips, each of which is the difference between the underling MBS pass-through coupon and the tranche's coupon prorated against the collateral based on its outstanding balance.

Building on the earlier sequential transaction, Table 17.1 illustrates the full sequential REMIC excecution. The IO tranche, because it represents the total IO exposure in the transaction, is priced and quoted on the notional amount of the underlying collateral ($200 million). Notice the following:

- The transaction's proceeds exceed that of the collateral resulting in a positive arbitrage of $28.5 million, or $0-4/32 .The deal economics are outlined in Table 17.2. Indeed, the IO proceeds of $40 million result

TABLE 17.1 REMIC Sequential OAS Analysis

	MBS 4.00%	Tranche A	Tranche B	Tranche C	Tranche IO
Net Coupon	4.00%	0.63%	1.41%	2.72%	Variable
Note Rate	4.75%	4.75%	4.75%	4.75%	4.75%
Term	360 mos.	360 mos.	360 mos.	360 mos.	360 mos.
Loan Age	0 mos.	0 mos.	0 mos.	0 mos.	0 mos.
Orig. Bal		$50mm	$75mm	$75mm	$200mm
Price	$105.75	$100.00	$100.00	$100.00	$20.00
Yield to Maturity	3.26%	0.63%	1.41%	2.70	7.26%
OAS	0.52%	0.00%	0.05%	0.31%	4.40%
ZV-Spread	1.28%	0.00%	0.00%	0.27%	4.23%
Spread to the Curve	1.52%	0.26%	0.11%	0.35%	4.03%
Effective Duration	7.13	1.78	8.97	13.7	−5.07
Effective Convexity	−15065	1377	−18941	−41132	12068

TABLE 17.2 REMIC Sequential OAS Analysis

	Asset Proceeds (Debit)	Deal Proceeds (Credit)
MBS 4.00%	$211.50	
Tranche A		$50
Tranche B		$75
Tranche C		$75
TrancheIO		$40
Deal Proceeds		$240
Gain/(Loss)		$28.5
Gain/(Loss) in 32_{nds}:		4.3

in a profitable deal arbitrage, highlighting the importance of derivative execution to a successful REMIC execution:

— The accounting of the transaction considers the underlying collateral as the asset, and the notes issued by the REMIC as the liabilities. Viewing the REMIC transaction in this manner yields a deeper understanding of the securitization process. Specifically, securitization allows issuers to secure term funding in the capital markets through the issuance of securities that either represent a beneficial interest in the underlying loans (grantor trust) or notes (owners trust) collateralized by the underlying loans which are paid via the asset's cash flows.

- The IO spread compresses as the transaction's tranches are retired. The IO stripped from Tranche A is 3.37% (4.00% − 0.63%) whereas the IO stripped from Tranche C is 1.28% (4.00% − 2.72%). The fact that the IO spread compresses as each tranche is retired plays a crucial role in the valuation of an IO stripped from a sequential transaction.

The bondlabSEQIO REMIC waterfall cash allocation rules may be expressed as follows:

- { Pay 100% of available interest to classes A, B, and C on a pro-rata basis, based on each class's respective accrued interest }
- { Pay remaining interest to class D }
- { Pay 100% of available principal in the following order: }
  - { Tranche 1 until the outstanding balance is reduced to zero, }
  - { Tranche 2 until the outstanding balance is reduced to zero, }
  - { Tranche 3 until the outstanding balance is reduced to zero }

CONCEPT 17.1

Unlike the IO presented in Chapter 14, which represents a 100% coupon strip, the IO stripped from a sequential transaction is somewhat contingent in nature due to the fact that it represents three unique strips, each with a different valuation reflecting the higher coupon rate paid by each sequential bond, changing the nature of the sequential *IO strip*.

17.1 KEY RATE DURATION ANALYSIS

Figures 17.1 and 17.2 illustrate the key rate duration profile of the 4.00% IO strip presented earlier versus those of the sequential IO tranche. Stripping the IO from a sequential transaction results in less stripped income given that a portion of the collateral's interest is committed to the coupon-paying tranches. The *sequential IO*'s shorter effective duration (−5.26 years) versus that of the stripped 4.00% IO (−7.55) reflects its lower relative coupon strip.

Examination of the key rate duration of each tranche provides the intuition to understand how the allocation of principal and interest alter the nature of the sequential strip. Each strip's key rate duration profile is altered by the presence of the tranche from which it is taken. The sequential IO strip

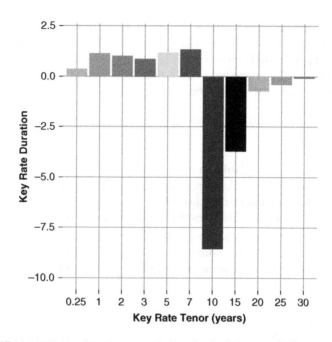

FIGURE 17.1 SMBS 4.00% Key Rate Duration

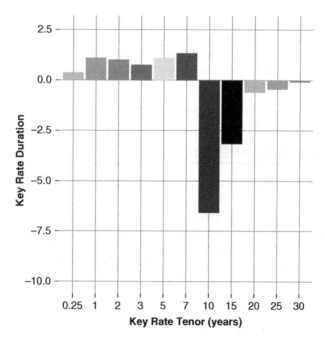

FIGURE 17.2 SEQ IO Key Rate Duration

provides a case study to investigate the interaction between the allocation of principal and interest across a transaction's capital structure. In this case, time tranching allocates principal, while the IO allocates interest in excess of that used to support the principal-bearing bonds.

- The front strip, taken off Tranche A, is the closest in nature to the MBS 4.00% strip. The front strip is 3.37%; thus, although somewhat lower, the sequential IO's shorter tenor key rate durations are close to those of the MBS 4.00% strip.
- The middle strip, that taken off Tranche B, is 2.59%. The middle strip is 65% of the MBS 4.00% and the middle key rate duration tenors reflect its lower strip exposure. For example, the sequential IO strip's 10-year key rate duration is −6.5 while that of the MBS 4.00% is −8.3 years.
- The last strip, taken off Tranche C, is 1.28%. The last strip is 32% of the MBS 4.00% and the longer key rate duration tenors, like those of the middle strip, are also lower than those of the MBS 4.00%.

In all, the sequential IO exhibits less overall sensitivity to changes in the level and slope of the yield curve. The sequential IO's key rate duration profile is altered from that of the MBS 4.00% due to the fact that it, by virtue of its structure, represents a combination of distinct IO tranches, each stripped off its respective principal-bearing tranche and thereby satisfying the specified portions test.

17.2   OAS DISTRIBUTION ANALYSIS

OAS price distribution analysis sheds additional light on the potential difference in price performance between the MBS 4.00% full IO strip and the sequential IO strip.

Figures 17.3 and 17.4 illustrate the MBS 4.00% IO price distribution and the sequential IO tranche. The option-adjusted spread price distribution is based on 200 rate paths (trajectories) and setting the random seed to 300. The OAS analysis supports the intuition presented in the previous section. That is, the sequential IO exhibits lower relative price sensitivity to simulated rate path trajectories than does the MBS 4.00% full IO strip.

- The sequential IO relative potential price upside is less than that of the MBS 4.00% IO. However, its relative potential price downside is also less than that of the MBS 4.00% IO.

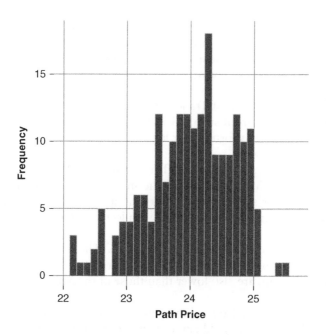

FIGURE 17.3 SMBS 4.00% IO Price Dist

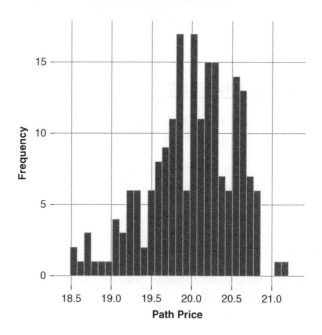

FIGURE 17.4 SEQ IO Price Dist.

- The relative price stability of the sequential IO is due to its lower IO strip, In particular:
  - The sequential IO strip reports a shorter effective duration (−5.07) versus (−7.55). The sequential IOs shorter effective duration relative to the full strip's longer effective duration implies a lower overall price volatility.
  - The key rate duration analysis shows the sequential IO strip carries less key rate exposure to the longer dated key rate tenors (10-year and greater) than the does MBS 4.00% IO strip, which serves to limit its price volatility.

In the case of the sequential IO strip, the division of principal (time-tranching) and interest (the coupon stripping of each sequential tranche) results in an IO cash flow and risk profile exhibiting greater overall stability relative to that of its comparable MBS 4.00% full IO strip.

CONCEPT 17.2

In the structured securities market tranches representing similar structuring techniques often do not yield similar performance. This dislocation is a result of the interaction between the allocation of principal and interest across the structure. Although conceptually the same in nature, each transaction due to its structural uniqueness fundamentally alters cash flows. Consequently, it is imperative the investor understand how the chosen structuring options express themselves in the performance of the security under consideration.

CHAPTER 18

PAC-Floater-Inverse Floater REMIC

A fixed-rate bond may be divided into both a floating- and an inverse floating-rate bond. This chapter finalizes the PAC-companion structure presented in Chapter 16, creating par execution across the capital structure by restructuring the companion bond into a floating and inverse floating rate bond, another example of the division of interest.

Singularly, the PAC-companion structure is an example of the division of principal. The PAC-floater-inverse floater structure is an example of both the division of principal (PAC-companion) and interest (floater-inverse floater). Chapter 16 outlined the division of principal required to create the companion bond whose cash flow is the input for the division of interest, which creates the floater-inverse floater structure. The "trick" is to create a structure including a floating and inverse floating rate bond from one that accrues at a fixed rate in such a manner that the PAC and floating rate bonds are priced at par and the REMIC arbitrage is profitable.

18.1 STRUCTURING THE FLOATER AND INVERSE FLOATER

In the case of the PAC-floater-inverse floater structure it follows from Chapter 16 that the first structuring step is the creation of the PAC bond payment and sinking fund schedule. In turn, the PAC bond's original balance determines the companion bond's original balance and the size of its cash flows. Both the PAC balance and its coupon define the companion cash flows that will be split into the floater and inverse floater. Extending the PAC-companion structure presented in Chapter 16 to create a floater-inverse floater companion bond is as follows:

- Establish the PAC bond.
  - The PAC bands are set at 75 and 250 PSA and the resulting original balance is $148.7 million.
  - The PAC coupon is set at 4.00%.

■ Establish the companion bond's original balance and its cash flows.
— The companion bond's original balance is $51.3 million.
— The companion coupon is set at 4.00%.

At first blush, setting the fixed-rate coupons of the PAC and companion bonds may seem counterintuitive. However, once the technique of splitting the companion bond into a floating and inverse floating rate bond is shown the reason for the initial fixed coupon strikes will become evident. After establishing the companion bond's principal balance and fixed-rate coupon it may be split into a floating and inverse floating rate bond as follows:

1. Determine both the floating rate bond's structure and inverse floater coupon multiplier.
2. Compute the floater and inverse floater principal split.
3. Establish the floater-inverse floater coupon structure.

18.1.1 Floater Structure

The floater cap is struck subject to the floater-inverse structuring rule set forth in 18.1. The floater margin used in rule 18.1 is set based on market pricing. In the forthcoming example the floater margin is struck at 0.30%:

$$\text{Floater cap} > \max(\text{Floater margin, Companion coupon}) \qquad (18.1)$$

while the inverse floater multiplier is determined by equation 18.2.

$$\text{Inverse floater multiplier} = \frac{\text{Companion coupon}}{\text{Floater cap} - \text{Companion coupon}} \qquad (18.2)$$

Equation 18.2 reveals the need for the structuring rule 18.1. If the floater cap is struck at a rate equal to or below that given by 18.1 then the denominator of equation 18.2 is zero or negative, respectively. Consequently, the inverse floater multiplier is either infinity or a negative value and as a result the inverse floater multiplier as an input to equation 18.3—the floater balance—produces a non-sensical result (infinity or a negative balance) and one is unable to split the companion bond into the floater and inverse floater combination. Thus far, structuring rule 18.1 and equation 18.2 illustrate the companion floater-inverse floater structure is dependent on the companion coupon and original balance, both of which are a function of the PAC bond's structuring bands.

Given a multiplier and floating rate bond margin one can solve for the floater cap. Assuming a 1.5 inverse floater multiplier the floater cap is.

$$1.5 = \frac{4.0}{\text{Floater cap} - 4.0}$$

$$\text{Floater cap} = 4.00 + \frac{4.0}{1.5}$$

$$= 6.66$$

Notice, as the PAC coupon is struck to lower levels the companion coupon increases. In turn, the floater cap also increases for a given multiplier. In this case, a par execution PAC bond coupon of 2.25% results in a companion coupon in excess of 9.00%, which implies a floater cap of 15.00%—too high for a reasonable execution in a low interest rate environment.

18.1.2   The Floater-Inverse Principal Split

The floater-inverse floater principal split begins with the determination of the floater balance given by equation 18.3.

$$\text{Floater balance} = \frac{\text{Inverse multiplier} \times \text{Companion bond principal}}{1 + \text{Inverse multiplier}} \quad (18.3)$$

The floater balance is derived from equation 18.3. An inverse multiplier 1.5× results in a floater balance is $30.7 million.

$$\text{Floater balance} = \frac{1.5 \times 51.3}{1 + 1.5}$$

$$= \frac{76.95}{2.5}$$

$$= 30.7$$

Once the floater balance is established, calculating the inverse floater balance is simple and given by equation 18.4.

$$\text{Inverse floater balance} = \text{Companion original balance} - \text{Floater balance} \quad (18.4)$$

In our example the inverse floater balance is $20.5 million.

18.1.3   The Floater-Inverse Coupon Structure

The inverse floater coupon is calculated as shown in equation 18.5.

$$\text{Inverse floater cap} = \frac{(CBC \times CBP) - (FM \times FB)}{IB} \qquad (18.5)$$

where: CBC = Companion bond coupon
CBP = Companion bond principal
FM = Floater margin
FB = Floater orig. balance
IB = Inverse floater orig. balance

Deconstructing 18.5 provides additional insight with respect to the inverse floater.

- **Companion bond coupon × Companion bond principal.** The first term in the numerator represents, absent principal amortization, the maximum annual interest available.
- **Floater margin × Floater principal.** The second term assumes the floating rate benchmark is zero and represents, absent principal amortization, the minimum interest paid to the floating rate bond.

Differencing the quantities in the numerator yields the maximum annual interest available to the inverse floater. Division by the inverse floater's original balance, the denominator, yields the maximum annual interest rate at which the inverse floating rate may accrue—its cap.

In our example, the inverse floater cap is:

$$\text{Inverse floater cap} = \frac{(4.0 \times 51.3) - (0.30 \times 30.7)}{17.1}$$

$$= \frac{205.2 - 9.21}{20.5}$$

$$= \frac{194.4}{17.1}$$

$$= 9.21$$

With the above structuring completed, both the floating and inverse floating bonds' coupon formulas can be written. The formula for each is:

- **Floating rate bond,** min(6.66, max((1 mo. LIBOR + 0.30), 0.30))
- **Inverse floating rate bond,** min(9.21, max((−1.5 × 1 mo. LIBOR) + 9.21, 0))

TABLE 18.1 REMIC PAC-PAC IO-Floater-Inverse Floater

	MBS 4.00%	Tranche A (PAC)	Tranche B (PAC-IO)	Tranche C (Floater)	Tranche D (Inverse)
Net Coupon	4.00%	2.25%	1.75%	0.55%	8.83%
Note Rate	4.75%	4.75%	4.75%	4.75%	4.75%
Term	360 mos.	360 mos.	360 mos.	360 mos.	360 mos.
Loan Age	0 mos.	0 mos.	0 mos.	0 mos.	0 mos.
Orig. Bal.		$148.7mm	$148.7mm	$30.7mm	$20.5mm
Price	$105.75	$100.00	$15.3125	$100.00	$102.00
Index (1 mo. LIBOR)				0.25%	0.25%
Cap				6.66%	9.21%
Floor				0.30%	0.00%

The one-month LIBOR rate used to set the floater and inverse floater coupons, assuming the Jan. 10, 2013, swap rate curve as the transaction's pricing curve, is 0.25%. Based on the one-month LIBOR rate the floater's initial coupon is 0.55% and the inverse floater's initial coupon is 8.83%. At this point, presumably both the floater and inverse floater should be priced at or near par, leaving a premium PAC bond with a 4.00% coupon. Therefore, assuming a par PAC bond coupon of 2.25%, the dealer must take a 1.75% IO strip from the PAC bond to achieve a par execution and thus complete the transaction. Figure 18.1 details the PAC-floater-inverse floater deal structure.

Because the collateral used in structuring the transaction is priced above par, the *interest only* derivative execution once again takes center stage in a successful arbitrage. By now, it should be readily apparent that derivative execution is often key to a profitable REMIC execution. The waterfall cash allocation rules are as follows:

- { Pay 100% of available interest to each class pro-rata, based on each class's respective accrued interest}
- { Pay 100% of the available principal in the following order:}
  1. Pay principal to Tranche A the minimum of:
     (a) The amount required to bring its period outstanding balance equal to the period target balance.
     (b) Tranche A's bond beginning balance.
  2. Pay the remaining principal received in each period pro-rata to Tranche C and Tranche D until each tranche's principal balance is reduced to zero.

3. Once Tranches C's and D's outstanding balances are reduced to zero, pay to Tranche A the minimum of:
(a) Tranche A period beginning balance.
(b) Tranche A beginning balance less the principal paid in (1) above, until tranche A's balance is reduced to zero.

CONCEPT 18.1

Notice the waterfall mirrors the PAC-Companion waterfall with the exception that the principal paid to the companion is now redistributed to the floater and inverse floater based on each tranche's pro-rata share of the underlying companion bond's cash flow.

18.2   A FRAMEWORK FOR FLOATING RATE SECURITIES

A pure floating rate security, that is one absent a margin, cap, or floor, is generally considered to be a zero or near-zero duration security. For example, consider a 10-year floating rate note indexed to one-month LIBOR which pays its coupon monthly. Recall from Chapter 2, the equivalent investment is a one-month LIBOR deposit and the investor reinvests each subsequent maturity in the same. This strategy replicates the 10-year floating rate note. Hence, it stands to reason the 10-year note's duration is equivalent to that of a one-month LIBOR deposit.

18.2.1   Deconstructing a Floating Rate Bond

- *Margin*: The introduction of a floater margin (spread), is added to the value of the index to determine the floating rate coupon. The margin gives rise to duration. That is, one may consider the floating bond's margin a fixed coupon based on the notional amount of a LIBOR deposit. Consider a floating rate Bond A issued at time t_0 with a margin of LIBOR + 0.25% and priced at par. Floating rate Bond B is issued at time t_1 with a margin of LIBOR + 0.35%. Thus, Bond A must price to an effective discount margin of 0.35%, which will cause its price to fall—the effect of spread duration. The investor often calculates *spread duration* to measure a floating rate bond's price sensitivity to changes in the spread (discount margin), holding the index constant.

- *Interest Rate Cap and Floor*: In practice, most floating rate securities are not "pure." Often they are structured with a *floor*—the minimum coupon the floater may pay, and/or a *cap*—the maximum coupon the floater may pay. The cap and floor are interest rate options. The floating rate investor is said to be "short the cap" and "long the floor." Once a floating rate note's coupon reaches its cap the floater's price will behave like that of fixed-rate bond. Thus, the presence of interest rate options also introduces duration. For example, as a floating rate note's coupon approaches the value of the cap its duration will increase.
- *Margin as Interest Only Strip*: Finally, in the case of a floating rate note collateralized by mortgages, one may think of the floater margin as an interest-only strip that is based on the notional amount of the floater. Recall from the previous chapters, interest-only strips exhibit a negative effective duration. Thus, it stands to reason that a floating rate bond collateralized by mortgages may also exhibit a modest amount of negative effective duration, the degree to which is dependent on the floating rate bond's embedded options (cap and floor) being sufficiently out of the money.
- *Inverse Floater Duration*: Given that both the floating rate and inverse floating rate bonds are created from a fixed-rate bond, in this case a companion bond, it follows that the combined dollar duration of the floating rate and inverse floating rate bonds should equal that of their parent bond.

$$\text{Companion } _{DD} = \text{Float } _{DD} + \text{Inverse } _{DD} \qquad (18.6)$$

where: $_{DD} = \text{Duration} \times \text{Curr. bal.} \times \text{Price}$

Dropping the float term (the zero duration term) and rearranging 18.6 yields the inverse floating rate bond's duration:

$$\text{Inverse duration} = \frac{\text{Companion duration} \times \text{Curr. bal.} \times \text{Price}}{\text{Inverse curr. bal.} \times \text{Price}} \qquad (18.7)$$

Rearranging equation 18.7, the inverse floater's duration can expressed as follows:

$$\text{Inverse duration} = \text{Comp. duration} \times \frac{\text{Comp. curr. bal.}}{\text{Inverse curr. bal.}} \times \frac{\text{Comp. price.}}{\text{Inverse price}}$$

— The ratio of the companion current balance to the inverse current balance is the leverage of the inverse floater and can be restated as 1 + Inverse multiplier, equation 18.2.
— In this example, the companion bond is the collateral from which the inverse floater is derived. Furthermore, the companion bond can be generalized to its underlying collateral.

With the above in mind and further assuming the duration of the floater is zero, which is often not the case, the equation for the effective duration of the inverse floater can be written as follows:

$$\text{Inverse dur.} = \text{Collateral dur.} \times (1 + \text{Multiplier}) \times \frac{\text{Collateral price}}{\text{Inverse price}}$$
$$(18.8)$$

Revising our example and substituting the known values into equation 18.8 yields an inverse floater effective duration:

$$\text{Inverse dur.} = 7.13 \times 2.5 \times \frac{105.75}{102}$$
$$= 16.63$$

18.3 OPTION-ADJUSTED SPREAD ANALYSIS

Table 18.2 illustrates the full execution of the PAC-PAC IO-floater-inverse floater transaction. The floating and inverse floating rate bonds' yield to maturity and spread to the curve are calculated using the forward LIBOR curve. Notice the floating rate bond reports a modestly negative effective duration while the inverse floater's effective duration is close to that estimated by equation 18.8.

Naturally, the average life profiles of the floating and inverse floating rate bonds will mirror that of the companion bond from which they are derived. The companion bond analysis was covered in Chapter 16 and will not be repeated. Rather, the remainder of the chapter will focus on key rate duration analysis to explore the sources of duration for both the floating and inverse floating rate bonds. Table 18.2 provides the OAS analysis used to explore the value of the cap and floor options embedded therein.

TABLE 18.2 REMIC PAC-PAC IO-Floater-Inverse Floater OAS Analysis

	MBS 4.00%	Tranche A (PAC)	Tranche B (IO)	Tranche C (Floater)	Tranche D (Inverse)
Net Coupon	4.00%	2.25%	1.75%	0.55%	8.91%
Note Rate	4.75%	4.75%	4.75%	4.75%	4.75%
Term	360 mos.	360 mos.	360 mos.	360 mos.	360 mos.
Loan Age	0 mos.	0 mos.	0 mos.	0 mos.	0 mos.
Orig. Bal.		$148.7mm	$148.7mm	$30.7mm	$20.5mm
Price	$105.75	$100.00	$15.3125	$100.00	$102.00
Yield to Maturity	3.26%	2.25%	2.91%	2.91%	5.42%
OAS	0.51%	0.31%	−0.16%	0.16%	2.91%
ZV-Spread	1.33%	0.28%	−0.32	0.13%	3.56%
Spread	1.46%	0.45%	−0.49	1.06%	1.83%
Effective Duration	7.13	7.11	10.7	−1.58	18.5
Effective Convexity	−15065	183	1917	510514	−539075

18.4 KEY RATE DURATION ANALYSIS

The *index strike* of a floating rate security is given by:

$$\text{Index strike} = \text{Interest rate cap} - \text{Margin} \qquad (18.9)$$

Consider Tranche C, its cap is 6.66%, and its margin is 0.30%. Its one-month LIBOR strike is 6.36%. Under the base case curve, Figure 18.1 shows the cap is forward *out-of-the-money* but given a +300 bps interest shift the cap is forward *in-the-money*. When investing in floating rate REMICs the investor should consider the following:

- *Forward index strike:* a lower forward strike reduces the value of the floating rate tranche relative to one with a higher forward strike.
- *Slower prepayments:* A longer average life (due to slower prepayments) increases the time value of the investor's short interest rate cap position thereby reducing the floating rate bond's value.
- If the floating rate bond's cap is in-the-money then the floating-rate bond's price will behave like that of a comparable fixed-rate bond in a rising interest rate environment.

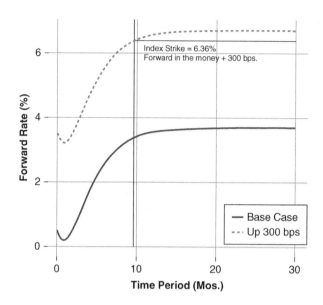

FIGURE 18.1   Interest Rate Cap Forward Curve Analysis

18.4.1   Floating Rate Bond

Figure 18.2 is an analysis of the key rate duration of Tranche C, the floating rate tranche. The effective duration of Trance C is −1.58. To most, a negative duration floating rate security seems counterintuitive. However, recall effective duration is the sum of each key rate duration. Thus, a negative effective duration implies a set of negative key rates, the degree to which is sufficient to shift the floating rate bond's effective duration from modestly positive to negative.

- The shorter key rate tenors are positive to seven years.
- The sum of the short and intermediate key rates—seven years or less—is 3.81, suggesting the floating rate bond's price declines as short and intermediate term interest rates go up. The intuition is as follows:
  - Higher short-term rates, all other tenors held constant, imply a flatter yield curve, lower forward rates, and a lower forward floating coupon, which is negative for the floater.
  - A wider spread between short and intermediate rates result in higher forward rates, which, although positive for the implied forward coupon is somewhat mitigated by the fact that the short cap position is now nearer to the money increasing its value and reducing the value of the floating rate bond.

    The extent to which these points influence the price of a floating rate bond is dependent on the index strike relative to the short-term rate.

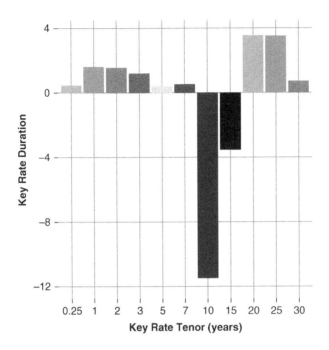

FIGURE 18.2 Key Rate Duration—Floating Rate Bond

- Both the 10- and 15-year key rate durations are negative. In fact, the floater exhibits a 10-year key rate duration rivaling that of an interest only class (Figure 14.2) and reflecting the companion bond's key rate durations from which it is derived.
  - A higher 10-year rate results in a slower prepayment expectation and a higher forward coupon. The higher forward coupon rate is positive for a floating rate REMIC. However, the longer average life increases the value of the short cap position, which could be a negative for the floating rate bond. In the case presented, a net higher 10-year is positive for the floater.
  - A lower 10-year rate results in a flatter yield curve and lower forward rates, which implies a faster prepayment expectation and lower forward coupon—negative for a floating rate REMIC.
- The longer key rate duration tenors (20-, 25-, and 30-year) are positive. Generally, these key rate tenors reflect the value of the short cap position. Specifically, as long-term rates rise and mortgage prepayments slow, the time value of the short option position increases while the floating rate coupon approaches its cap strike.

Key rate duration analysis highlights an important point when investing in floating rate bonds collateralized by mortgage-backed securities. Namely, the REMIC floater's value is tied to both the level and slope of the yield curve in unique ways apart from those of a plain vanilla floating rate bond that pays its principal at maturity. The unique nature of a REMIC floating rate bond principally arises from the interaction between expected prepayments and the value of the embedded cap and floor options. Indeed, in the case of a bullet maturity floater the time value of the short interest rate cap declines linearly with the maturity of the bond. However, in the case of a floating rate REMIC the time value of the short interest rate cap changes as the overall prepayment environment changes, complicating relative value analysis beyond that of simply considering the discount margin.

Indeed, recall from Chapter 16, a lower PAC-Companion ratio increases the stability of the companion bond. Thus, not only do the underlying collateral, margin, cap, and floor strikes influence the value of a floating rate REMIC, but so do the structural choices made. For example, all else equal, a floating rate REMIC structured to a lower PAC-Companion ratio should trade to a narrower discount margin or option-adjusted spread than one structured to a higher PAC-Companion ratio, due to the greater certainty of its average life and hence the value of its embedded short cap position.

Clearly, a REMIC floating rate bond is more complicated than it first appears. Option-adjusted spread analysis may help the investor untangle the myriad of embedded options in the REMIC floating rate bond. The LIBOR OAS of a floating rate bond, like its fixed-rate cousin, reflects the asset swap spread, or the spread the investor would expect to earn over LIBOR after hedging costs. In the case of a floating rate bond, the option cost is:

$$\text{Floater option cost} = \text{Option-adjusted spread} - \text{Margin} \qquad (18.10)$$

In our example presented, the floating rate bond's (Tranche C) option cost is 14 bps (16 − 30). That is, after hedging both the cap and prepayment risk, the investor expects to earn LIBOR + 16 bps (the OAS) yielding an option cost of 14 bps.

18.4.2 Inverse Floating Rate Bond

Figure 18.3 presents the key rate duration analysis of tranche D—the inverse floating rate tranche. The effective duration of the inverse floating rate tranche is 18.5. The high effective duration is largely a product of the inverse floater's leverage relative to the underlying collateral (equation 18.8).

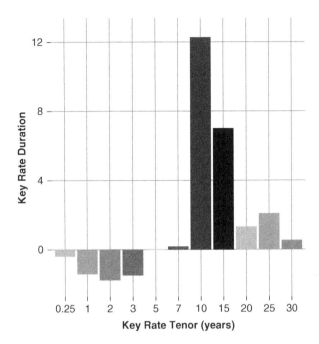

FIGURE 18.3 Key Rate Duration—Inverse Floating Rate
Bond

Notice the following:

- The shorter tenor key rate durations are negative up to the three-year tenor while the intermediate key rate durations are positive.
- The sum of the short and intermediate key rates −4.96, suggesting the inverse floating rate bond's price increases as the short- and intermediate-tenor rates go up. The intuition is as follows:

  — Higher short-term rates resulting in a flatter yield curve, which implies lower forward rates and a higher forward coupon for the inverse floating rate bond.
  — Higher intermediate rates result in a steeper forward curve and higher forward rates. The higher forward rates imply a lower coupon for the inverse floating rate bond.

- Unlike the floating rate bond, the inverse floater's 10- and 15-year key rate durations are positive. A higher 10-year rate results in a higher forward curve and slower prepayment expectation. For the inverse floater, this means a lower coupon on a forward rate basis and a longer average life.

- Like the floating rate bond, the inverse floater's longer key rate duration tenors are positive. The positive duration of the longer tenors implies that as the long tenor rates rise, each tranche approaches its respective cap (floater) or floor (inverse floater) at which point their interest rate sensitivity (duration) converges to that of the fixed-rate companion bond from which they are derived.

The key rate duration analysis provides greater intuition with respect to the influence of changes in both the level and slope of the term structure on the value of an inverse floating rate bond collateralize by MBS. Namely, the companion inverse floating rate bond is leveraged against both the short-term rate via its floating coupon formula, and prepayment rates via its exposure to the 10-year tenor and by extension the mortgage rate. For example, as the PAC:Companion bond ratio increases the inverse floating rate bond from which it is created will exhibit greater leverage relative to the ten-year note. Conversely, a lower PAC:Companion ratio will reduce the inverse floating rate bond's leverage relative to the 10-year note.

The PAC-PAC IO-floater-inverse floater structure is an example of the division of principal used to create a prepayment protected class—the PAC bond—as well as the division of interest. The inclusion of the PAC IO, which was created to facilitate the par execution of the PAC bond, completes the REMIC arbitrage. IO classes were evaluated earlier, and consequently, the PAC IO presented herein was not reviewed. However, the reader is encouraged to analyze the PAC IO using Bond Lab. The PAC IO, floater, and inverse floater allow the investor to express her view with respect to the evolution of the forward rate curve. For example, the PAC IO and floating rate bond allow her to follow the forward rate curve, while the inverse floater allows her to fade the forward rate curve.

CHAPTER 19

Accrual REMIC *Z-Bond*

An accrual class is used to manage the average life profile of another class in the structure. The accrual bond's ability to manage the average life profile of another class is achieved by redirecting its interest payment due as principal paid to that class whose average life it supports. To accomplish the redirection of its interest payment the accrual bond's principal balance increases—accrues—at the stated coupon rate. Once the targeted class's balance is reduced to zero the accrual bond's outstanding principal balance is paid down to zero. Thus, the *accrual bond* is conceptually similar to that of a zero coupon bond; hence, its acronym *Z-bond*.

A Z-bond is typically used in either a sequential structure or a PAC-Companion structure to manage extension risk. However, more often than not the Z-bond is viewed by the dealer as a structural enhancement that is used to clean up tail cash flows as well as manage extension risk.

Structurally, the Z-bond is an example of the division of principal. At first blush, considering the Z-bond as an example of the division of principal seems somewhat counterintuitive since its payment waterfall rule is based on the redirection of interest. However, the redirected interest is used to accomplish the following:

- Pay down the principal balance of the targeted class.
- Determine the amount by which the Z-bond's principal balance is accrued.

The Z-bond structure achieves the division of principal through the redirection of interest. Further, the Z-bond represents a subtle truism of structuring; once the collateral's cash flow is deposited into the trust, both principal and interest become mutually interchangeable.

The Z-bond example builds on the earlier PAC-Companion structure. The BondLabPACZ transaction illustrates the use of a Z-bond to manage the companion bond's average life profile. The BondLabPACZ waterfall rules may be written as follows:

- { Pay 100% of available interest to each class pro-rata, based on each class's respective accrued interest}

- { Pay 100% of the available principal in the following order:}
  1. Pay principal to Tranche 1, the PAC bond, the minimum of:
     (a) The amount required to bring its period outstanding balance equal to the period PAC target balance.
     (b) The PAC bond beginning balance.
  2. Pay to Tranche 2, the companion bond, as principal from the accrued interest to be paid to the Z-bond.
  3. Tranche 3, the Z-bond, beginning balance is increased up to the interest amount used to pay as principal to Tranche 2, the companion bond.
  4. Pay the remaining principal received in each period to Tranche 2 until its balance is reduced to zero.
  5. Pay to Tranche 3, the Z-bond, from the remaining collateral principal until its adjusted balance (Adjusted balance = Beginning balance + Amount paid in step 3) is reduced to zero.
  6. Once the companion bond balance in reduced to zero, pay to the PAC bond the minimum of:
     (a) The PAC bond period beginning balance.
     (b) The PAC bond beginning balance less the principal paid in (1) above,
     until the PAC bond balance is reduced to zero.

Recall, in the BondLabPAC transaction the companion bond is sized to $52.2 million. In our example, the companion classes consist of both the companion bond and the Z-bond, which is sized to an original balance of $15 million. The Z-bond manages the average life profile of the companion bond and cleans up its tail cash flows. Figure 19.1 summarizes the PAC-companion-Z structure.

Notice, neither the PAC nor companion class is structured to a "market" or par coupon execution. Rather, all classes are structured such that the class coupon is equal to that of the underlying collateral (Table 19.1). In addition, the PAC class price required to make the REMIC arbitrage is $108, significantly above par. Further, both the PAC and companion class OAS valuations are relatively low, suggesting efficient execution of the Z-bond structure requires a relatively rich valuation of the PAC class. Additionally, the dealer would likely strip the PAC class to achieve par execution. From Chapter 14, coupon stripping, given an IO price of $24, the dealer may strip 125 bps, bringing the PAC price down to $100.5, creating an IO with a minimum value of $7.50.

As stated earlier, the purpose of the Z-bond is to manage the average life of the companion bond as well as clean up its tail cash flows. Figure 19.1 illustrates a comparison between the principal cash flow of the companion

TABLE 19.1 REMIC PAC-Companion-Z OAS Analysis

	MBS 4.00%	Tranche A (PAC)	Tranche B (Companion)	Tranche C (Z-bond)
Net Coupon:	4.00%	4.00%	4.00%	4.00%
Note Rate:	4.75%	4.75%	4.75%	4.75%
Term:	360 mos.	360 mos.	360 mos.	360 mos.
Loan Age:	0 mos.	0 mos.	0 mos.	0 mos.
Orig. Bal.		$148.7mm	$36.3mm	$15.0mm
Price	$105.75	$108.00	$103.00	$101.00
Yield to Maturity	3.26%	2.97%	3.31%	3.86%
OAS	0.52%	0.06%	−0.40%	1.21%
ZV-Spread	1.33%	1.06%	1.21%	1.29%
Spread	1.52%	1.24%	1.70%	—%
Effective Duration	7.13	7.01	3.71	16.8
Effective Convexity	−15056	862	810	3325

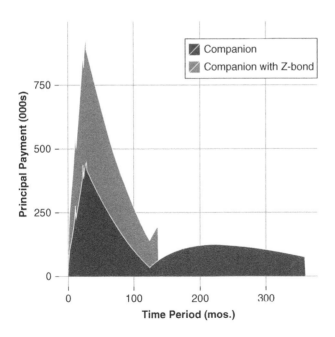

FIGURE 19.1 Comparison of Companion Bond Execution

bond presented in Chapter 16 absent the Z-bond execution and the companion bond cash flow given the Z-bond execution. Notice the following:

- The companion with Z-bond execution reports greater principal received in each period. Recall the Z-bond interest is redirected to the companion bond as principal. Consequently, the companion with a Z-bond reports greater principal paid in any given period than that of a comparable companion bond without a Z-bond.
- The companion with Z-bond execution also reports a shorter principal payment window. The presence of the Z-bond cleans up the companion cash flow relative to that of a comparable companion bond without a Z-bond execution.

  The net effect of this structuring strategy:

  — The companion receives more principal earlier.
  — As a result, the companion bond's average life is reduced because its tail cash flows are eliminated by the Z-bond.

The remainder of this chapter focuses on analysis of the Z-bond. In the PAC-companion-Z bond structure, the Z-bond serves as the companion bond of last resort to the PAC bond. Given the intent of the Z-bond is management of the companion bond's average life profile, and the purpose of a companion bond is the management of the PAC's sinking fund schedule, the Z-bond should exhibit greater average life variability than either the PAC or companion bond.

Figure 19.2 compares the average life profiles of the PAC, companion, and Z-bond from 50 to 350 PSA. It shows that the PAC bond offers a stable average life across the full range of the PSA scenarios analyzed. The companion bond exhibits slightly more extension and call risk across the PSA scenario range than that of the PAC bond while the Z-bond exhibits the greatest average life variability across the PSA scenarios.

Indeed, under the slowest prepayment scenarios (50 and 100 PSA), the average life of the Z-bond is greater than that of the underlying collateral. At first blush, one may ask, how can the Z-bond report a greater average life than that of the collateral?

- Z-bond interest payments are deferred and capitalized as principal. Thus, the amount of principal returned is greater than original face amount.
- A slower prepayment assumption extends the timing of the return of principal, increasing the time weight used in the average life calculation.

Together, these principles produce an average life exceeding that of the underlying collateral. Of course, one may argue that the average life may

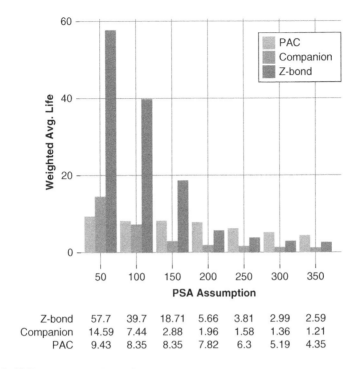

FIGURE 19.2   Average Life Analysis

	50	100	150	200	250	300	350
Z-bond	57.7	39.7	18.71	5.66	3.81	2.99	2.59
Companion	14.59	7.44	2.88	1.96	1.58	1.36	1.21
PAC	9.43	8.35	8.35	7.82	6.3	5.19	4.35

be calculated based on the maximum accrued current balance—or principal returned—thereby reducing the average life and bringing it in line with the expectation relative to the underlying collateral. Recall, from equation 3.4 the average life calculation is based on the face value or total principal of a bond. Indeed, at new issue the face value of the Z-bond presented is $15 million. However, its principal accrues at the coupon rate. Thus, at the time of the return of principal to the investor, the Z-bond's face value has gone up. Consequently, if one were to calculate the average life of the Z-bond based on the sum of the principal returned as opposed to its original principal amount, the conceptual equivalent of its face amount, the average life of the Z-bond falls to 24.4 years—still longer than that of the collateral.

Nonetheless, for purposes of exposition and to further illustrate the impact of the redirection of principal as capitalized interest the Z-bond's average life is reported, in its strictest sense, using the original principal balance at issuance. Consequently, the Z-bond's average life as reported in Figure 19.2 is, at least in its strictest sense, correct and highlights the Z-bond's average life variability as the companion of last resort.

CONCEPT 19.1

The Z-bond interest paid as principal to target tranches is capitalized as principal and as a result the Z-bond is conceptually similar to that of a Treasury zero coupon bond. However, unlike a zero coupon bond the principal balance of the Z-bond increases over time, whereas that of a traditional zero coupon bond remains constant at the stated face value or notional amount.

19.1 KEY RATE DURATION ANALYSIS

Figure 19.3 illustrates the Z-bond's key rate duration profile and further shows how the deferral of interest payments and their capitalization as principal influences the Z-bond's weighted average life, and by extension its effective duration. Overall, the Z-bond exhibits an effective duration similar to that of its conceptual cousin the zero coupon bond. In this case, the Z-bond's effective duration is 16.8 versus that of its average life of 24.4.

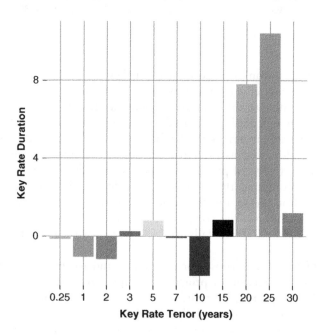

FIGURE 19.3 Z-Bond Key Rate Duration Analysis

The Z-bond, like the companion bond from which it was derived, exhibits mixed key rate durations through the five-year tenor—the sum of which is −1.36. The short tenor key rates suggest that the Z-bond's price behavior moves positively with changes in the short end of the curve. The intuition is straightforward. A bear flattening of the curve with the short end twisting up results in lower forward rates and slower future prepayment expectations. The Z-bond reports mixed intermediate key rate durations (7-, 10-, and 15-year), the sum of which is −1.30. Although lower than those of the companion from which the Z-bond is structured the key rate durations along these tenors reflect the callable nature of the Z-bond. Specifically, as a last cash flow tranche the Z-bond is least callable bond within the structure.

The Z-bond's 20-, 25- and 30-year key rate durations are 7.8, 10.4, and 1.2, respectively. In all, these key rate durations sum to 20.2 years, accounting for 122% of the Z-bond's overall effective duration. The heavy key rate durations between the 20- and 30-year tenors reflect the capitalization (accrual of the redirected interest).

19.2   OPTION-ADJUSTED SPREAD ANALYSIS

Option-adjusted spread analysis can be used to further quantify the Z-bond's risk characteristics. The following sections examine the average life and spread distributions of both the underlying collateral and the Z-bond.

19.2.1   OAS Weighted Average Life Distribution

Figures 19.4 and 19.5 compare the average life of the underlying collateral to that of the Z-bond. The deferral of interest, which is capitalized as principal, results in a significantly longer average life than that of the underlying collateral. The Z-bond exhibits an OAS average life distribution ranging between a minimum of 13 and 55 years (in the strictest sense), significantly greater than that of collateral that ranges between 8 and 12 years. Not only is the Z-bond's average life longer than that of the underlying collateral, reflecting the fact that it represents last collateral cash flow, but the Z-bond's average life range is also greater, reflecting the greater prepayment risk inherent in both its last cash flow priority and companion bond nature.

19.2.2   OAS Spread Distribution

Figures 19.6 and 19.7 show that relative to the underlying collateral, the Z-bond reports a wider overall spot spread distribution, with more negative observations than those of the underlying collateral. Further, the Z-bond

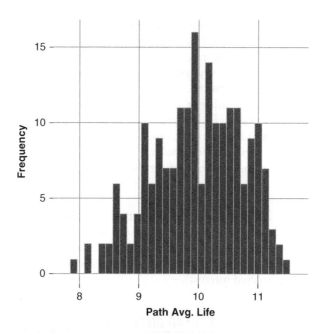

FIGURE 19.4 MBS 4.00% Avg. Life Dist.

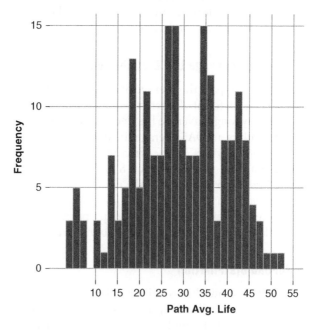

FIGURE 19.5 Z-bond Avg. Life Dist.

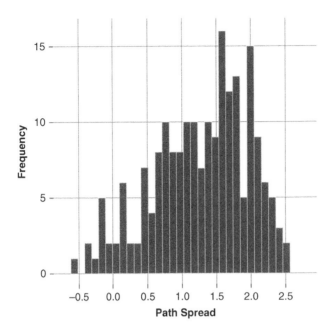

FIGURE 19.6   MBS 4.00% Spot Spd. Dist.

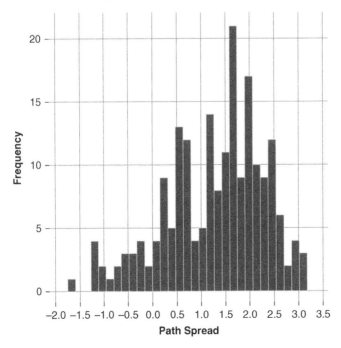

FIGURE 19.7   Z-bond Spot Spd. Dist.

also reports some modestly higher spot spread observations at the extreme right of the distribution. The tail distribution of the Z-bond relative to the collateral is due to the fact that the Z-bond principal accrues at the fixed coupon rate. Consequently, across higher short-rate trajectories the Z-bond is expected to underperform while lower short-rate trajectories favor the Z-bond. Naturally, the level at which the Z-bond's coupon is struck in relation to the long-term forward rate will influence its relative performance. For example:

- Given a rising interest rate environment,
  - A Z-bond whose coupon is struck above the expected long-term forward rate will perform better than one whose coupon is struck below the long-term forward rate.
- Given a falling interest rate environment,
  - A Z-bond whose coupon is struck above the expected long-term forward rate will perform better than one whose coupon is struck below the long-term forward rate.

  Simply said, a higher coupon is preferable to a lower coupon because the investor has, by investing in a Z-bond, locked in her reinvestment rate until such time the Z-bond begins to pay interest and return principal.

Further, notice the average life profile of the PAC bond using a Z-bond structure relative to that of the PAC-Companion structure presented in Chapter 16.6. The PAC bond's average life profile also exhibits less extension and call risk relative to that of the PAC-Companion structure. The re-direction of interest, paid as principal, to the companion stabilizes the PAC bond. Thus, it follows that the presence of a Z-bond also alters the valuation of the PAC bond. The reader is encouraged to use Bond Lab to construct a relative value analysis between the PAC-Companion and the PAC-Companion-Accrual bond classes.

Mortgage Credit Analysis

Mortgage Default Modeling

*Worm or beetle—drought or tempest—on a farmer's land may
fall, each is loaded full o' ruin, but a mortgage beats em' all.*
— *Will Carleton*

Up to this point, the focus of this book has been the evaluation of securities
whose credit enhancement is external to the structure. The most common
and well known is the corporate guarantee of the government-sponsored
enterprises Fannie Mae (FNMA), Freddie Mac (FHLMC), and the Government National Mortgage Association (GNMA). Only GNMA securities
carry the full faith and credit pledge of the U.S. government—an explicit
guarantee. Both FNMA's and FHLMC's guarantees are corporate. However,
the U.S. government acts as a credit backstop, and both FNMA and FHLMC
securities are said to carry an implicit government guarantee.[1]

MBS structures that rely on an internal credit enhancement mechanism
are self-insuring and are often referred to as private-label MBS (PLMBS) or
non-agency MBS. The terms *private-label* and *non-agency* MBS are used to
differentiate those MBS transactions whose credit enhancement is internally
created from those whose credit enhancement relies on either a direct or
indirect government guarantee.

A mortgage default arises from the following:

- Poor underwriting standards are used.
- The borrower experiences a life event such as:
  - Long-term unemployment
  - Illness or disability
  - Family break-up
- Home prices decline precipitously and the borrower finds himself in a
  negative equity position, leading to a strategic default.

---

[1]As of this writing both FNMA and FHLMC are in conservatorship of the U.S.
Treasury.

Modeling the mortgage default rate will follow the general framework of modeling of voluntary prepayment rates. However, in this case we will employ logistic regression analysis—a parametric modeling technique rather than the proportional hazards approached outlined in Chapter 8. Other potential modeling strategies include:

- Cox proportional hazards model
- Competing risks proportional hazard model
- Multinomial logistic regression model

Both the competing risks and multinomial models are usually designed to include delinquency transition rates as a predictor in the *default model*, a topic addressed later in this chapter. To begin the analysis of mortgage default (involuntary prepayment) a survival function is used to extract the hazard rate and translate it to a default curve—event code 2 in the data set. Figures 20.1 and 20.2 present the cumulative survival rate and its translation to the conditional default rate CDR. In aggregate, the conditional default rate begins at 0.0 CDR in the first month and increases to around 2.5 CDR by month 48. The CDR remains at or above 2.5 through month 60, after which

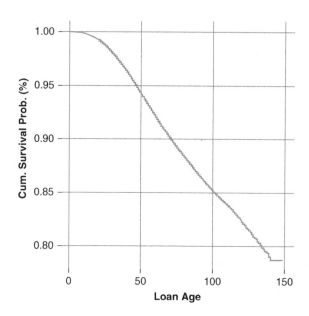

FIGURE 20.1   FH 30-yr. Cum. Survival

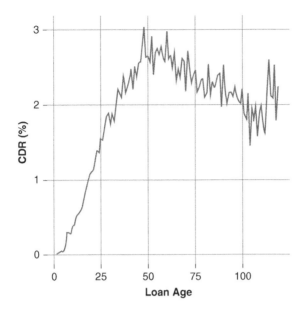

FIGURE 20.2 FH 30-yr. CDR

the CDR begins to gradually decline. Thereafter, the conditional default rate stabilizes around 1.5 CDR.

The standard default rate assumption SDA curve used to value both agency and prime credit borrower private-label mortgage-backed securities assumes the default rate begins at 0.02 CDR in the first month and increases linearly by 0.02 CDR up to month 30, where it reaches its maximum value of 0.60 CDR. Thereafter, the SDA curve assumes a flat default rate through month 60, after which it declines linearly to a minimum of 0.03 CDR per month.

CONCEPT 20.1

The analyst when evaluating non-standard or non-qualified residential mortgage (QRM) loans like subprime or Alt-A loans will often employ a multiple, much like a PSA assumption, of the SDA curve because mortgage default, irrespective of loan type, tends to functionally follow the SDA curve.

20.1 CASE STUDY FHLMC 30-YEAR DEFAULT ANALYSIS

This case study uses FHLMC's sample loan level data set as of August 2013. The sample data set contains contains 50,000 loans randomly selected from each full vintage year from 2000 through 2011 and a proportionate share of loans from each partial vintage year 1999 and 2012. In all, the data set used for this case included 675,000 loans originated between January 1999 and July 2012.

The updated loan-to-value ratio is calculated using the Federal Housing Finance Agency (FHFA) state home price index. To measure home price appreciation and therefore updated LTV, each loan is referenced to the home price index value reported in the quarter corresponding to its origination date. This becomes the loan's base home price index value. The home price is updated quarterly based on the current home price index relative to its starting value. The equation used to compute the updated loan-to-value ratio is:

$$\text{Updated loan-to-value ratio} = \frac{\text{Updated home price}}{\text{Current loan balance}} \quad (20.1)$$

$$\text{where: Updated home price} = \frac{HPI_{t+n}}{HPI_t} \times \frac{\text{Orig. loan amount}}{\text{Orig. LTV}}$$

$$t = \text{Loan origination period}$$

$$t + n = \text{Current period}$$

The case study highlights the analysis of involuntary prepayment rates (borrower default) based on the following predictor variables:

- Loan age
- Original loan-to-value ratio
- Home prices—measured via the borrower's updated loan-to-value ratio
- Borrower's credit score
- SATO

20.1.1 Influence of Loan-to-Value Ratio on the Expected Default Rate

Default modeling begins with an analysis of borrower's original and updated loan-to-value ratio (recall from Chapter 8.5 the three data types: categorical, continuous, and time dependent):

- The borrower's original loan-to-value ratio is a continuous variable.
- The borrower's updated loan-to-value ratio is a time-dependent variable.

Departing somewhat from the modeling techniques presented in Chapter 8, the functional form of the original and updated loan-to-value ratios are explored by transforming both from continuous to categorical variables by "binning" the data into discrete values. To summarize, the modeling techniques presented in this chapter differ from those presented in Chapter 8 in the following manner:

- A fully parametric model is used (logistic regression) rather than the semi-parametric Cox proportional hazard model.
- The functional form of the continuous variables are explored by transforming those variables to categorical variables rather than via residual analysis.

Figure 20.3 presents default frequency by original loan to value. Notice default rates tend to go up as the original loan-to-value ratio increases, suggesting the following:

- A borrower that is able to make a substantial down payment represents a superior credit risk relative to one unable to make a significant down payment.

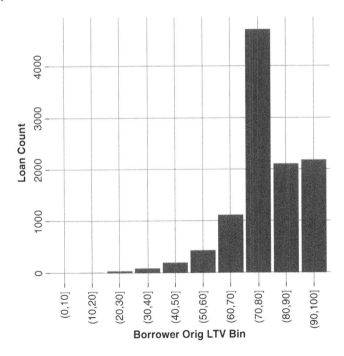

FIGURE 20.3 Default Freq. Orig. LTV

■ A borrower with little to no equity is more likely to default than one with a significant equity share, particularly in a declining home price environment.

Figure 20.4 is a histogram of borrower default given the updated loan-to-value ratio. The distribution is skewed right indicating that a borrower in a negative equity position is more likely to default than one in a positive equity position. The fact that the borrower default declines as homeowner's equity increases suggests the following:

■ Rising home prices and the wealth effect associated with home equity gains act to reduce default rates
  — A borrower facing default is more likely to sell to realize a gain than a loss. Consequently, the default becomes a voluntary repayment.
  — Positive home equity suggests a borrower with greater financial flexibility, thereby reducing the probability of default.

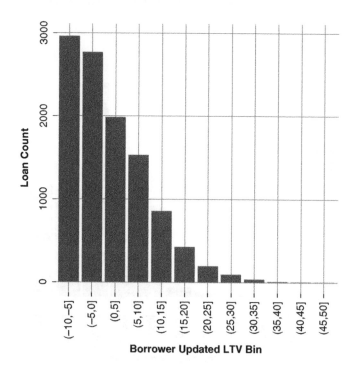

FIGURE 20.4   Default Freq. Updated LTV

■ Declining home prices may trigger a strategic default on the part of the borrower. That is, a borrower transitioning from a positive to negative equity position due to declining home prices may decide to simply default and walk away from his obligation.

Figures 20.3 and 20.4 provide a visual representation of default. Unfortunately, one is unable to determine relative risk—a comparison of risk between the levels of updated and original loan-to-value ratios. Table 20.1 summarizes the results of a *logistic regression* of original and updated loan-to-value ratio. Loan age is a predictor in the model and as before a spline is used to model its functional form. The borrower's updated loan to value is measured by the change from the original to the current loan-to-value ratio.

TABLE 20.1 Logistic Default Model

	Estimate	Std. Error	Z value	Pr($>$|Z|)
(Intercept)	−5.0277	0.5861	−8.58	0.0000
ns(LoanAge, df = 3)1	1.8378	0.0558	32.94	0.0000
ns(LoanAge, df = 3)2	2.1245	0.1227	17.32	0.0000
ns(LoanAge, df = 3)3	−0.4304	0.0987	−4.36	0.0000
OrigLTVBin(10,20]	−1.1203	0.6571	−1.70	0.0882
OrigLTVBin(20,30]	−1.1060	0.6069	−1.82	0.0684
OrigLTVBin(30,40]	−0.7438	0.5921	−1.26	0.2091
OrigLTVBin(40,50]	−0.5201	0.5877	−0.88	0.3762
OrigLTVBin(50,60]	−0.1379	0.5854	−0.24	0.8137
OrigLTVBin(60,70]	0.4592	0.5842	0.79	0.4318
OrigLTVBin(70,80]	0.7016	0.5836	1.20	0.2293
OrigLTVBin(80,90]	1.5922	0.5839	2.73	0.0064
OrigLTVBin(90,100]	1.8274	0.5839	3.13	0.0017
OrigLTVBin(100,110]	−5.4311	40.2717	−0.13	0.8927
ChgLTV(−5,0]	−0.4350	0.0276	−15.75	0.0000
ChgLTV(0,5]	−1.1050	0.0313	−35.29	0.0000
ChgLTV(5,10]	−0.8213	0.0333	−24.67	0.0000
ChgLTV(10,15]	−0.8203	0.0405	−20.28	0.0000
ChgLTV(15,20]	−0.9736	0.0534	−18.23	0.0000
ChgLTV(20,25]	−1.1243	0.0747	−15.04	0.0000
ChgLTV(25,30]	−1.3568	0.1025	−13.24	0.0000
ChgLTV(30,35]	−1.8167	0.1591	−11.42	0.0000
ChgLTV(35,40]	−2.2390	0.2702	−8.29	0.0000
ChgLTV(40,45]	−2.5544	0.4510	−5.66	0.0000
ChgLTV(45,50]	−1.5626	0.5115	−3.05	0.0023

- Both the intercept and the loan age are significant at the 99.0% confidence level.
- An original loan-to-value ratio below 80% is not a significant predictor of borrower default at the 99% confidence level. The astute observer will notice an original loan-to-value ratio greater than 100% is not significant due to the low loan count within the category.
- The borrower's updated loan-to-value ratio is a significant predictor of default at the 99.0% confidence level across all categories.

The model indicates original loan-to-value ratios greater than or equal to 80% are significant predictors of default, while lower loan-to-value ratios are not significant predictors of default.

Figures 20.5 and 20.6 are an examination of the odds ratios and their standard errors, which are obtained by exponentiation of each. The confidence interval of many of the odd ratios overlap, suggesting they may not be significantly different. For example, at the 95% confidence level $Z = 1.96$, the OrigLTVBin(80,90] and OrigLTVBin(90, 100] odds ratios overlap; thus, these ratios (coefficients) may not be significantly different.

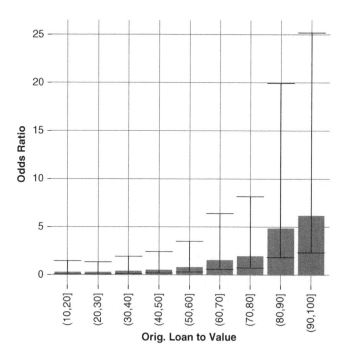

FIGURE 20.5   Orig. LTV Odds Ratio

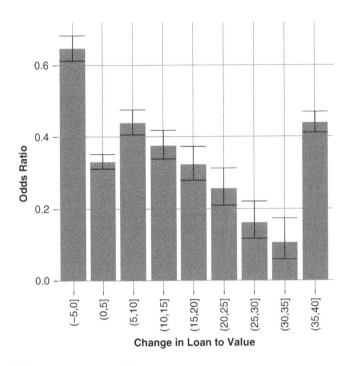

FIGURE 20.6   Updated LTV Odds Ratio

The change in borrower equity is also a significant predictor of the default. Despite the lower standard errors of the coefficients, they still overlap, suggesting the bins used are not significantly different. For example, the (10,15], (15,20], (20,25] odds ratios overlap, indicating a potential lack of statistical difference between the coefficients.

Both the original loan-to-value ratio and the updated loan-to-value ratio, after adjusting for loan seasoning (loan age), are significant predictors of default. Nonetheless, the analysis of the significance of these predictors and their standard errors suggests combining and reducing the number of transformations of both original and updated loan-to-value ratios into fewer categorical variables. Specifically:

- The original loan-to-value ratio is binned using cut-points of 0%, 80%, 90%, and 110%, creating the following three levels within the original loan-to-value categorical variable (0,80], (80,90], and (90,110].
- The change in loan to value is binned, creating the following levels within the updated loan-to-value categorical variable (−10,5], (−5,0], (0,15], (15,30], and (30,50].

The idea is simple; the analysis presented in Table 20.1 suggests some bins are not significantly different in terms of their influence on borrower default rates, nor is the number of observations (loan count) within the bin sufficient to determine a reliable coefficient. The strategy of combining bins achieves the following:

- The number of levels within each categorical variable is reduced.
- The statistical significance of each bin (level) increases.
- Each bin (level) is significantly different relative to the others.

Once a proper transformation of a continuous variable to a categorical variable is complete, the model is refit and the investor may extract the functional form of those variables under investigation. The functional form is determined by examining and plotting the odds ratio of the levels within each explanatory variable.

Table 20.2 presents the results of the model after combining levels within each categorical variable. The predictive variables of the model are significant beyond the 99% confidence level, with the exception of the ChgLTV(20,35] categorical variable—which is significant beyond the 90% confidence interval. Notice, the levels of each categorical variable have been ordered such that the referent or baseline defines a borrower with an original loan to value between 80% and 90% and a change in the borrower's loan-to-value ratio between 0% and 15% (recall section 8.5.1). Once the model is fit, the functional form of both original loan to value and updated loan-to-value ratios may be explored by plotting the odds ratio of each level with the predictive variable.

TABLE 20.2 Logistic Default Model

	Estimate	Std. Error	z value	Pr(>|z|)
(Intercept)	−4.4335	0.0532	−83.26	0.0000
ns(LoanAge, df = 3)1	1.8286	0.0558	32.76	0.0000
ns(LoanAge, df = 3)2	2.2912	0.1200	19.09	0.0000
ns(LoanAge, df = 3)3	−0.3292	0.0970	−3.39	0.0007
OrigLTVBin(0,80]	−1.1517	0.0260	−44.21	0.0000
OrigLTVBin(90,110]	0.2342	0.0320	7.32	0.0000
ChgLTV(−10,−5]	0.9377	0.0259	36.18	0.0000
ChgLTV(−5,0]	0.4535	0.0254	17.85	0.0000
ChgLTV(15,30]	−0.0847	0.0413	−2.05	0.0406

20.1.2 Original Loan-to-Value Odds Ratio

Figure 20.7 plots the original loan-to-value odds ratios and their respective confidence intervals. The confidence intervals around the odds ratios do not overlap, indicating they are significantly different.

The interpretation of the odds ratio is straightforward, relative to the referent borrower (original loan to value between 80% and 90%).

- A borrower with a loan-to-value ratio less than 80% is 0.30 times as likely to default.
- A borrower with a loan-to-value ratio greater than 90% is 1.26 times as likely to default.

20.1.3 Updated Loan-to-Value Odds Ratio

Figure 20.8 plots the combined updated loan-to-value odds ratios and their respective confidence intervals. The updated loan-to-value ratio is an example of an external time dependent variable, described in section 8.5.3. The figure indicates that the updated loan-to-value ratio is a

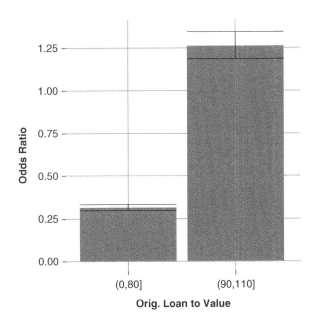

FIGURE 20.7 Orig. Loan-to-Value Odds Ratio

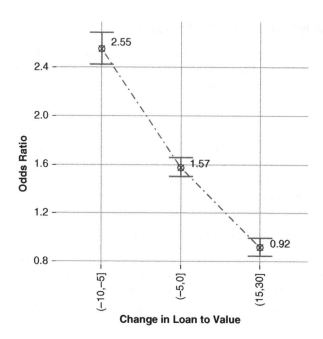

FIGURE 20.8   Change in Loan-to-Value Odds Ratio

decreasing exponential function. That is, the likelihood of default decreases exponentially as the borrower's updated loan-to-value ratio declines. The interpretation of the odds ratios is as follows:

- A borrower with a loan-to-value ratio between 80% and 90% who experiences a negative change between −10% and −5% is 2.5 times more likely to default than a borrower who experiences a positive change in equity between 0% and 15%.
- A borrower with a loan-to-value ratio between 80% and 90% who experiences a negative change between −5% and 0% is 1.5 times more likely to default than a borrower who experiences a positive change in equity between 0% and 15%.
- A borrower with a loan-to-value ratio between 80% and 90% who experiences a positive equity change between 15% and 30% is .90 times less likely to default than a borrower who experiences a positive equity change between between 0% and 15%.

Clearly the risk of default increases as the borrower's equity position deteriorates. At first blush, one may be tempted to attribute the increased risk of default to strategic defaults—the case when a borrower in a negative equity position simply walks away from the home. The strategic default conclusion is too simplistic. Typically, a decline in home prices is symptomatic of a broader economic decline. Consequently, the default may have been triggered by an event such as a job loss, which—although it could be related to the decline in the borrower's equity position—is not a strategic default.

20.2 OTHER VARIABLES INFLUENCING BORROWER DEFAULT

The investor may choose to add additional variables to the default model, such as:

- The quality of the issuer's loan underwriting process. Generally, the quality of the issuer's loan underwriting process, either easy or conservative, will manifest itself as a higher or lower baseline default curve. The investor may choose to adopt an individual default model for each issuer, or alternatively, she may choose to subjectively score each issuer's underwriting process, thereby including her judgment in the model.

  The loan origination channel includes the following:

  — *Retail*: The issuer may originate loans through its own trained employees.
  — *Correspondent*: A correspondent agrees to underwrite loans in accordance with the issuer's underwriting matrix and practices (acts as the issuer's agent). In return, the issuer agrees to purchase loan packages from the correspondent.
  — *Broker*: A broker may submit a loan package to a number of lenders.
  Simply from a standpoint of quality control, one would expect the retail channel to exhibit the highest level of credit quality, followed by the correspondent channel, then the broker channel. Consequently, one would think the retail channel may exhibit the lowest frequency of default, while the correspondent and broker channels may exhibit higher ones.

- Measures of borrower financial flexibility, these include:
  — The borrower's credit score, which may be assigned by the loan underwriter according to an internal credit model or simply a credit score reported by any of the credit monitoring/reporting services. A borrower with a high credit score exhibits a willingness to pay—the first key underwriting standard—and as a result, one would expect those borrowers with higher credit scores to exhibit a lower incidence of default.

— A borrower with a lower debt-to-income ratio has greater financial flexibility than one with a higher debt-to-income ratio and exhibits a greater ability to pay—the second key underwriting standard. Consequently, one would expect a borrower with a lower debt to income ratio to exhibit a lower incidence of default.

- Property occupancy—either owner or investor. One would expect investor owned properties to exhibit a higher incidence of default than those that are owner occupied as the former may be subject to a greater risk of strategic default.

20.2.1 Borrower Credit Score

Including the borrower's credit score in the default model follows the method previously outlined. The borrower's credit score is binned and the model is refit. The coefficients are translated to odds ratios. Both the odds ratios and standard errors are plotted and examined. Figure 20.9 plots

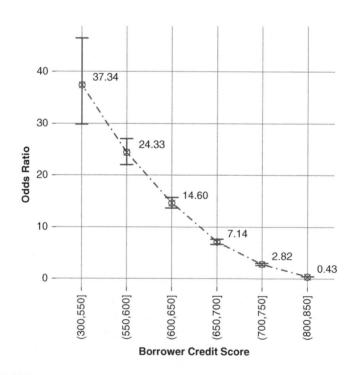

FIGURE 20.9 Borrower Credit Score Odds Ratio

the odds ratios of borrower original credit score and their associated confidence intervals:

- The baseline borrower credit score is (750,800]. Thus, the model's baseline borrower possess the following characteristics:
  — The original loan to value is between 80% and 90%.
  — The change in loan to value is between 0% and 15%.
  — The original credit score is between 750 and 800.
- The confidence intervals around each coefficient do not overlap each other, indicating the coefficients are significantly different.
- Credit score is decreasing exponential function. For example, all else equal:
  — A borrower with an original credit score between 300 and 550 is 37 times more likely to default than the baseline borrower, suggesting the borrower is almost certain to default.
  — A modest downward drift in borrower credit score increases the likelihood of default. For example, underwriting a borrower with an original credit score between 700 and 750 increases likelihood of default by 2.8 times.
  — A borrower with an original credit score between 800 and 850 is less than half as likely to default as the baseline borrower.

20.2.2 Borrower Debt to Income

The borrower's debt to income ratio at origination is binned and the model is fit again. Figure 20.10 plots the borrower's debt to income odds ratio and their associated confidence intervals. Addition of the borrower's debt to income ratio improves the overall model fit by a modest amount. However, most likely the borrower's debt to income ratio will be somewhat correlated to his credit score, as a lower ratio indicates a lower level of debt service and by extension implies a borrower with a stronger credit profile.

The borrower's debt to income ratio appears linear with a kink at the (40,50] cut point. Beyond the (40,50] cut point the slope increases, suggesting a higher relative frequency of default beyond a 40 debt to income ratio. The increase in the slope of the function beyond a 40 debt to income ratio is likely due to the lower overall financial flexibility of the borrower.

20.3 SPREAD AT ORIGINATION (SATO) AND DEFAULT

Recall, from Chapter 11, spread at origination (SATO) captures the spread or premium paid by the borrower above the current "prime" lending rate at the time of origination. A high SATO implies a borrower with a weaker credit

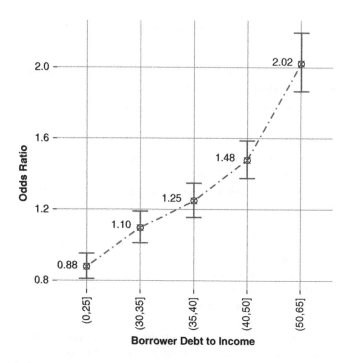

FIGURE 20.10   Borrower Debt to Income Odds Ratio

profile, which results in lower relative turnover rates and less responsiveness to economic incentives to refinance. Given a higher SATO is associated with lower voluntary repayments it stands to reason that SATO may also act as a predictor on the frequency of default.

SATO is a significant predictor of default and the initial investigation of the model suggests a SATO-based model is preferable over a model including borrower credit score and debt to income because measuring the premium paid by the borrower over the "prime" mortgage lending rate at the time of origination captures the combination of factors that determine his credit profile. SATO is an exponentially increasing function on a borrower's expected default rate:

- A borrower required to pay an additional 25 to 75 basis points above the prime lending rate is 1.4 times more likely to default than one who is able to finance at the prime lending rate.
- The expected default rate increases exponentially as SATO increases. A borrower required to pay 125 to 175 basis points over the prime lending rate is 2.5 times more likely to default than one who is able to finance at the prime lending rate.

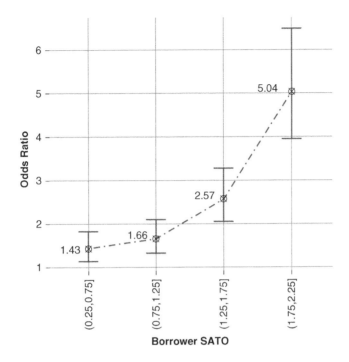

FIGURE 20.11 Borrower SATO Odds Ratio

20.4 DEFAULT MODEL SELECTION

Figure 20.12 compares the credit score (720) and debt to income ratio (25) model versus the SATO model (75 basis points). The average SATO of the borrower cohort with a 720 credit score and 25 debt to income ratio is 75 basis points, suggesting each model should return similar predictions—as is the case.

A *confusion matrix*, Table 20.3, is calculated and used to decide which model to deploy.

- The accuracies of the models are comparable, suggesting that either model may be useful to predict the incidence of default.
- The sensitivities of both models are comparable. Sensitivity, in this case, measures the model's ability to correctly identify the incidence of default.
- The specificity of the DTI and credit score model is higher than that of the SATO model. Specificity relates to a model's ability to exclude the incidence of default correctly.

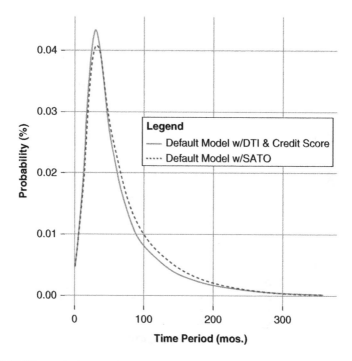

FIGURE 20.12 Default Model Comparison

TABLE 20.3 Confusion Matrix Model Comparison

	Model w/ DTI			Model w/ SATO		
Pred./Ref.	0	1		Pred./Ref.	0	1
0	213.694	8,616		0	213,975	9,099
1	496	970		1	215	487

Accuracy	0.953	0.958
95% CI	(0.958, 0.960)	(0.957, 0.959)
No Information Rate	0.957	0.958
Sensitivity	0.997	0.999
Specificity	0.101	0.050
Pos. Pred. Value	0.961	0.959
Neg. Pred. Value	0.661	0.693
Prevalence	0.957	0.957
Detection Rate	0.954	0.956
Detection Prevalence	0.993	0.996
Balance Accuracy	0.549	0.524

The analysis suggests the SATO model overstates the incidence of default and results in a higher number of false positives (defaults when there is no default). That is, the SATO model has a higher level of sensitivity and lower level of specificity. However, both models seem comparable in performance and the analysis suggests SATO can be used effectively to predict the frequency of default. The advantages of the SATO model are:

- It requires fewer inputs than the DTI and credit score model. Thus, from a data management standpoint the model is easier to maintain.
- It does not rely on the issuer's loan level disclosure. Often loan level disclosure data may be incomplete or inaccurate due to human error or fraud whereas the SATO model relies on market inputs, the "prime" mortgage lending rate at the time of origination and the borrower's note rate.

Figure 20.13 illustrates the model's projection given the baseline SATO (75 basis points) and a high SATO (300 basis points) notice the influence of a higher SATO on the incidence of default.

- The higher SATO odds ratios begin at 0.01 in the first month compared to the lower SATO odds ratios whose odds begin at 0.0 in the first month.
- By month 30, the higher SATO odds ratio reaches a peak of 0.10 compared to that of the lower SATO odds ratio that reaches a peak of 0.04.
- Throughout most of the life of the loan, the higher SATO exhibits a higher expected default rate, indicating the borrower's weaker overall credit and lack of financial flexibility relative to the lower SATO borrower.

The analysis presented indicates a default model based on the following variables:

- *Loan seasoning.* The expected default rate starts relatively low and increases as the loan seasons reaching a peak around month 30. Thereafter, the expected default rate begins to decline.
- *Borrower's initial equity or down payment.* A higher down payment suggests a financially stronger borrower than one with a lower down payment.
- *Change in the borrower's equity.* A borrower migrating from a positive equity position to a negative equity position is 1.5 to 2.5 times more likely to default than a borrower remaining in a positive equity position.
- SATO or spread to the prime lending rate at the time of origination. A higher SATO suggests a borrower with a weaker credit profile and by extension a higher expected default rate.

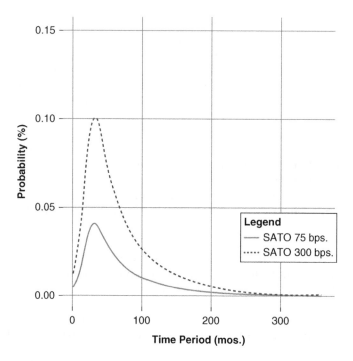

FIGURE 20.13 Default Model SATO Comparison

This chapter presented the analysis of mortgage default using logistic regression as an a alternative to the Cox proportional hazard model presented in Chapter 8. The modeling differences are:

- The functional form of the predictor variables are explored by plotting the odds ratio rather than through residual analysis presented in Chapter 8.
- The logistic regression model is parametric and can be used to predict beyond the last observed point.

The Predictive Default Model

*To know yet to think that one does not know is best; not to know
yet to think that one knows will lead to difficulty.*
Lao Tzu, 6th Century Chinese Poet

Chapter 21 extends the concepts presented in Chapter 20 and illustrates a
framework for the implementation of a predictive residential mortgage
default model. The model presented in Chapter 20 is parametric; thus one
could simply extend the regression model. However, doing so substitutes
convenience for flexibility. When considering borrower default it is important to note that technically, a borrower having missed one payment is in
default. However, practically, the borrower is considered delinquent. Thus,
in the context of the MBS under consideration, a default may represent either
a buyout or liquidation of the mortgage loan following a prior delinquency
such as 120 days past due (as is the case with agency MBS) or a liquidation
following foreclosure proceedings (as is the case with private-label MBS).

Unlike the voluntary prepayment model, which is additive in nature, the
default model is multiplicative on the hazard function. One might question
why one would employ a multiplicative model to predict default given the
alternative choice of an additive model to predict voluntary repayment. The
answer is simple; the choice of a multiplicative model to predict default is
made to illustrate the application of the modeling strategy. Certainly, one
could easily refactor the voluntary repayment model from that of an additive
model to a multiplicative model.

The functional form of the monthly default rate model is:

$$\text{MDR} = (\lambda)(\exp(\beta_1 + \beta_n)) \tag{21.1}$$

where: λ = Baseline default assumption
β = ln (Odds ratio)

Decomposing borrower prepayment between voluntary and involuntary (default) repayment adds to the mortgage lexicon:

- The constant repayment rate (CRR) generally refers to the mortgage pool's annualized voluntary repayment rate.
- The term constant default rate (CDR) generally refers to the mortgage pool's annualized involuntary prepayment rate—its default rate.
- The term constant prepayment rate (CPR) refers to the mortgage pool's total annualized prepayment rate, inclusive of both voluntary and involuntary repayments.

The CDR, an annualized measure, is converted to an MDR the conceptual equivalent of the single monthly mortality (SMM) rate as follows:

$$MDR = 1 - (1 - CDR)^{(1/12)} \qquad (21.2)$$

CONCEPT 21.1

It is important to note, when deriving mortgage cash flow projections using both a voluntary repayment and a defaults model, the applicability of each with respect to the derivation of the overall cash flow differs. The voluntary repayment cash flow is projected based on the period beginning balance after giving credit to scheduled principal, whereas the defaulted cash flow is projected based solely on the period beginning balance. Since both cash flow projections, voluntary and default, are based on the beginning balance, the order of operation is irrelevant when simply calculating prepaid and defaulted principal in a given period.

Naturally, a mortgage default implies a prior mortgage delinquency. However, for the purpose of the valuation of an MBS whose guarantee is that of timely payment of interest and principal, delinquency assumptions are not required. In other cases, the investor may further require a delinquency assumption. Thus, the investor faces a choice. Model the default rate as a function of delinquency—a roll rate model approach—or model delinquency as a function of default—work the roll rate backward.

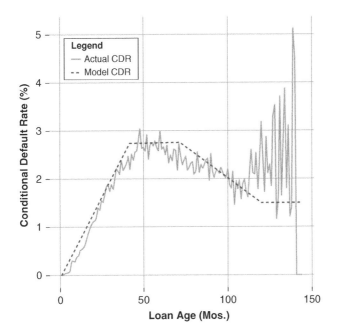

FIGURE 21.1 Baseline Agency Default Assumption

21.1 CONSTANT DEFAULT RATE

The baseline agency MBS CDR curve is shown in Figure 21.1 and defined as follows:

- The model's default rate begins at 0.0 and increases linearly over 42 months to a maximum value of 2.75.
- The default rate is then flat over the next 30 months, after which it declines linearly over the next 48 months (to loan age 120). Beyond month 120, the default rate holds constant at 1.0. Typically, a borrower default assumption is not applied to the last 12 to 6 months of cash-flow projections.

21.2 BORROWER ORIGINAL LOAN-TO-VALUE DEFAULT MULTIPLIER

The original loan-to-value variable is a step function. Recall from Chapter 20, a borrower with a loan-to-value ratio less than 80% is less likely (0.30 times) to default than a borrower with a loan to value between

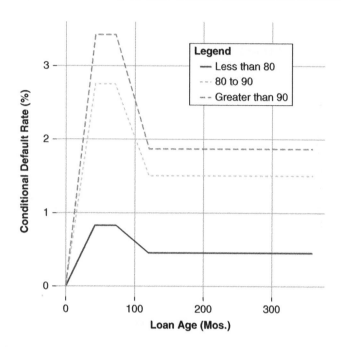

FIGURE 21.2 Baseline Agency Default Assumption

80% and 90%, whereas a borrower with an original loan to value greater than 90% is more likely to default (1.26 times, which in this case is passed to the model as 1.25). The step from the lowest multiplier (0.30) to the highest multiplier (1.25) results in a parallel shift of the default curve (down or up) based on the original loan-to-value ratio. The original loan-to-value multiplier step function is straightforward:

$$\begin{cases} 0.30 & x \leq 80 \\ 1.00 & \nleq 80 \leq 90 \\ 1.25 & 90 \nleq x \end{cases}$$

Figure 21.2 illustrates the change in the default curve given the original loan-to-value ratio. Given a loan-to-value ratio less than 80%, the peak default rate is 0.83% versus a loan-to-value ratio greater than 90% whose peak default rate is 3.42%.

21.3 UPDATED LOAN-TO-VALUE DEFAULT MULTIPLIER

The loan-to-value ratio may change over time due to principal amortization, partial principal repayment (curtailment), and the valuation of the home.

Of the three, principal amortization and partial principal repayment gradu-ally reduce the value of the homeowner's mortgage (liability), while a change in the valuation of the home alters the value of the asset. A decline in the value of the home relative to the outstanding mortgage balance exponen-tially increases the risk of default. The updated loan-to-value default risk multiplier is given by the following equation:

$$\text{Default risk multiplier} = \exp^{\beta \times \delta LTV} \qquad (21.3)$$

Figure 21.3 illustrates the default multiplier for a borrower whose original loan to value is 80%. A borrower experiencing an equity decline of 50%; that is, the borrower's loan to value increased to 130%, is more than nine times more likely to default than one whose equity remains unchanged. Similarly, a borrower experiencing an equity increase of 50%, that is the borrower's loan to value fell to 30%, is about 0.08 times less likely to default than one whose equity remains unchanged. Thus, as the loan-to-value ratio approaches 0%, the likelihood of default also approaches zero.

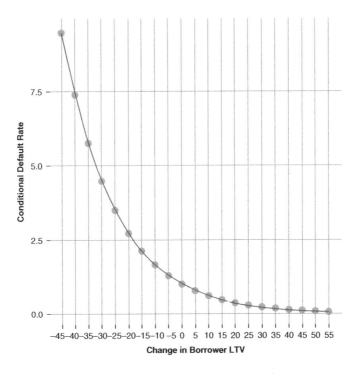

FIGURE 21.3   Updated Loan-to-Value Ratio Default Multipliers

21.4   SPREAD AT ORIGINATION (SATO) DEFAULT MULTIPLIERS

The spread at origination (SATO) is a proxy for the borrower's credit profile. The intuition is straightforward. A negative or zero SATO represents a "prime" credit borrower while a higher SATO is likely an "impaired" borrower in one way or another. Irrespective of the reason for a premium to the "prime" mortgage lending rate, a borrower exhibiting a higher SATO is one with less overall financial flexibility and thus more likely to default.

Figure 21.4 depicts the relationship between SATO and the default multiplier. A loan originated with negative SATO (−0.50%) is 0.6 times as likely to default as a loan originated at the prime mortgage rate (a zero SATO). A negative SATO indicates the borrower "bought down" his loan rate rate by paying additional points, an indication not only that the borrower intends to

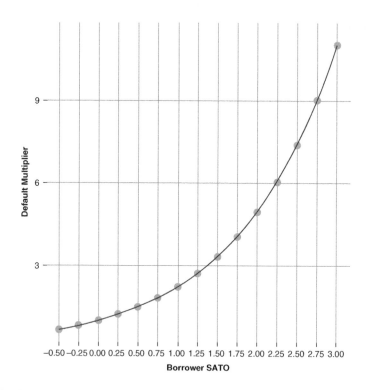

FIGURE 21.4   Borrower SATO Default Multipliers

remain in the home for a period at least equal to the buy-down breakeven but also that the borrower has greater financial flexibility. Conversely, a higher SATO reflects a weaker credit borrower. In the model, a loan with a 2.50% SATO is six times more likely to default than one whose note rate reflects the prime mortgage rate at the time of origination.

Figures 21.5 and 21.6 illustrate the default model applied to an MBS 4.00% pass-through. Figure 21.5 illustrates the mortgage pool's expected default across updated LTV scenarios assuming the SATO and original LTV are 0.25% and 80.0%, respectively. Notice the model's predicted default rate increases exponentially as the borrower's update loan-to-value increases (home prices decline). Thus, a period of declining home prices followed by a recovery would result in higher default rates, followed by a decline in the predicted default rate, as home prices recover, the extent to which defaults rise and fall is also influenced by the original loan-to-value ratio and SATO. For example, Figure 21.6 illustrates the predicted default rate given a SATO of 1.25% and an original loan to value ratio of 100%. The expected maximum default rate under the same updated LTV scenario is more than 60 CDR, twice as great as the maximum expected default rate presented in Figure 21.5.

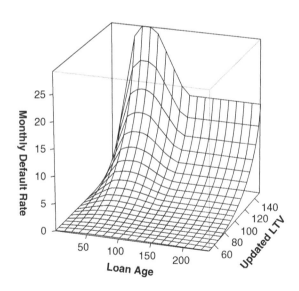

FIGURE 21.5 Predicted Default 80% LTV and −0.50% SATO

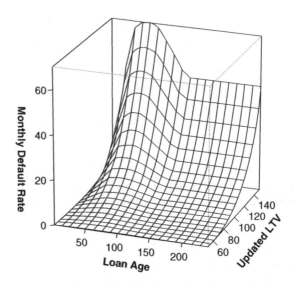

FIGURE 21.6   Predicted Default 100% LTV and
1.25% SATO

21.5 COMPLETING THE PREPAYMENT MODEL

The default model is now ready to be integrated into the prepayment model.
The model now predicts both voluntary prepayments (Chapter 9) as well
as involuntary repayments (borrower default). In addition, the analyst may
input a *loss severity* assumption. Each cash flow vector is reported separately: voluntary repayment, defaulted balance (involuntary repayment),
severity (loss given default), and recovered balance.

Table 21.1 presents an OAS comparison of the MBS 4.00% and 5.50%
prior to and inclusive of the default model. In the case of agency MBS,
which carry the guarantee of the agency, the loss severity realized by the
MBS investor is zero and, as a consequence, default cash flows (buyouts)
pass through as a prepayment with no principal loss. Thus, the change
in OAS presented in Table 21.1 is attributable to the inclusion of the
default vector. The OAS of both the MBS 4.00% and 5.50% go down

TABLE 21.1   OAS Analysis

MBS Pass-Through	OAS w/o Default	OAS w/ Default	Difference
MBS 4.0%	0.56%	0.54%	−0.02%
MBS 5.5%	0.24%	0.22%	−0.02%

TABLE 21.2 OAS Analysis

MBS Pass-Through	OAS w/ 100% Recovery	OAS w/ 80% Recovery	Difference
MBS 4.0%	0.54%	0.51%	−0.03%
MBS 5.5%	0.22%	0.19%	−0.03%

by 2 bps. The lower OAS reported by each reflects the faster expected overall prepayment rate as a result of including the default vector in the prepayment model.

Naturally, the option-adjusted spread of each MBS example declines given that both are priced at a premium. Nonetheless, the OAS analysis presented in Table 21.1 highlights the fact that default cash flows alter the timing of the cash flow returned to the investor and thereby influences the valuation of a mortgage-backed security. The OAS decline simply represents the earlier return of principal. To the extent defaulted principal is not covered by a 100% principal guarantee, losses passed through to the investor will place further downward pressure on OAS.

Table 21.2 presents an OAS comparison of the MBS 4.00% and 5.50%, assuming a 20.0% loss severity. The MBS 4.00% OAS declines to 51 bps, while the MBS 5.50% OAS declines to 19 bps. Clearly, the loss given default, if passed through to the investor, negatively influences the value of mortgage-backed securities. Indeed, the private-label MBS market was conceived to allocate credit risk among investors whose loss tolerances varied. The structuring techniques used in the private-label MBS market allow dealers to create MBS classes, in the absence of external credit enhancement, ranging from triple-A down to below investment grade or not-rated classes.

One may argue that any MBS relying on a third-party guarantee other than that of the U.S. government, as is the case with GNMA, may be rated no higher than that of the third-party guarantor. However, in practice and leading to the financial crisis of 2008, many MBS investors relied on the following assumptions:

- The implicit government guarantee of FNMA and FHLMC, which, following the financial collapse of each, turned out to be correct.
- The bond insurance provider, when employed in a transaction, exercised the appropriate loan level due diligence—an assumption that turned out to be incorrect.
- The behavior of the bond credit rating agencies is mostly agnostic with respect to market share. Thus, one assumes each rating agency

correctly assigned credit enhancement levels without regard to the market share or revenue implications of their assigned ratings. Simply stated, investors assumed the rating agencies acted as agent on their behalf—an assumption that also proved incorrect.

When investing in private-label MBS the investor must understand both the allocation of principal and interest, outlined in the previous section, and the allocation of credit risk across the MBS transaction's capital structure or its impact on the balance sheet of a third-party bond guarantor, the extent of which is measured by simulating both an interest rate and home price process. Chapters 22 and 23 outline the basics of private-label MBS and the process by which the investor may determine credit enhancement levels.

CHAPTER 22

The Basics of Private-Label MBS

Things are not always as they seem; the first appearance deceives many.

Phaedrus 444–393 BC

*P*rivate-label or *nonagency MBS* are mortgage-backed securities issued without the guarantee of Fannie Mae, Freddie MAC, or Ginnie Mae. To achieve the credit ratings that are assigned to each class or tranche and to protect the investor from losses, private-label MBS (PLMBS) rely on internal credit enhancement. Typically, this enhancement employs a combination of the following:

- *Excess spread*, the difference between the interest paid to the liabilities (notes issued) and the interest earned on the assets (mortgage loans)
- *Overcollateralization* (OC), the difference between the principal amount of the notes issued and the principal amount of the underlying collateral
- *Subordination*, bonds subordinated in priority of principal repayment

Losses due to *defaults* are absorbed in reverse priority through the capital structure (Figure 22.1) first by excess spread, then by write-down of the overcollateralization (OC) account, and finally via the principal write-down of the subordinated bonds.

The collateral used in a private-label transaction may consist of either fixed-rate collateral, adjustable-rate collateral, or a mixture of both. In order to accommodate the different groups of collateral used in a transaction several credit enhancement structures have been designed. These structures are known as I, H, or Y structures.

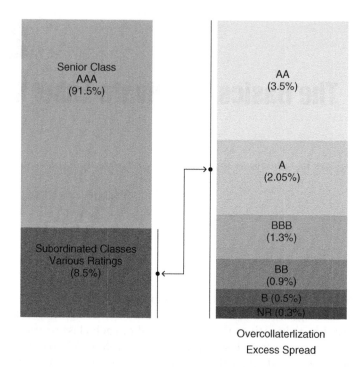

FIGURE 22.1 Prime MBS Credit Enhancement at Deal Inception

22.1 I STRUCTURE

The type I credit enhancement structure (Figure 22.1) accommodates a single collateral group of either fixed-rate, adjustable-rate, or mixed loan types. Although the issuer may mix loan types in an *I structure*, normal practice implies a single loan type that is either fixedrate or adjustable rate. The benefit of the I structure is largely the absence of cross collateral credit enhancement, which serves as a credit subsidy between collateral groups.

22.2 H STRUCTURE

The *H structure* (Figure 22.2) can be thought of as a group of distinct transactions, with the exception that the excess interest between each of the collateral groups is shared in order to maintain the targeted overcollateralization of each group. The H structure is often referred to as a crosscollateralized transaction, since the credit support is subsidized between between collateral groups via the redirection of excess interest.

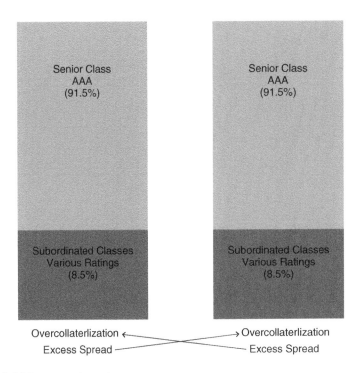

FIGURE 22.2 H Credit Enhancement Structure

Consider the following scenario. Group 1's excess interest is insufficient to cover losses and maintain the collateral group's target OC level. However, group 2 excess interest is sufficient to cover its losses and maintain its target OC level. In this case, the remainder of group 2's excess interest after absorbing losses, if any, is used to bring group 1's OC to its target level.

22.3   Y STRUCTURE

The *Y structure* also allows for two distinct collateral groups and takes its name from the fact that the diagram of the credit enhancement of the structure resembles the letter "Y." Unlike the H structure, the Y structure employs a single subordination scheme to support the senior classes of both groups 1 and 2. Due to the co-mingling of the assets that fall below the AAA rating level, the Y structure, like the H structure, subsidizes losses between both collateral groups.

Figures 22.1 though 22.3 present the structures used to achieve a AAA credit rating across the nonagency (private-label) MBS sector. The most

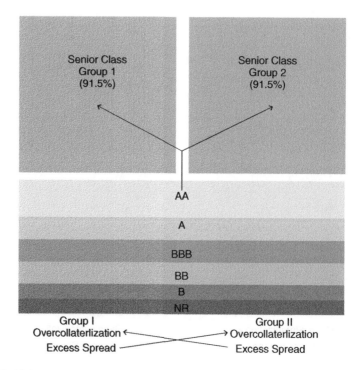

FIGURE 22.3   Y Credit Enhancement Structure

direct structure (the I structure) subordinates losses of a single collateral group. Both the H and Y structures allow for each collateral group to subsidize the losses of another. A transaction allowing for the subsidy of losses between collateral groups complicates the credit analysis of private-label MBS. The complexity arises due to the fact that the investor must analyze the credit of all collateral groups and determine the extent to which one collateral group may subsidize the other.

For example, consider an H structure consisting of a fixed-rate collateral group (1) and an adjustable-rate collateral group (2). To the extent that losses are greater in group 2 and excess interest from group 1 is reallocated to build OC in group 2, the overall credit risk of group 1 increases because the return of excess interest as principal to group 1 is delayed due to its redirection to group 2. As a result, the group 1 investor must provide a default and loss assumption for both groups 1 and 2 in order to adequately assess the overall credit exposure and expected loss of the notes backed by group 1.

Notice that the subordination is often tranched, creating AA, A, BBB, BB, B, and a non rated class, creating six distinct credit tranches. Credit tranching, as described above, is often referred to as a six-pack transaction in deference to the number of credit classes that are created.

At this point, it is important to note that both the H and Y structures may be used to securitize more than two distinct collateral groups. Each of these structures, unlike the I structure, socializes losses across a transaction.

- The H structure partially socializes losses across the collateral groups at the level of the excess interest and over collateralization, whereas the Y structure completely socializes losses.
- The Y structure, socializes losses at the level of excess interest, over collateralization, and the subordinated classes.

CONCEPT 22.1

The H and Y structure, unlike the I structure, socializes losses between collateral groups. The investor should consider the dealer and issuer motivation of any transaction—maximizing proceeds and achieving the lowest cost of funds. As a result, the stronger collateral group subsidizes the weaker collateral group, suggesting the stronger collateral group is priced rich relative to the weaker collateral group. As a general rule, the investor should command a premium in subsidized transaction relative to one that is not subsidized.

22.4 SHIFTING INTEREST

Private-label MBS transactions employ a *shifting interest* mechanism designed to increase the credit enhancement available to the senior classes. Early in the life of the transaction, typically the first 36 months, principal collections and in some cases, excess interest is paid to the senior classes only and the subordinated classes are locked out from receiving principal pay-downs.

For example, assume an I structure like that depicted in Figure 22.1. The AA, A, BBB, BB, B, and not rated classes account for at least 3.5%, 2.05%, 1.3%, 0.9%, 0.5%, and 0.3% of the capital structure, respectively, during the lockout period.

- The triple-A class is paid down faster than the credit support classes and its relative percentage interest in the underlying mortgage pool decreases.

■ Concurrently, the relative percentage interest of the subordinated classes in the mortgage pools increases, affording greater loss protection to the triple-A class.

Generally, subordinated classes are locked out from receiving principal collections in the first 36 months of a transaction or until the credit enhancement level supporting the senior classes has doubled, whichever occurs later. The stepdown date is the point at which the subordinated bonds are no longer locked out and begin to receive principal collections. It refers to the reduction (stepdown) of the dollar amount of subordination as credit enhancement. With respect to the I structure under consideration, at the step down date, the mezzanine (double-A) and subordinated classes would receive their pro rata share of principal collections and begin to amortize.

The 36-month lockout period is based on the historic mortgage default experience. Figure 22.4 illustrates a cumulative default curve based on FHLMC's loan level data. The figure shows a mortgage pool consisting of prime borrowers will experience around 40% of its total expected

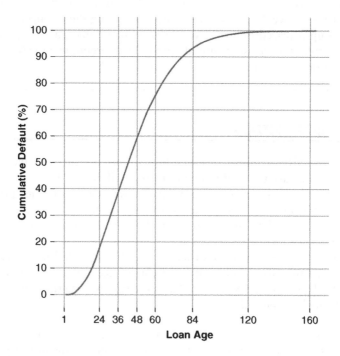

FIGURE 22.4 Agency Mortgage Default Timing Curve

cumulative defaults by month 36 and by month 48 the pool will likely experience the majority (60%) of its total expected cumulative defaults, most occurring between months 24 and 36. Given the expected timing of the defaults, the early lockout of the subordinated bonds maximizes the amount of credit support available concurrent with the peak in the default timing curve. Provided the transaction passes the stepdown test at month 36 the subordinated classes will begin to receive principal collections. However, should the transaction fail its stepdown test the subordinated classes will continue to be locked out from principal collections until such time the transaction passes its stepdown test.

22.5 DEEP MORTGAGE INSURANCE *MI*

The issuer may purchase mortgage insurance at the time of securitization as a form of credit enhancement. Recall from Table 6.2 the presence of mortgage insurance minimizes the investor's realized loss given default. Consequently, the credit rating agencies view deep MI as a source of external credit enhancement which, in the rating agency view, reduces the amount of upfront credit support needed to achieve the desired credit ratings on those classes relative to senior/subordinated structure, which does not have issuer paid deep MI. Naturally, the investor must consider the issuers motivation—the lowest cost of funds. Thus, an issuer is willing to purchase deep MI when its cost is less than that of the capital cost of the subordinated notes—a capital structure arbitrage. In a transaction supported by deep MI the issuer pays a premium, which may come out of the cash flow of the securitization for an MI policy that covers losses on a portion of the pool. It is important to note the following with respect to deep MI as a form of credit enhancement:

- Loan level deep MI differs from a monoline wrap. A monoline wrap from a bond insurance company is an unconditional guarantee of timely payment of interest and the ultimate repayment of principal. Consequently, the investor's credit risk exposure is directly linked to the monoline insurer.
- In a deep MI transaction the loans must meet the insurer's criteria. The MI insurer specifies the characteristics of the loans such as the minimum and maximum LTV, property type, minimum and maximum borrower credit score, etc. When a covered loan defaults, the issuer must submit a claim to the insurer. The insurer may choose to cover all or a portion of the claim or may reject the claim altogether if the insurer determines that its underwriting guidelines have been violated.

From the above description, it should clear that a transaction employing deep MI is not, in the strictest sense, a self insuring structure because the overall credit enhancement levels are determined by the presence of the deep MI policy and as a result the investor bears credit risk exposure to a second party external to the transaction. A deep MI policy covers a portion of the principal balance of the loan to a pre-specified LTV ratio, typically 60% to 65%. Additionally, a deep MI policy will cover accrued interest and expenses incurred during the foreclosure and liquidation process. Conceptually, deep MI takes a second loss position behind the borrower's equity, and to the investor the liquidated loan appears to have a lower LTV ratio.

22.6   EXCESS INTEREST

Excess interest is the difference between the collateral pool's weighted average mortgage rate and the weighted average cost of the liabilities, net of fees and expenses. Generally, the underlying pool of mortgage loans (assets) is expected to generate more interest than what is paid to the classes (liabilities).

- To the extent excess interest net of fees, expenses, or derivative payments is positive, it is used to absorb losses incurred by the underlying mortgage pool.
- Once the financial obligations of the trust are met, excess interest is used to maintain overcollateralization at its target level. Factors influencing the extent to which excess interest is available to maintain overcollateralization include:
  — Full or partial voluntary repayments and defaults may reduce the amount of excess spread because those borrowers with a higher mortgage rate have a greater tendency to voluntarily repay or default. In turn, the weighted average loan rate of the underlying mortgage pool declines over time, a phenomenon commonly referred to as WAC *drift*.
  — If the realized delinquencies, defaults, and losses are greater than expected, the transaction's excess interest is reduced by the amount necessary to compensate for the cash flow shortfalls required to make a full principal distribution to the senior and mezzanine certificates in any period.

22.7   OVERCOLLATERALIZATION

Overcollateralization is the excess of the principal balance of the pool of mortgage loans (assets) over the principal balance of the issued notes (liabilities). It is a form of internally created credit support. Excess spread, also internally created, is used to pay down and maintain the outstanding classes' principal balance below that of the pool of mortgage loans.

Overcollaterlization is either fully funded at the transaction's closing or builds over time using excess interest to pay down the principal balance of the senior liabilities until the OC reaches its targeted amount. In the case of the latter, the target OC amount is usually achieved in the early months of the transaction's life, whereas in the case of the former excess interest is used to maintain the target OC amount. Generally, the target OC amount is established as a percentage of the transaction's original principal balance and varies from one transaction to another depending on the underlying collateral composition, structure, and the rate (coupons) paid on the liabilities.

A transaction using overcollateralization as credit enhancement can sustain losses in any period equal to the amount of the currently available excess spread and overcollateralization before the subordinated classes incur a principal writedown. For example, assume an I transaction presented in Figure 22.1 and a fully funded target OC amount of 1.0%. Once the transaction's cumulative losses exceed the targeted OC amount, and if the excess spread is insufficient to cover the losses in a given period, then the lowest rated subordinated class whose principal balance is greater than zero will experience a principal writedown.

22.8   STRUCTURAL CREDIT PROTECTION

In addition, structural credit protection in the form of trigger events is also used. These include delinquency and overcollateralization triggers. For the most part, trigger events are based on seriously delinquent loans and cumulative losses. A seriously delinquent loan is a loan that is 60+ days past due (dpd), in foreclosure, or real estate owned (REO). These triggers are considered in effect on or after the stepdown date if either or both the delinquency and cumulative loss test(s) are not passed.

22.8.1   Delinquency Triggers

There are two types of delinquency triggers: soft trigger and hard trigger. In either case, the goal of the trigger is to manage the transaction's stepdown.

22.8.1.1   Soft Delinquency Trigger　A soft delinquency trigger dynamically links the credit enhancement to the credit performance of the underlying collateral. There are two types of soft delinquency triggers:

- *A trigger based on the credit enhancement of the senior classes.* This trigger specifies a target value of delinquencies as a percentage of the senior classes' credit enhancement and for the most part protects the senior class bondholders. However, because the trigger is specified as a percentage of the senior classes' credit enhancement, it becomes mechanically weaker as the senior classes pay down. In fact, under a fast prepayment scenario, the trigger may weaken to the point that it may no longer be effective.

- *A trigger based on the credit enhancement of the most senior outstanding class.* A trigger of this type will not allow the stepdown if the percentage of seriously delinquent loans exceeds a target level that is tied to the credit enhancement available for the most senior outstanding class. Structurally, this trigger partially addresses the shortcomings of the delinquency trigger discussed above.

22.8.1.2 Hard Delinquency Trigger A hard delinquency trigger is not tied to the senior classes' credit enhancement percentage. Rather, a hard delinquency trigger is stated as a fixed percentage of the mortgage pool's current collateral balance. A hard delinquency offers the following advantages over a soft delinquency trigger.

- A hard delinquency trigger mitigates adverse selection risk due to faster than expected prepayments.
- A hard delinquency trigger's ability to prevent stepdown does not weaken with an increase in subordination to the senior classes.

22.8.2 Overcollaterlization Step-up Trigger

The overcollateralization step-up trigger increases a transaction's target OC amount, rather than stopping the release of OC to a higher level if the mortgage pool's cumulative losses exceed a specified amount. The OC step-up trigger provides the advantage of causing the OC target to increase during the later stages of the transaction's life. However, due to the phenomenon of WAC drift, it is possible that when cumulative losses cross the specified level excess spread may be insufficient to build the additional overcollateralization called for by the trigger event.

22.8.3 Available Funds Cap

The term *available funds cap* (AFC) refers to the singular truism of MBS investing: a bondholder may only be paid interest up to the amount of the net interest that is generated by the underlying pool of mortgage loans. The AFC arises when a transaction's liabilities are floating and it is collateralized by hybrid adjustable-rate loans. Most hybrid adjustable-rate loans have a fixed-rate period, commonly from one to five years, which limits the interest available to the trust. All adjustable rate loans have both a periodic and a life cap. Both of these limit the interest available to the trust needed to meet class interest payments after trust fees and transaction expenses. Together, they give rise to the available funds cap.

Most floating rate MBS classes are indexed to one-month LIBOR and reset monthly. The note rate on adjustable- and hybrid adjustable-rate loans in MBS transactions often reference several interest rate indexes like six-month LIBOR or the one year Constant Maturity Treasury (CMT) and their note rates do not reset monthly. This difference creates both an index and rate reset timing mismatch. The differing indexes used to set the interest rate on the pool of mortgage loans (assets) versus the one-month LIBOR index used to determine the classes' (liabilities') interest rate creates additional risk, which is commonly referred to as *basis risk*.

The calculation of the initial available funds cap is relatively straight forward. First, subtract expenses (servicing fees, trustee fees, IO strip, and net swap payments) from the original weighted average coupon on the underlying pool of mortgage loans. Once the cost of the liabilities have been accounted for, the available excess spread can be calculated as outlined in Table 22.1. Consider the following:

- A transaction collateralized by a mortgage pool of 7/1 hybrid ARM loans with a current rate of 3.125% and a life cap of 8.125%
- Current one-month LIBOR of 0.25%
- No swap hedge used in the transaction

TABLE 22.1 Available Funds Cap Calculation

	Initial AFC(%)		Life AFC(%)
Wtd. Avg. Gross WAC	3.125	Weighted Avg. Life Cap	8.125
Less Servicing Fee	0.25	Less Servicing Fee	0.25
Less Trustee Fee	0.05	Less Trustee Fee	0.05
Less IO strip (if any)	0.00	Less IO strip (if any)	0.00
Less Deep MI	0.25	Less Deep MI	0.25
Less Net Swap Pmts. (bps)	0.00	Less Net Swap Pmts. (bps)	0.00
Net Initial AFC	2.575	Net Life AFC	7.575
Weighted Avg. Bond Spread	0.10	Weighted Avg.Bond Spread	0.10
Current 1-Mo. LIBOR	0.25		
Weighted Avg. Bond Coupon	0.35		
Initial Excess Spread	2.25		

The initial available funds cap is 2.575%, the initial excess spread is 2.25%, and the net life cap is 7.575%. The LIBOR strike, first introduced in Section 18.4, can also be calculated from Table 22.1 as follows:

$$\text{LIBOR strike} = \text{Net life AFC} - [\text{Index} - \text{Weighted avg. bond spread}]$$

$$(22.1)$$

22.9   HEDGING ASSET/LIABILITY MISMATCHES

Hedging the basis risk in a PLMS transaction can be done using either interest rate caps, interest rate swaps, or a combination of both. Asset/liability hedges are required in a transaction for the following reasons:

- The available funds cap refers to the fact that the coupon on a floating rate bond (liability) is limited to the weighted average note rate on the underlying loans (assets), less the expenses of the trust. The trust's expenses may include any or all of the following: trustee fees, surety fees, bond surety fees, IO strip, and mortgage insurance fees. Furthermore, the timing mismatch between adjustments to the liability rate (generally monthly) and the asset rate (generally semi-annual or annual) may create a temporary interest shortfall due to the presence of periodic caps that may limit the weighted average loan rate on the mortgage pool relative to the weighted average rate of the classes.
- A mortgage securitization may include hybrid ARM loans with fixed-rate periods ranging from 2 to 10 years, as well as term fixed-rate loans. In turn, the nature of the underlying collateral may create an asset/liability mismatch of floating-rate classes (liabilities) and fixed-rate assets (the mortgage pool). Consequently, the mismatch must be hedged to preserve the excess spread in a rising interest rate environment.

22.9.1   Hedging with Interest Rate Caps

Hedging with an interest rate cap (Figure 22.5) requires the issuer to purchase a cap in order to hedge the asset/liability mismatch thus incurring an upfront cost. The cap contract is not an asset of either the lower or upper tier REMICs. Rather, cap payments are made to a distribution account after fees. The hedge is straightforward: At the closing of the transaction, the trust enters into a cap contract with a cap provider. The cap contract states the LIBOR strike and the notional balance on which the contract is based.

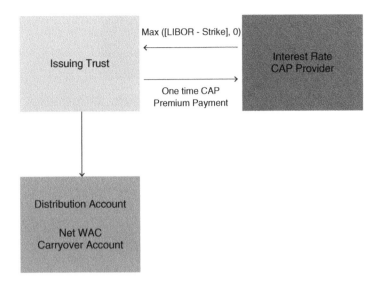

FIGURE 22.5   Hedging with an Interest Rate Cap

In addition, the cap contract may specify a maximum LIBOR rate beyond which the cap will not pay—a cap corridor.

Generally, the cap contract is struck to cover the hybrid ARM fixed-rate period. For example, a transaction collateralized by 7/1 hybrid ARM loans may enter into a cap contract covering the first 84 distribution dates of the transaction. Under the agreement, the cap counterparty agrees to pay the trust the excess of the LIBOR strike up to a maximum value based on an actual/360 basis. The cap payment, if made by the cap counterparty, is deposited to the Net WAC carryover account and made available to pay the interest to each class.

22.9.2   Hedging with Interest Rate Swaps

If the transaction is hedged with an interest rate swap (Figure 22.6), it is held in a supplemental interest trust which is not considered an asset of either the lower-or upper-tier REMICs. The swap payments become fees and expenses of the trust and net swap payments by the trust are withdrawn from amounts on deposit in the distribution account.

On the distribution date, the supplemental interest trust pays the swap provider a fixed rate and the swap provider pays the supplemental

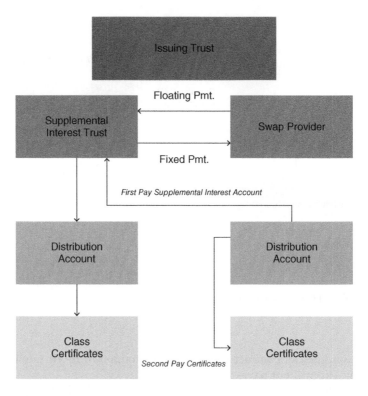

FIGURE 22.6 Hedging with an Interest Rate Cap

interest account a floating payment equal to one-month LIBOR. The swap payments are based on the amount of the outstanding balance of the senior and mezzanine classes. A *net swap payment* is made on the distribution date as follows:

- If the fixed payment is greater than the floating payment, the supplemental interest trust pays the swap provider.
- If the fixed payment is less than the floating payment the swap provider pays the supplemental interest trust.

If the supplemental interest trust is required to make a payment to the swap provider because the fixed payment is greater than the floating payment, the trust is required to make a payment from the distribution account to the supplemental interest account. In this case, the payment to the supplemental interest account is made before interest distribution to the class certificates.

From the discussion above, it should be apparent that a PLMBS transaction which relies on either a cap agreement or an interest rate swap to hedge basis risk is not, in the strictest sense, a self-insuring structure. Indeed, the timely payment of interest to the class certificate holders is dependent on the performance of the cap or swap counterparty. Thus, by extension the trust is exposed to the creditworthiness of the cap or interest rate swap provider—a third party to the transaction.

CHAPTER 23

Sizing Mortgage Credit Enhancement

The hardest thing to do is to find a black cat in a dark room, especially if there is no cat.

Confucius

Home prices [Stanton and Wallace 2005] are assumed to follow a geometric Brownian motion given by the following equation:

$$\Delta r = (r_t - \theta) \times \Delta t + \sigma\sqrt{\theta} \times \Delta W(t) \tag{23.1}$$

where: r_t = short-term rate
θ = housing risk premium
σ = the variance of home prices
$\Delta Wt(t)$ = a Weiner process

Further, we can deduce from Cox [John C. Cox 1985] if $2\theta \geq \sigma_2$ the upward drift is sufficiently large as to make the zero inaccessible. The home price model is calibrated assuming the housing risk premium is a constant 2.5% and the volatility of home prices is 8.6% (annualized). Figures 23.1 and 23.2 illustrate the result of home price simulation assuming the short-term rate is 0.25% and 20.00%, respectively. The model assumes home prices are correlated to interest rates via the housing risk premium.

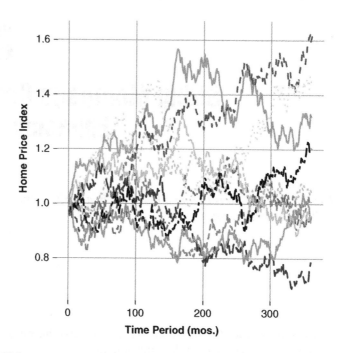

FIGURE 23.1   Home Price Paths Short Rate = 0.25%

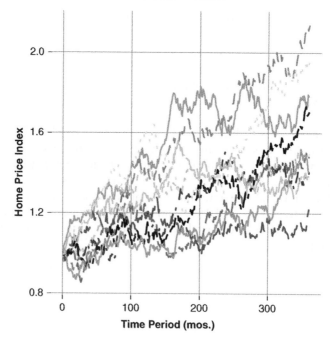

FIGURE 23.2   Home Price Paths Short Rate = 20.00%

23.1 SIMULATING BORROWER DEFAULT RATES

The simulated home price paths are passed to the default model outlined in Chapter 21 and the pool's updated loan to value is calculated based on the simulated change in home prices and principal reductions related to amortization of the loan. Figure 23.2 illustrates the expected default vector based on 1,000 interest rate and home price simulations. The home price simulation assumes a long-term home price appreciation rate of 2.50% and annualized home price volatility of 5.2%; the random seed is set to 300. The simulation produces the following results:

- The minimum peak default rate is around 2.75 CDR.
- The expected default rate begins to reach its peak near month 48. Thereafter, default rates generally trend down though month 120.
- Beyond month 120, the expected default trends down; however, some home price simulations result in a resurgence of borrower default beyond the 120-month mark. The subsequent resurgence in the expected borrower default rate is generally less than that shown in the peak months. The lower default rate is a result of:
  - *The borrower's tenure in the home.* Recall, the default model outlined in Chapter 21. The expected borrower default rate declines as the tenure in the home increases beyond month 72.
  - *The increase in borrower equity.* The borrower's equity increases due to principal amortization and home price appreciation. As a result, the expected default rate due to a decline in home prices later in the borrower's tenure is less than that earlier in the borrower's tenure.

23.2 ESTIMATION OF CUMULATIVE DEFAULT RATES

Mortgage default rates are often quoted either as a percentage of the pool's original balance or of its current balance. For the purpose of *credit enhancement*, defaults are measured as percentage of the pool's original principal balance. In addition, notice when establishing a pool's credit enhancement level, voluntary repayments are not passed through the prepayment model. Indeed, when the analyst seeks to establish the credit enhancement of a pool of mortgage loans she assumes the voluntary repayment rate is 0.0 CPR. The assumption stresses a mortgage pool's credit performance in that the borrower either remains current and remits timely payment of

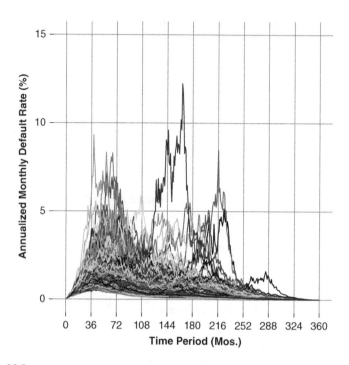

FIGURE 23.3 Simulated Annualized Default Rate

the mortgage payments due, or defaults, which subjects the trust (investor) to a loss.

CONCEPT 23.1

Private MBS credit enhancement levels are determined assuming the voluntary repayment rate is 0.0 CPR. If the analyst allowed voluntary repayments she would credit those repayments representing positive selection (the exit of borrowers prior to default), which would result in a lower level of credit enhancement.

Figure 23.4 illustrates the cumulative principal default rates across the home price simulations presented above. The simulated principal losses range between 10% and 40%. Naturally, the investor will incur a loss severity given borrower default as outlined in Tables 6.1 and 6.2.

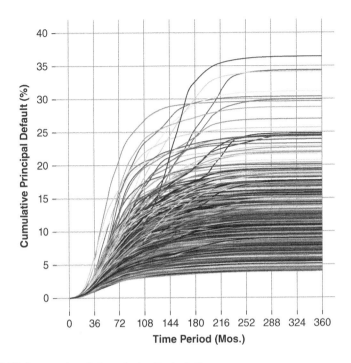

FIGURE 23.4 Simulated Cumulative Default Rates

Generally speaking, the credit rating agencies assume the following when establishing a transaction's credit enhancement level:

- The expected cumulative default rate
- Loss severity given borrower default
- In some models, a triple-A coverage ratio

Given these assumptions, a transaction's credit enhancement (subordination) level is set. Equation 23.2 generalizes the formula for setting the credit enhancement level.

$$\text{Credit enhancement} = \left[\sum_{t=1}^{n} \times CPD_{t=n} \right] \times \frac{1}{n} \times S \times CR \qquad (23.2)$$

where: CPD = Cumulative principal default
  n = Number of simulations
  S = Loss severity
  CR = Coverage ratio

For example, the simulation results presented in Figure 23.4 yield the following observations:

- The expected cumulative principal default stated as a percentage of the original balance is 9.9%. Given a 35% *loss severity*, the *expected loss* is 3.46%.
- Assuming a credit enhancement level similar to that presented in Figure 23.1 the implied coverage ratio is 2.45.
- Further, the astute reader will notice in the simulation presented, the cumulative default rate reaches 35%. Under this scenario, the *cumulative loss*, assuming a 35% severity, is 12.2%. Thus, under the worst-case scenario, the implied coverage ratio of 81% (9.9/12.2) is insufficient to protect the triple-A investor against "tail risk" losses.

Figure 23.5 illustrates the prime mortgage loss distribution. It suggests an 8.5% enhancement level will protect the triple-A investor in most cases. The cumulative density distribution presented in Figure 23.6 provides greater clarity. Given an 8.5% subordination, the triple-A investor is protected against 99% of the potential outcomes.

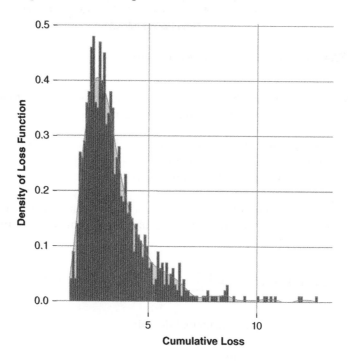

FIGURE 23.5 Prime Mortgage Cumulative Loss Distribution

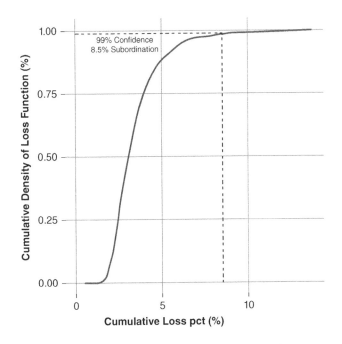

FIGURE 23.6 Prime Mortgage Cumulative Density Loss Function

23.3 TRANSLATING CREDIT ENHANCEMENT TO A THIRD-PARTY GUARANTEE FEE

Returning to the example of the GSEs (FNMA, FHLMC, GNMA), one can easily translate the required credit enhancement level to an implied guarantee fee. The average life of the 4.00%, 30-year mortgage used in the above example is 17.9 years. The implied guarantee fee is calculated according to equation 23.3.

$$\text{Implied GSE guarantee fee} = \frac{EL \times CR}{AL} \qquad (23.3)$$

where: EL = Expected loss
CR = Coverage ratio
AL = Avg. life absent voluntary repayments

One simply divides the expected loss × the required coverage ratio by the average life of the mortgage absent voluntary repayments.

For example, given the expected loss of 3.46% and a loss coverage multiplier of 3, the annual guarantee fee is 58 basis points ((3.46 × 3) ÷ 17.9).

23.4 ROLE OF THE CREDIT RATING AGENCIES (NRSROs)

A credit *rating agency* may apply to the Securities and Exchange Commission for registration as a Nationally Recognized Statistical Rating Organization (NRSRO). A credit rating agency establishes mortgage credit enhancement levels based on statistical models that are not fully available or disclosed to the investor. Additionally, the investor who relies solely on a credit rating agency must recognize the following:

- The credit rating agency does not act as agent on the investor's behalf. Rather, the credit rating agency charges the investment bank a fee for rating a transaction. The investment bank passes the fee to the transaction as part of the "deal fees" charged by the investment bank. The deal fees are then subtracted from the transaction's proceeds before remittance to the issuer—the rating agency is engaged in a transaction by the investment bank on behalf of the issuer.
- Historically, the credit rating agencies, when assigning credit enhancement levels, have tended to act counter to the business cycle. The counter-cyclic behavior of the rating process results in the assignment of lower credit enhancement levels at the peak of a business cycle and higher credit enhancement levels at the trough of a business cycle.

The weight given by the investor to the rating assigned by a credit agency must take into account the above factors. The rating assigned by an NRSRO may provide a helpful starting point. However, it is in the investor's best interest to model both the transaction's credit waterfall and assess the sufficiency of the transaction's credit enhancement level based on her own models.

About the Website

Investing in Mortgage-Backed and Asset-Backed Securities comes with a companion website at www.wiley.com/go/investinginmbs (passcode: schultz16).

Available for download is source code for the BondLab R package as well as an Introduction to BondLab.

INTRODUCTION TO BONDLAB

Companion2IMBS_1.0.tar.gz provides a gentle introduction to BondLab. The companion provides source code calling BondLab functions and illustrates how one may, using BondLab, create proprietary valuation models.

SOURCE CODE FOR THE BONDLAB R PACKAGE

BondLab_0.0.0.9000.tar.gz is the source code for the BondLab R package. The analysis presented in the book *Investing in Mortgage- and Asset-Backed Securities* using R and Open Source Analytics was done using the BondLab R package. The BondLab R package allows the reader to replicated the analysis and valuation models outlined in the book.

INSTALLATION INSTRUCTIONS

To install BondLab and R, download the following:

Windows Users

Download R
https://www.r-project.org

Download R studio IDE Free Open Source Edition
https://www.rstudio.com

Download Rtools
https://cran.r-project.org/bin/windows/Rtools/

Mac Users

Download R
   https://www.r-project.org

Download R studio IDE Free Open Source Edition
   https://www.rstudio.com

Download Quartz
   http://xquartz.macosforge.org/landing/

Bibliography

Arnholz, John, and Edward Gainor. 2006. *Offerings of asset backed securities*. Aspen Publishing.

Corporation Federal Home Loan Mortgage. No date. http://www.freddiemac.com/debt/pdf/fixed-income-glossary.pdf.

Crawley, Michael J. 2013. *The r book second edition*. John Wiley & Sons, Inc.

Cox, John C., Stephen A. Ross, and Jonathan E. Ingersoll Jr. 1985. A theory of the term strucuture of interest rates. *Econmetrica*.

Downing, Chris, Richard Stanton. and Nancy Wallace. 2005. A empircal test of a two-factor mortgage valuation model: how much do home prices matter. *Real Estate Economics*.

Ferstal, Robert, and Josef Hayden. 2010. Zero-coupon yield curve estimation with the package termstrc. *Journal of Statisical Software*.

Fisher, Lawrence, and Roman Weil. 1972. Coping with the risk of interest-rate fluctuations: returns to bondholders from naive and optimal strategies. *The Journal of Business*.

Governors of the Federal Reserve System, Board of. No date. http://www.federalreserve.gov/datadownload/Choose.aspx?rel=H15.

Hayre, Lakhbir. 2006. *Modeling of mortgage prepayments and defaults*. Technical report. Citigroup Global Markets.

Ho, Thomas. 1992. Key rate durations: measures of interest rate risks. *The Journal of Fixed Income*.

Hosmer, David W., and Stanley Lemeshow. 1998. *Applied survival analysis, regression modeling of time to event data*. John Wiley & Sons, Inc.

Iacus, Stefano M. 2011. *Option pricing and estimation of financial models with R*. Wiley.

Internal, Revenue Service. 2012a. *Irc 1.806d-1*. Technical report. Internal Revenue Service.

James, Gareth, et al. *An introduction to statistical learning with applications in R*. Springer.

Jones, Jonathan D. 1999. Total return analysis. *Risk Management Series, Office of Thrift Supervison*.

Keynes, John Maynard. 1936. *The general theory of employment, interest, and money*. Palgrave Macmillan.

Macaulay, Fredrick R. 1938. *Some theoretical problems suggested by the movements of interest rates, bond yields and stock prices in the united states since 1856*. NBER.

McDonald, Daniel J., and Daniel L. Thorton. 2008. A primer on the mortgage market and mortgage finance. *Federal Reserve Bank of Saint Louis Review*.

Michale, Michael, Marschoun LaCour-Littlem, and Clark L. Maxam. 2002. Improving parametric mortgage prepayment models with non-parametric kernel regression. *JRER*.

Muth, John F. 1961. Rational expectations and the theory of price movements. *Econmetrica*.

Nash, John C. 2014. On best practice optimization methods in R. *Journal of Statistical Software*.

Nash, John C., and Ravi Varadhan. 2011. Unifying optimization algorithms to aid software system users: optimx for R. *Journal of Statistical Software*.

Paul Emrath, Ph.D. 2009. *How long buyers remain in their homes*. Technical report. National Association of Home Builders.

Peristiani, Stavros. 1998. Modelling the instability of mortgage-backed prepayments. *Federal Reserve of New York Research Paper 9804*.

R Core Team. 2013. *R: a language and environment for statistical computing*. Vienna, Austria: R Foundation for Statistical Computing. http://www.R-project .org/.

Sack, Refet S., Gurkaynak Brian, and Jonathan H. Wright. 2006. The U.S. treasury yield curve: 1961 to the present. *FEDS*.

Schultz, Glenn M. 1986. Duration, immunization, and the management of interest rate risk. *Undergraduate Independent Study, University of Louisville*.

Schwartz, Eduardo S., and Walter Torous. 1992. Prepayment default, and the valuation of mortgage pass-through securities. *The Journal of Business*.

Schwartz, Eduardo S., and Walter N. Torous. 1989. Prepayment and the valuation of mortgage backed securities. *The Journal of Finance*.

———. 2012b. *Irc 1.806g-2*. Technical report. Internal Revenue Service.

Smith, W.N., Veneables, D.M., and the R Core Team. 2013. *An introduction to R, version 3.0.1*. R Foundation.

Spahr, Ronald W., and Mark A. Sunderman. 1992. The effect of prepayment modeling in pricing mortgage backed securities. *Journal of Housing Research*.

Stanton, Richard. 1995. Rational prepayment and the valuation of mortgage-backed securities. *Review of Financial Studies*, 677–708.

Therneau, Terry M., and Patricia Gambash. 2000. *Modeling survival data: extending the cox model*. Springer.

Vayanos, Dimitiri, and Jean-Luc Vila. 2009. A preferred-habitat model of the term structure of interest rates. *NBER Working Paper Series, Working Paper 15487*.

Waring, M. Barton, and Laurence B. Siegel. 2006. The myth of the absolute return investor. *Financial Analysts Journal 62*.

Index

Note: Page references followed by f and t indicate an illustrated figure and table, respectively.

Printed and bound by CPI Group (UK) Ltd, Croydon, CR0 4YY

23/04/2025

14660999-0004

—